THE WORD IN
BLACK AND WHITE

The Word in Black and White

Reading "Race" in American Literature, 1638–1867

DANA D. NELSON

New York   Oxford
OXFORD UNIVERSITY PRESS

Oxford University Press

Oxford   New York   Toronto
Delhi   Bombay   Calcutta   Madras   Karachi
Kuala Lumpur   Singapore   Hong Kong   Tokyo
Nairobi   Dar es Salaam   Cape Town
Melbourne   Auckland   Madrid

and associated companies in
Berlin   Ibadan

First published in 1992 by Oxford University Press, Inc.,
200 Madison Avenue, New York, New York 10016

First issued as an Oxford University Press paperback, 1994.

Library of Congress Cataloging-in-Publication Data
Nelson, Dana D.
The word in black and white : reading "race" in American
literature, 1638–1867 / Dana D. Nelson.
p. cm.
Includes bibliographical references (p.   ) and index.
ISBN 0-19-506592-1
ISBN 0-19-508927-8 (pbk.)
1. American literature—Colonial period, ca. 1600–1775—History
and criticism.   2. American literature—White authors—History and
criticism.   3. American literature—19th century —History and
criticism.   4. American literature—1783–1850—History and
criticism.   5. Minorities in literature   6. Race in literature.
I. Title.
PS173.E8N45   1992
810.9'355—dc20   91-8513   CIP

2   4   6   8   10   9   7   5   3   1

Printed in the United States of America
on acid-free paper

To John and Cathy

Preface

On February 14, 1989, while delivering a lecture at Princeton University, Pulitzer Prize–winning novelist Toni Morrison questioned the odd circumstance that she is often asked to come to campuses where there have been ugly racial incidents in order to address primarily white audiences on the nature of racism. Her difficulty with this, she explained, is that implicit in such requests is an attitude that "we [blacks] are a problem and it is our job to solve ourselves." She pointed out that "the survivor [of racism] is assumed to be both patient and physician," so that in many ways the victim is held responsible for his or her continued suffering. The accountability for the phenomenon of racism in American culture, however, lies elsewhere, and Morrison's suggestion here is pointed: "Why ask the victim to explain the torturer?"

Given the resurgence of racially motivated hate crimes throughout the United States and the increased visibility of and support for openly racist media and political figures, it is obvious that racism is not a problem that went away or even diminished in the sixties and seventies. It is, apparently, part of the deep structure of U.S. culture. And it seems that Morrison might be right: Americans concerned about racism could begin by looking at the "white" historical record on race. In fact, it is becoming increasingly clear that understanding the role of the dominant culture is elemental to an examination of racism. Benjamin Ringer and Elinor Lawless argue that the actions of the larger society have a basic influence on the "structure and character" of the minority group (18). For this reason, we cannot begin to explain the continuing *effects* of racism in the United States without first explaining how members of a dominant culture first created the *idea* of "race" — how they evoked "race" as a means for delineating and oppressing groups of people, and how the idea of "race" has circulated and evolved through Anglo culture in the United States.

While there is evidence of racism throughout recorded history, institutionalized racism coincides with the era of American colonization and is, some argue, built into the very structure of our country's society and politics.[1] The idea itself has assumed many different shapes in U.S. history. Taken variously to stand for cultural, evolutionary, moral, metaphysical, and biological difference, "race" has never been a stable idea or a fixed concept. Moreover, its most enduring representation—as a scientifically documentable kind of difference—has now been thoroughly debunked: "race" is no longer recognized as a valid scientific category.[2] That being so, we can perhaps enter into a more critical understanding of "race." One approach might be to consider it in terms of what Michel Foucault defines as an "apparatus," namely, "a formation which has as its major function at a given historical moment that of responding to an urgent need" (*Power/Knowledge*, 195).[3] That urgent need came early in the American colonial period, and was complexly shaped by the religious, economic, social, political, and psychological exigencies of early Anglo-American colonists. Looking at it from this angle, we can see how "race" has proved to be a remarkably resilient, persistent, and flexible formation, responding to various urgent needs of the Anglo-American majority for centuries.

We can also see from this perspective that "race" will be simultaneously ever-changing and adaptive. As an apparatus that circulates through culture, through the "discourse, institutions, architectural forms, regulatory decisions, laws, administrative measures, scientific statements, philosophical, moral and philanthropical propositions—in short, the said as much as the unsaid," "race" must be flexible in order to maintain its currency (Foucault, *Power/Knowledge*, 194). It is a concept that is dispersed through every level of culture, insistently but silently structured into our political system and permeating our conscious and unconscious lives. So we can see that "race" cannot be productively studied as some kind of essence that inheres to certain individuals who "possess" it.

But neither is it productive to think of it as mere illusion. Saying "race" does not reside within the individual, does not make the individual's experience of it less real, so we need to understand how "race" is socially constructed as a reality that affects various groups of people differently. Arguing for their theory of racial formation, Michael Omi and Howard Winant insist that effort must be made to understand race as an "unstable and 'decentered' complex of social meanings constantly being transformed by political struggle" (67, 69). Foregrounding the dynamic quality of "race" is crucial. While our culture, education, and experience teach us to accept race as a *fact*, it is important—if we hope productively to analyze "race"—to study it as a *fiction*. The difference is not that one is true and the other false, but rather that, as Donna Haraway observes, "fiction is an *active* form, referring to a present act of fashioning, while fact is a descendant of a past participle, a word form which *masks* the generative deed or performance" (*Primate Visions*, 4; my emphasis). Considering "race" as a fiction reminds us that before notions of different races could become "common sense," the idea of "race" had to be invented, described, promulgated, and legislated by those who would benefit as a group from the concept. For the idea to be maintained, all those activities must be continuously maintained. And to the extent that ideas of "race" are developed and adapted to different historical, political, and economic circumstances, they are also fictive.

To put this another way, "race" as a knowable object does not preexist itself but is constituted by every expression of that idea. To acknowledge this fictional dimension is not to discredit actual, material effects of "race" in society nor to discredit the political efficacy of the concept[4] but to highlight its arbitrary constructedness.[5] In this way "race" can be viewed in a literary sense as a viable, active metaphor that serves to inscribe and naturalize (as well as to subvert) power relationships being constantly reproduced in cultural texts as well as in human relationships. (I intend my frequent bracketing of the term, along with perceptually invalid racial markers like "white," "black," and "red" to serve as a reminder of this principle. My own preference is for bulkier but more accurate geopolitical descriptors such as Anglo, African, and Native American, which distance us from perceptually invalid and essentializing markers for "race.")

My project in this book is to examine the deployment of "race" in a variety of literary texts by "white" authors, from colonization through the Civil War. Taking culture and, concomitantly, literature as a contested site, I consider a wide variety of texts, fictional and nonfictional, canonical and noncanonical, which assume a variety of positions on the issue of "race." These texts help us see how literature represents as well as presents strategies for an ongoing debate over "race," and how it replicates the provisional nature of "race." I am not interested in why particular individuals might want to dominate others through "race" but how the idea of "race" works at the level of ongoing cultural subjugation. For that reason I focus on how these texts strategize "race" for their larger culture, how their strategies are determined by, as well as how they *add* to, the ongoing debate over "race." I read, in other words, how these texts read "race."

One of my most specific theoretical assumptions is that literature is symbolic action with reference to a real world and, as such, should not be abstracted from its material and cultural contexts. My method is a bricolage of "sociological criticism(s)"[6] through which I examine how these various texts produce racial subjects ("black" and "red," *and* "white"), how "race" is organized and administered, and conversely, how it is disrupted, made less oppressive or differently relevant. My historical interest is motivated by my contemporary concerns over continuing racism and I am interested in exploring the various ways we can be critical about "race" now. If each of the primary texts in my study presents some kind of strategy for dealing with the problem of race, I am testing how various kinds of contemporary theories congenial to my general method can strategically read those prior strategies. For this purpose, I variously adapt and utilize the tactics of many related theorizations, related through their attention to the historical, material, and political dimensions of literature, through their adoption of disruptive, adversarial reading strategies—approaches often strategic to the purposes of nondominant cultural groups under the rubrics of race, class, and gender.

I have not tried to write a continuously progressing history because fictions of "race" seem to me neither continuous nor progressive. However, history and cultural criticism are inevitably narrativized. One of my major emphases here is how powerful story is in delimiting as well as projecting the way we know. Each chapter is therefore internally constructed as an ongoing story that finally interrelates to the others through an aggregate of arguments.

Chapter 1 makes explicit the focuses of a sociological criticism of literature, as I apply them in this study. It explores a broad historical outline, focusing on how colonial literature serves to justify the colonial endeavor at (at least) two levels: culturally and economically. It considers epistemological history immediately preceding the age of Anglo-European exploration and colonization, arguing that the seeds of oppressive colonization were germinating even before actual "discovery," taking root during early Renaissance paradigm shifts. I argue that the Copernican revolution, which displaced Western "Man" from his solipsistic centrality in the universe and made him ancillary to a heliocentric universe, spawned a compensatory epistemology that insisted on an aggressive sense of superiority finding its best expression in the Great Chain of Being. We can see how theories about the *hierarchical* ordering of the universe developing during the era of colonization predicted gradations not just between "Man" and other creatures, but *among* "Mankind" as well. Having offered these speculations about the groundings of what I call the superiority story, I turn to my literary subject, analyzing two texts that are paradigmatic of colonial literature: John Underhill's promotional pamphlet *Newes from America* and the slavery passages from Thomas Jefferson's *Notes on the State of Virginia*.

Chapter 2 takes up two more colonial texts: Cotton Mather's "The Negro Christianized," and William Byrd's *Histories of the Dividing Line*. Like the previous chapter, it contrasts a text generated in the northern colonies to one produced in the southern. But unlike those discussed in chapter 1, both texts considered here make a self-conscious effort to intervene in early racist attitudes and policies. In keeping with my own commitment to adversarial reading, I begin by questioning their most explicit project, focusing on what plays out as textual economies of morality and power, and weighing the imaginative hold of racial tropes of difference—what Abdul JanMohamed discusses as "manichean allegory"—which effectively undermine these writers' explicitly stated attempts to support African and Native Americans.

Next I examine explicitly fictionalized literature, but a literature with a conflicted relationship to its own fictionality: historical romance novels of the frontier. In chapter 3 I turn to James Fenimore Cooper's *The Last of the Mohicans*, Robert Montgomery Bird's *Nick of the Woods*, and William Gilmore Simms's *The Yemassee*. Here I discuss the sociological and textual dimensions of colonial representations of "race," and the actual usefulness of those representations in displacing social frictions among "whites," as well as in displacing their collective guilt for a policy that was only obliquely represented as but fairly culminated in the genocide of Native American populations. Although these texts are formulated around a historical past, they still offer strategies of attitude and actual policy toward the continuing frontier, then farther west (or even overseas). Lastly I explore the politics and implications of using the novel to embody the Anglo colonial "tradition." In light of Mikhail Bakhtin's discussion of the ideological function of language in the novel, I explore how the novel, as "double-voiced discourse," in some ways resists the ideological drives present in these frontier novels.

Chapter 4 turns again to literature that self-consciously attempts to intervene in racist attitudes and/or behavior and here I look to "sympathetic" constructions of "race." Catherine Maria Sedgwick's *Hope Leslie* and Lydia Maria Child's *Romance of the Republic* focus on Native Americans pressed by the Anglo frontier and African Americans impressed into slavery. My interest here is in the "sentimental" strategies deployed in each text to present empathetic versions of the racial Other, as well as the explicit focus of each novel on the politics of narrating history. Distinguishing, after Tzvetan Todorov, between prejudice of superiority and prejudice of equality, this chapter explores the efficacy of these sympathetic texts in developing different versions of Native and African American cultures and socially transforming and/or ameliorating strategies. These aspects of the novels are finally weighed against the metafictional/metahistorical intervention that each raises in terms of representing "race."

Chapters 5 and 6 counterpose two canonical texts not ordinarily paired, but which both participate in colonialist exploration, and in explorations of racialist epistemologies. First, chapter 5 presents a reading of Edgar Allan Poe's *Narrative of Arthur Gordon Pym* as a text that at its most conspicuous level purports to affirm white superiority. Studying the narrative and imaginative structures of *Pym*, this chapter proposes that a marginalized level of the text deconstructs its foregrounded racialist epistemology. (As a side note, I briefly consider the poststructuralist playground that this text now provides, and I question the political implications of discovering "indeterminacy" in Poe's attitudes towards race). Next, chapter 6 turns to Herman Melville's "Benito Cereno," demonstrating that the text provides an incisive analysis of the ideological and dominative underpinnings of racism. "Benito Cereno"— like *Pym*, and even more explicitly—undermines the real value of racial certainty (or racialism). But its radical potential is abbreviated by a kind of imaginative paralysis that stands in helpless horror at the effects of domination and violence, and can neither voice nor envision an escape from the literally vicious cycle.

Finally, the conclusion summarizes my theoretical concerns by considering Harriet Ann Jacobs's *Incidents in the Life of a Slave Girl*. I posit this text as a counterpoint to "Benito Cereno" and to the other texts considered. Of all the texts in the study, *Incidents* offers the most radical challenge to the cultural dialogue on "race," and presents the most incisive analysis of how *variously* "race" can intersect with power. It reconfigures the sympathetic model to provide a way of honoring and validating differences of experience and perspective between "whites" and "blacks." It offers this reformulation of sympathy to challenge its readers by presenting a better means of achieving an end to slavery and racial prejudice. But at the same time it registers a prediction of the ways in which its message might be ignored or misappropriated by its "white" audience.

Throughout, my interest in these texts is unified by what Nancy Armstrong and Leonard Tennenhouse have termed the "violence of representation" that occurs in texts about race, the oppressive reduction of the apparently infinite diversities among humans to an oppositional binary, always hierarchically figured. My most basic point is that while the *word* is black and white, people most certainly are not. There is, I would argue, an essential violence embedded in the very concept of "race"; and I use "essential" in both its senses, elemental and necessary. The ideological figuration of "race" is structurally violent in its reductiveness, denying the perceptual evidence of multitudes of colorations among "whites," "blacks," and "reds" for the continuance of its own cultural agenda. At the same time, the notion of "race" is necessary for a certain kind of violence, established and promulgated to justify the domination of one group of human beings over another.

In my analysis, however, I try to avoid forcing these diverse texts into a preconceived thesis. I am more interested in their differences than their similarities. The most general conclusion I will cautiously put forward is this: Power is seductive, and the power that "whites" have staked in marking others "black" or "red" often subverts their best intentions to give it up. Yet on the other hand, as Foucault has insisted and I try to highlight, it is wrong to see power as only oppressive.[7] It can be productive and progressive—both by the intentions of those who exercise it, and unintentionally, in the gaps left by its constant failure to create a total, seamless system. We can see evidences of both kinds of productivity in the texts I present in this study, and so they remind us that there is something both to hope for *and* to work for, always self-critically.

I have been conscious throughout of Houston Baker's impatience with "white" theorists who engage in guilty and self-indulgent confessionals on the subject of racism and narcissistically ignore what he terms the "native" sound. Part of what I hope to establish here is the importance—recognized explicitly in *Hope Leslie* and *Romance of the Republic* and ironically suggested by Babo's silence in "Benito Cereno"—of listening to the voice of that oppressed Other. Yet, on the other hand, "whites" in the United States historically have been extraordinarily good at *not* looking inward. Race is something that has always belonged to "them." "We" have always been absolved of looking to ourselves in this matter, which is precisely the challenge Morrison offered to her Princeton audience. Another aspect of my study tries to suggest the need for vigilant and constant self-scrutiny in this regard, something that "we" need to do before we can be honest about our motives, and more authentically humble about our position.[8] Such self-scrutiny seems to me a prerequisite for listening to those whom "we" have constituted as "Other," and is precisely the lesson that *Incidents in the Life of A Slave Girl* suggests "whites" might productively learn.

To this end, I urge my reader to think about the relevance of my readings to our own particular moment. As Cary Nelson has recently observed:

> [I]f writing literary history necessitates enacting our own historical moment it also offers the possibility of coming to know more of our place in history. . . . To argue that such knowledge—provisional knowledge of our own time—is either trivial or contaminating, preferably to be rejected in favor of some more permanent truth, is, curiously, to deny any significance to our own historical moment or to our lives within it. (10)

I began this project out of concern over contemporary racism; I constructed this study to see how race in the United States had been narrativized and strategized in the past. I was alternately surprised and dismayed, encouraged and challenged by what I found. I discovered that while I critically deconstructed the texts I studied, I was also instructed by them. The recognition that undergirds Lydia Maria Child's *Romance of the Republic* similarly charges my study: all "whites" (myself included) benefit from institutionalized racism in the United States, and this means that all "whites" (myself included) must take responsibility for the effects *and* the elimination of racism. As an Anglo-American, an academic, an educator, I realize that there is no vantage from which I can speak or know or act outside of the "contamination" of power. Aldon Nielsen rightly observes that "the signifier of whiteness continues to rewrite itself as a discourse into our institutions, including our literature, and we, as racial subject, continue to read it, to recognize it, to privilege it, and to enjoy its power" (5). We should accept that neither our guilt nor good intentions will free us from this fact. Just as we now can understand how Child's optimistic program of white benevolence toward blacks, through supervision and education, did not replace but simply underwrote racial hierarchy in a different way, we must be willing to turn the analysis against ourselves. As Armstrong and Tennenhouse put it, we are variously "condemned to power" (26) and so the challenge is to understand as critically as possible how that is so, and how we can position ourselves in relation to that power in order to work for social justice. Ultimately I hope with Nielsen that "reading 'race'" can be a relevant and productive critical activity, an activity that could allow Anglo-Americans to rethink their stance in relation to "race" and "whiteness" *now*. I can't think of any other reason to proceed, professionally or personally.

Baton Rouge, La.   D.D.N.
October, 1990

Acknowledgements

I've learned a good deal while writing this book. After the years of work, I'm certain of one thing: you don't complete a project like this by yourself. I am indebted to many individuals for their support—financial, scholarly, and personal. Thanking all these wonderful people seems the best preface to the book.

Louisiana State University's College of Arts and Sciences provided me with a generous summer fellowship to facilitate my revision of the manuscript. Members of my department, particularly the chair, John R. May, and the graduate chair, Jim S. Borck, were unstinting in their encouragement and last-minute help. Many of my colleagues at LSU helped me work through ideas in this book at various stages. In this regard, I would particularly like to thank Emily Toth, Bainard Cowan, John Lowe, Frank de Caro, and Rosan Jordan. Thanks to Richard Moore for his careful research assistance and to Susan Kohler for her endless patience and limitless expertise.

For their insightful reading and comments on sections of the manuscript I thank Veronica Makowsky, Michelle Massé, Elsie Michie, J. Gerald Kennedy, Nancy Bentley, Shirley Samuels, and Lora Romero. Carolyn Karcher offered encouragement and shared scholarship in a way that inspired me. I am especially grateful to Wai-Chee Dimock, who gave my manuscript the kind of attention that every writer dreams of and offered criticism that enriched my approach and, I hope, my book. Thanks also to Roberta Waddel, of The New York Public Library, for her help in finding jacket illustrations.

From the "deep history" of this manuscript, I would like to thank Arnold E. Davidson and Linda Wagner-Martin. They have been good friends and mentors, and I hope my career is a tribute to them.

I am grateful for William Sisler's initial support of my project. While it is disconcerting to "lose" an editor in midstream, I couldn't have dreamt up a better replacement than Liz Maguire, whom I admire as a professional and enjoy as a friend.

I have friends to thank for putting up with my whining and worrying, friends who called and wrote to distract and soothe me and to share their lives with me, particularly Marcy Bauman, Nadine Romero, and Rafia Zafar. Somehow saying thank you doesn't seem a gesture equivalent to the energy they've offered, but there it is. And heartfelt thanks to the modest friend who pushed me through the last months of revisions when the going was tough for many reasons.

Thanks to my family, which has believed in me and let me know it: Edith Moore Nelson, Katherine Louise Ewin, Delana and Jim Nelson, Julie, and especially Jim. John Salvino has stood behind this project and beside me all the years I have worked on it, from the first spark of excitement to the last heave of exhaustion. I owe him quite a bit, gratitude for his support here being among the least — and the best.

Finally, I want to thank Cathy N. Davidson. My debts to her are of the deepest sort, and my words here seem inadequate for the task. She has read versions of this manuscript early and late, and her numerous critiques taught me my most important lessons about writing. Annette Kolodny once outlined an ideal mentor in a National Women's Studies Association session, a model Cathy surpassed. Her guidance has led me from student to professional; her example has inspired me to be both a better scholar and a better person.

Contents

THE WORD IN
BLACK AND WHITE

They have often asked mee, why we call them Indians Natives &c. And understanding the reason, they will call themselues Indians, in opposition to English, &c.
Roger Williams, *A Key into the Language of America*, 1643

So at this day, they are named Negroes, as them, whome no men are blacker.
George Abbot, 1599

1

An Uncommon Need: "Race" in Early American Literature

The Function of Colonial Literature

Narrative, as a process of representation, provides a powerful tool for conceptualization. As Thomas Leitch notes, "stories imitate a world of potential, of coming-to-be" (16), and nowhere more than in the discovery of the "New" World did the role of story as "coming-to-be" operate formatively. Well before Europeans set sail for the newly discovered worlds, they were reading, hearing, and telling about what they would find. And even when what they found —as in Columbus's case—baffled their expectation, inevitably, as Tzvetan Todorov points out, they fit it into familiar representative modes. Native Americans became "Indians," the unknown brought in line with the known. In this way, Columbus's early accounts of "Cyclops and mermaids, [of] Amazons and men with tails," do not reflect observed phenomena, but rather Columbus's "finalist strategy of interpretation," the conclusions he formed *before* beginning his travels (*Conquest*, 15). Todorov underscores the importance of prior conceptualization to interpretation and representation: "In the course of the third voyage, Columbus wonders about the origin of the pearls the Indians sometimes bring him. The thing occurs before his eyes; but what he reports in his journal is the explanation given by Pliny," that oysters grow on trees by the shore and pearls result from the falling dew (*Conquest*, 17).[1]

Like Columbus, the English colonists who contemplated a voyage to the New World over a hundred years later sought the comfort of previous knowledge to shape their expectations of their future destiny, to tell their "coming-to-be" narrative of life in America. Significantly, as Mary Louise Pratt observes, promotionalist frontier literature operates as a "normalizing force" which "serves, in part, to mediate the shock of contact on the frontier" (121). Facing the unfamiliar, colonial literature gained a measure of control by relying on the familiar to explain it. Promotional tracts served in this way a normative function, offering the writer a sense of mastery and authorship over

3

the often as yet unseen New World, and modeling for the reader/explorer methods for gaining control of an alien environment. Colonial literature both offered strategies and served as a strategy for dealing with life in the New World.

British promotionalists grounded their exploration narratives in two inter-locking discourses, religious mission and capital accumulation. The twin goals functioned symbiotically, one justifying and supporting the other. We can see this dual enterprise in narratives about the New World that preceded actual voyage. For instance, as John Cotton elaborates in his "God's Promise to His Plantations":

> Some remove and travail for merchandise and gain-sake: *Daily bread may be sought from far*, Proverbs 31:14. Yea our Savior approveth travail for merchants. . . . The comparison from the unjust steward, and from the thief in the night is not taken from the injustice of the one, or the theft of the other; but from the wisdom of one and the suddenness of the other; which in themselves are not unlawful. (8)

Cotton conflates religious and economic discourse, referring to the familiar (biblical) to elaborate a code of action for the unfamiliar (frontier). It is strik-ing, too, that his ethical code tantalizingly offers material gain, justifying actions that his own account suggests might be *un*ethical ("unjust . . . thief") with an obfuscating cloak of biblical rhetoric.[2]

As "God's Promise" highlights, religious mission provided a certain security and justification to the colonists. As they took, promotionalists reasoned, they would also give: "We shall come in with the good leave of the natives," speculated John Winthrop of his future neighbors, "who finde benefitt already by our neighborhood and learne of us to improve part to more use then before they could doe the whole, and by this meanes we come in by valuable pur-chase: for they have of us that which we will yield them more benefitt then all the land which wee have of them" (1629, 423). Despite its apparent promise of reciprocal profit, Winthrop's tract nonetheless registers a more unilateral "purchase." The native inhabitants of America may gain by their social trans-action with the Puritans. But, conversely, the pecuniary imagery alongside the apologetic reason for the tract itself traces the much greater commodity value of the "purchase" for the Puritans.

Promotionalists recognized the importance of America's original inhabit-ants to the colony's spiritual and financial success. Yet even though Native Americans stood in a positive relation to the former, they presented a signifi-cant barrier to the latter. Consequently, as Robert Berkhofer has detailed, promotional discourse constructed a bifurcated Indian, at once "tractable" and "trecherous" (see esp. 27–28). John Smith's *A True Relation* documents the typically split stance of the colonists toward the native inhabitants of America. In the space of two paragraphs at the opening of his narrative, Smith portrays the local natives as vigilant and ruthless attackers and, conversely, as generous and attentive followers (see pp. 5–6, paras. 3 and 4). Similarly, though Winthrop portrays the natives of New England as willing neighbors in his promotional pamphlet, the suggestion he obliquely offers in his "Model of Christian Charity," the famous sermonic exhortation delivered on the *Arbella*, contrasts sharply with his earlier message. On the ship Winthrop speaks of enemies first as those to be loved according to the dictates of the Old and New Testaments, as well as by nature: "The law of nature could give no rules for dealing with enemies, for all are to be considered as friends in the state of innocency, but the Gospel commands to love an enemy" (1630, 9). If the laws of nature do not clearly dictate ethics toward enemies, the New Testament does, Winthrop underscores, employing the more anaesthetized connotations of "enemy" as "stranger." Yet later, as he reaches a high emotional pitch in his sermon, he uses "enemy" in its most violently oppositional sense, apparently discarding his New Testament references and promising his listeners in the sonorous tones of the Old Testament that "we shall find that the God of Israel is among us, when ten of us shall be able to resist a thousand of our enemies" (20). His final message to his auditors is a mixed testament: enemies are at once to be loved and resisted.

It is difficult to be precisely sure of how Winthrop intended his comments. Certainly they are generally appropriate to the dual stance the Puritans maintained toward Native Americans, as an object for conversion, read through New Testament imperatives to "love thine enemy," and as an object for annihilation, read through Old Testament precedent of righteous vengeance. It is more likely, in this specific reference, however, that Winthrop is referring obliquely to two specific sets of enemies. The friendlier version of "enemy" arguably pertains to fellow colonists. The latter use of "enemy" is apparently intended with reference to those outside the colonial community, and as such dictates a stance toward the enemies "out there," establishing thereby a certain boundary between Self and Other. While it might be argued that Winthrop's latter use of "enemy" refers to non-Puritan, *British* antagonists, we can also recall that the Massachusetts Bay mission did not proceed—overtly at least—under the same antagonistic circumstances as did the Plymouth Company. Winthrop may have been referring, then, to British enemies, but his words also provided a strategy, a standpoint toward Others most immediately present to the new colonists—those "tractable" natives. As Winthrop's famous sermon suggests, the sense of religious destiny that the Puritan colonist created for himself placed him in direct and violent opposition to anyone who interfered with his mission—religious or economic. Although the natives became the focus of the Puritans' religious errand to the New World (enemies to be loved), they also became an important obstacle, one that rightly had to be overpowered to make way for the New Canaan.

The fictional contact between colonists and native inhabitants which occurred in promotional and frontier literature shaped the expectations of voyagers to the point that actual contact, however much it contradicted the promotional tracts, managed only to confirm their speculations. A member of Christopher Newport's expedition up the James River in 1607 reported in "A Breif [*sic*] description of the People": the Indians "are naturally given to trechery, howbeit we could not find it in our travell up the river, but rather a most kind and loving people" (qtd. in Nash, "Image," 44). Like Columbus's obstinate refusal to see the real source of pearls, American explorers and colonists refused to see anything but the Indian they had fictively created in advance of contact with him.[3] Thus the natives' friendliest gestures could be represented only as evidence of their devious (non-English) nature.

Alongside its justificatory purposes, promotional literature sought to fix a concept of the Self in relation to the peoples already inhabiting the discovered world. Perhaps influenced by the earlier stories of Spain's conquest and geno- cide, afraid for their own survival in the colonies, and concerned with the maintenance of an English sense of self in an unfamiliar, un-English environ- ment, English colonists seized on the difference of the natives in order to establish firmly their positional superiority.[4] This position of superiority promulgated in the literature at once justified their presence, predicted their success and confirmed their English identity. So in 1620 Thomas Peyton could confidently represent the Englishman's relative status in the colonies:

> The Libian dusky in his parched skin,
> The Moor all tawny both without and in,
> The Southern man, a black deformed Elfe,
> The Northern white like unto God himselfe.
>   qtd. in Vaughan, "White Man," 920

The strategies of interpretation and representation that the English colo- nialists brought to bear on relations with Native Americans in many ways duplicated those employed to justify growing involvement in slave trade. At the same time that Plymouth colony was established, the first Africans were landing in Jamestown, to work as servants and slaves.[5] Although actual poli- cies toward natives and Africans varied widely—one race was to be assimilated and, failing that, exterminated, the other separated and cultivated—they could be explained in similar terms. Like Indians, Africans were depicted as lacking in culture and religion, and the English formulated their exploitation as a humane enterprise, offering Africans a chance at figurative, if not literal, enlightenment.

The evolution of the concept of "race," of Indianness and Blackness, in Anglo-colonial usage is instructive. Racialism did not emerge in full flower until the mid-nineteenth century; indeed, as many carefully note, early Euro- pean representations of Native Americans had much more to do with cultural, rather than so-called racial, differences. Textual and artistic representations from the period of early contact reflect much more interest in personal orna- mentation and social organization than a physiognomy.[6] Although European representations of Africans had virtually always drawn attention to the dark- ness of African skin, which increasingly carried a host of negative connotations in European thought, still, early observers depicted African darkness as some- thing of a marvel, even accepting the fact that the Africans themselves found their so-called blackness beautiful.[7] In European speculations that the hotter sun, or red-colored oils were the cause for differences in skin color, is a search for commonality—even if that commonality is the ethnocentric assumption that "we all start out white." "Black" and "red" at this early juncture desig-nated a superficial, metaphoric difference between groups of human beings.

Somewhere, though, that emphasis on commonality changed. Michel Fou-cault has argued for a crucial epistemological shift in Europe during the seven-teenth century, from a study of similitude and resemblance to a study of difference and identity:

> During the period that has been termed . . . the Baroque, thought ceases to move in the element of resemblance. Similitude is no longer the form of knowledge, but rather the occasion of error, the danger to which one expuses oneself when one does not examine the obscure region of confusions. . . . The activity of the mind . . . will therefore no longer consist in drawing things together, in setting out on a quest for everything that might reveal some sort of kinship, attraction, or secretly shared nature within them, but, on the contrary, in discriminating, that is, in establishing their identities, then the inevitability of the connections with all the successive degrees of a series. (*Order*, 51, 55)

This epistemological rupture affected the evolving conception of "race" in the British colonies. During the mid-seventeenth century, representations of both African and Native Americans began a shift from theories of cultural and climate-imposed physiological difference, grounded in assumptions of original commonality, to speculations about profound and ineradicable racial differ-ence that derived not from climate, but from the moral condition of Indians and Africans, thereby creating a focus on fundamental difference in identities, histories, and futures.[8]

During this period in the American colonies the tobacco enterprise began to boom; southern colonists needed more land and a fixed supply of labor to work it. It is not coincidental that in the frontier and colonial literature of this period, the Indian becomes *instinctively* hostile, and the African begins to seem *metaphysically* black. The European thus created a sense of religious justification for definitive and harsh action. Winthrop Jordan establishes that a new usage of the term "white" arose as the Europeans began to see them-selves in exact opposition to the "black" slave, now defined not by social status, but by moral condition (95). Alden Vaughan convincingly demon-strates a similar lexical shift in the use of "red" and "tawny" as adjectives *describing* the native to nouns that *define* the Indian during that period.[9] Thus, colonial literature at once reflects the changing attitudes toward Indians and Africans at the same time it provides a means for inscribing—making possible and permanent—that mark of difference.[10]

Superiority Story

As many scholars have observed, race relations in the New World were influ-enced by many factors, and can be fruitfully, if not conclusively, viewed from legalistic, economic, philosophic, sociologic, and scientific perspectives.[11] All these perspectives combine in colonial American and U.S. history in telling what would become the Ur-narrative of white racial superiority. As Reginald Horsman explains in his weighty study *Race and Manifest Destiny*, these attitudes would reach their fruition in the mid-nineteenth century. But an important model for the story formed in the scientific revolution of the middle Renaissance.

In 1543 Copernicus published *Of Celestial Motions*. This work upset the cosmography that showed man as the focus of the beautifully orchestrated, crystalline spheres. Until Copernicus, astronomy had worked together with theology in establishing man as the physical and moral center of the universe. Dissatisfied with the inconsistencies of the Ptolemaic system and the elaborate compensations that it forced on astronomers, Copernicus devised a new interpretation of the skies which upset every supposition of heavenly hierarchies, moving Intelligences and divine schemes to date. Placing the stars at a distance beyond imagination, Copernicus implied without explicitly positing an infinite universe (Giordano Bruno was soon to burn at the stake for pursuing the logical implications of this concept). Conceivably, Copernicus's alternate map was the overturning of the way Europeans represented Man's place in relation to the World, the Heavens and God. This was perhaps the most radical and devastating effect of all.

But Europeans were *not* devastated by Copernicus's theory. In pointing out the fundamental conservatism at the heart of Copernicus's motivations and discoveries, Herbert Butterfield emphasizes that "it would be wrong to imagine that the publication of Copernicus's great work in 1543 either shook the foundation of European thought straight away or sufficed to accomplish anything like a revolution" (67).[12] Copernicus himself, Butterfield notes, relied more for his revision on Ptolemy's *representation* of the heavens than on his own *observation* of the skies in devising his own system, which was actually only a "modified form of the Ptolemaic system" (36–39; Butterfield's emphasis).[13] Hampered in his theorizing by reluctance to abandon what he had learned to be "true" of the Ptolemaic/Aristotelian universe, the revolutionary astronomer failed, along with others, to pursue the most radical implications of his heliocentric theory. Nearly three quarters of a century passed before Kepler was able to add his mathematical genius to the chaos of interpretations and data, devising a more advanced theory for a heliocentric universe.

Even after Kepler, the Ptolemaic system maintained currency among the Europeans. Well over a century after *Of Celestial Motions*, it was possible for Milton's *Paradise Lost* to depict a geocentric universe, and mention heliocentricity only in passing.[14] More than a substitution of maps, the heliocentric universe required a literal revolution in thought before it could gain acceptance, which, opposed to the ornate and satisfying aesthetics of the crystalline schemes, was especially difficult to achieve. All of history had been devoted to placing Man at the center of God's creation. Suddenly, European Man was to understand that he was not the nucleus, and was required to search for other means of self-definition.

Kepler's insight and Galileo's work became more widely recognized early in the 1600s, an age known, perhaps not coincidentally, for its "Jacobean melancholy." Renaissance man reluctantly set about redefining his place in the new order. In a process of thought parallel to that which had attached epicycles and eccentric circles to compensate for the inconsistencies of the Ptolemaic system, Europeans began working to reconcile heliocentricity with their desire to be the focus of existence. It was an age of caution: radical theorists like Bruno and Galileo met opposition and persecution. Although geocentricity was abandoned, it was eventually replaced by the Great Chain of Being.[15] Seventeenth-century philosophers reassembled forces and turned their confusion into an ode to the complexity of the world, which God had created for their use and glory.[16] The eighteenth-century Enlightenment kept Man rationally and squarely at the top rung of the ladder, and the story of (European) man's hierarchical superiority became "common sense."[17]

It is this constructed notion of superiority that was crucial to the way in which the European perceived himself, and his role in this world. It is this attitude that brought him to the "new" world, seeking to inscribe physically and textually his mastery over the globe he claimed in his story of superiority. As V. Y. Mudimbe argues, colonialism becomes the project of scientific authority and "can be thought of as a duplication and fulfillment of the power of Western discourse on human varieties" (16).[18]

The foundation of the superiority story was a pervasive conservatism that revolved, as Mudimbe further observes, on two "main and complementary paradigms . . . the inherent superiority of the white race, and . . . the necessity for European economies and structures to expand into the 'virgin areas' of the world" (17). European action and representation sought new frontiers to confirm and assert the old—the same superior sense of Self. But their enterprise on all fronts was always threatened by a sense of change, a sense of difference from their own constructed identity. As Pratt succinctly summarizes, "nowhere are the notions of normal, familiar action and given systems of difference in greater jeopardy than on the [colonial] frontier. There, Europeans confront not only unfamiliar Others, but unfamiliar selves" (121). Karen Kupperman comments on the more specific challenge to social order that the colonial enterprise presented: "Not only did the colonial effort raise questions about the relevance of traditional skills, particularly those of a 'better sort,' it also appeared to offer a chance for new individuals and groups within English society to rise" (151). The high ratio of "gentlemen" to common workingmen in the Jamestown settlement marks top-level concern for the continuance of the social order.[19] All the colonies instituted policies to punish individuals who threatened governmental stability: commoners who spoke out against those of higher class were often punished (154). Despite strict sanctions, there were numerous threats. Nash notes the "frightening rapidity" of challenges to hierarchy issued by "Mortonites, Gortonites, Hutchisonians . . . and Quakers," all rapidly taken up and defeated with little damage to existing communal paradigms" (Great Fear, 6).

While French and Spanish colonists adopted social policies of assimilation, English settlers in America worked quickly to duplicate traditional family arrangements. Colonial authorities shipped in boat loads of British women for the frontiersmen to marry, hoping to lend stability by establishing familiar social patterns. Seeking to ground themselves in a sense of permanence and custom, the colonists were particularly disconcerted by the transitory habits of the natives, who were apt to abandon camp, disappear, and reappear with little warning. As Axtell sums up, "surprise was the last thing the English wanted in the New World" (138).

Some early writers, however, found much to admire in the social arrangements of the natives. Alarmed by the growing trends of mercantilism and commerce, these writers turned to native life as model. Thomas Morton, one of the earliest to laud the Indian way, established the general pattern that would culminate in the cult of the noble savage:

> In the yeare since the incarnation of Christ, 1622, it was my chance to be landed in the parts of New England, where I found two sortes of people, the one Christians, the other Infidels; these I found most full of humanity, and more friendly then the other. . . . I have observed they will not be troubled with superfluous commodities. Such things as they finde they are taught by necessity to make us of, they will make choise of, and seeke to purchase with industry. So that, in respect that their life is so voyd of care, and they are so loving also that they make use of those things they enjoy, (the wife onely excepted), as common goods, and are therein so compassionate that, rather than one should starve through want, they would starve all. Thus doe they passe awaye the time merrily, not regarding our pompe, (which they see dayly before their faces,) but are better content with their owne, which some men esteeme so meanely of. (123, 178)

Thomas Morton was no friend to the authorities of Plymouth Bay, and it should be noted that his account was concerned primarily with provoking and contradicting his Puritan enemies. Yet as Richard Drinnon convincingly argues, it was Morton's very respect for native customs that initially triggered his prosecution by the Puritans. Morton's *New English Canaan*, Drinnon says, "represented an authentic and almost singular effort of the European imagination to extract a sense of place from these new surroundings or, better, to meet the spirit of the land halfway. . . . Like the Indians, [Morton] loved the wilderness the Saints hated" (*Facing West*, 17). Thomas Morton's respect for the "Infidels" was real and profound.

But even such obvious admiration needs to be seen in context. If the "cult of the noble savage" was different in sentiment from the "cult of the ignorant savage," it was not so different in its final vision. Despite the various exhortations to the virtues of savage life, it was clear that Morton and later writers of the "cult of the savage" never intended to model their society on that of the natives. What these tracts harked back to was the Rousseauistic "presocial" state, a state precisely from which European society was perceived as having descended. The reforms suggested were not a matter of adopting native social patterns, but recapturing desireable traits that the English had previously exhibited (see Kupperman, 147–48). This backward-yearning was less a radical than a fundamentally conservative gesture.

If colonists' attitudes toward natives were governed in part by a profound need to maintain traditional social order, so too, argues Edmund Morgan, were their attitudes toward slavery. The practice came into currency as a recourse to the flood of poor indentured servants sent by England who increasingly threatened the social order (i.e., the supremacy of the landed class). Recounting the struggle of the landed class to deal with a growing populace of "freedmen" (ex-bondsmen who were "without house and land"), Morgan suggests that the best available remedy was to stem the influx of English lower-class servants by relying instead on black slavery ("Slavery and Freedom," 20).

While most Africans were shipped to America as slaves in the early years of the colonies, "it is equally clear that a substantial number of Virginia's Negroes were free or became free," says Morgan (see esp. 17–18). Freed blacks redoubled the number of indentured English servants who had finished their term, and together presented a mounting problem for the ruling class. The landed gentry needed a steady supply of labor to work their land, yet their social position was threatened by this growing number of freedmen, African and British who without land or property were becoming increasingly restive. One solution was to put those without property back into forced labor. The landed class realized, however, that "to have attempted the enslavement of English-born laborers would have caused more disorder than it cured." The "common-sense" path, then, was to "keep as slaves black men who arrived in that condition," instead of granting them the "natural" rights of the English-men. Thus, argues Morgan, Virginia's magnates arrived at a "solution which strengthened the rights of Englishmen and nourished that attachment to liberty which came to fruition in the Revolutionary generation of Virginia statesmen. . . . The rights of the English were preserved by destroying the rights of Africans" ("Slavery and Freedom," 25, 24).[20]

Morgan's argument does highlight how the fundamentally protective worldview of the English colonialist planted the seeds of liberal reform and democracy, but it does not adequately account for why the English, who heretofore had treated Africans as indentured servants, found them especially available for this new, racial category of lifetime slavery.[21] Morgan insists that slavery grew as a result of economic necessity, not of racial persecution: "Winthrop Jordan has suggested that slavery came to Virginia as an unthinking decision. We might go further and say that it came without a decision. It came automatically as Virginians bought the cheapest labor they could get" ("Slavery and Freedom," 24–25). In support of this argument, Morgan points to the Virginians' liberal treatment of African slaves during the early years of colonization, when freed blacks were allowed to take a place in the community at a social and legal level apparently on par with that of freed white men.

The point to be made in response to Morgan's thesis is that something made the Africans *conceptually* available as a solution for economic necessity. Morgan's point that it was a recourse to "common sense" to "keep as slaves black men who arrived in that condition" overlooks the ideological machinations that *made* it "common sense" to enslave African men *and* women. Economic interest coincided with psychological need and social position; the seeds of racism made the economic solution of racial slavery "sensible." If, as Morgan argues, Africans were treated more liberally during the early colonial period, they were, as Morgan is himself careful to observe, never regarded as potential equals—certainly not to the aristocracy, and never consistently to the lower classes, as we know from more punitive legal sentences and indenture terms. Morgan's conclusion that economic pressure, not racism, led to development of a slave institution cannot account for the fact that the "white" oppressors in the mid-1600s began to count "black" Africans not as human objects, but as exchange objects, which is precisely what made them conceptually available as slaves. It may be quite true that economic possibilities and social demands gave impetus to racial persecution and enslavement. But it was a cultivated and deep-seated sense of European (*cum* "white") superiority that suggested African slavery as a "natural" solution to Anglo/English economic woes.

As this discussion has suggested, the genesis of racial discrimination rose out of both psychological and economic factors, the two complexly intertwined. Anglo attitudes toward the racial Other were defined by a need for superiority at once physical and metaphysical. Two texts, John Underhill's *Newes from America* and sections XIV and XVIII of Thomas Jefferson's *Notes on the State of Virginia* foreground alternately material and psychological motivations of Othering. Both serve as "frontier literature" in a colonialist setting in that each operates in differing ways to codify racial borders. Each offers insight into the process of Othering that we will see in subsequent Anglo-American texts.

Mercy Did They Deserve for Their Valor

John Underhill's promotional pamphlet *Newes from America* is an extraordinary historical document that seldom receives attention by literary critics. At once an account of the Pequot War, and a promotion of the scenic Connecticut countryside, *Newes from America* emerges as textualized violence and appropriation, much as the Pequot War itself emerged materially. The two levels of Underhill's text, like the war, operate synergistically: the need to vanquish antagonistic natives ostensibly for self-protection, and admiration for the geography of the Connecticut valley that the Pequots inhabit.

Francis Jennings argues that the Puritan concern with the Pequots was not one of self-defense but solely economic and proprietary. Jennings traces in detail how the burgeoning Connecticut settlement was looking for a chance to commandeer land that the Pequots refused to relinquish (see 207–27). In fact, Underhill's account foregrounds the colonialists' direct interest in the land. He begins his text:

> I shall not spend time (for my other occasions will not permit) to write largely of every particular, but shall, as briefly as I may, perform these two things; first, give a true narration of the warlike proceedings that hath been in New England these two years last past; secondly I shall discover to the reader divers places in New

England, that will afford special accommodations to such persons as will plant upon them. (49)

According to the explicit plan for Underhill's narration, these two diverse accounts will be "interw[oven] . . . in the following discourse." Inseparable issues in the colonialist mind, the account of a brutal massacre and promotion of the paradisiacal setting for English colonists dovetail for Underhill.[22]

The captain details how, on their way to the village Mystic, the "few feeble instruments, soldiers not accustomed to war" systematically "burn . . . and spoil" the very land that he invites, in the next breath, his brethren Englishmen to settle (54). "The truth is," asserts Underhill, "I want time to set forth the excellence of the whole country; but if you would know the garden of New England, then you must glance your eye upon Hudson's river, a place exceeding all yet named" (64). Proceeding to chronicle the various locations that would afford abundant accommodation, he reluctantly concludes:

> In regard of many aspersions hath been cast upon all the country, that it is a hard and difficult place for to subsist in, and that the soil is barren, and bears little that is good, and that it can hardly receive more people than those that are there, I will presume to make a second digression from the former matter, to the end I might encourage such as desire to plant there.
>
> There are certain plantations, Dedham, Concord, in the Mathethusis Bay, that are newly erected, that do afford large accommodation, and will contain abundance of people. (65–66)

Pointedly, the Connecticut colony, a paradise depleted of Pequots, is now ready for settlement.

The vigor with which Underhill promotes "the garden of New England" ironically traces the real aggressor in the Pequot War. Ann Kibbey explains in her excellent study of Puritan rhetorical practice and its consequence for their actual policies and governance, that "despite the Puritan claim of self-defense, the evidence strongly implies that the Pequots, far more than the Puritans, acted in self-defense. Even the governor of Plymouth colony observed at the time . . . that the Puritans had "occasioned a war, etc., by provoking the Pequods" (100).[23] One of the charges made against the Pequots by the Puritans was against their murder of two traders, John Stone and John Oldham. But as the Puritans clearly knew according to their own records, Niantics had killed Stone, Narragansetts, Oldham (see Jennings, 202–27).[24]

The events leading up to the "war," as well as the British colonial restructuring of that war in colonial texts highlights the ruthless quality of identity politics and "race" in early America. The war that ensued against the Pequots to "avenge" Stone and Oldham's deaths was characterized, Kibbey asserts, by the "frequent refusal of Puritan men to distinguish among 'Indians,' combined with their declared intent to exterminate the Pequots" (101). Underhill's text highlights the strategic nature of such confusion. In his account of Oldham's death, where it is important to blur tribal boundaries in order to pin the blame on the Pequots, Underhill refers only to "Block Islanders," and "Indians." Yet he seems perfectly comfortable elsewhere in the text distinguishing between the various groups, for instance when he relates his dispassionate observation of "Pequeats, Narragansets and Mohigeners changing a few arrows together" after the Puritans have completed their slaughter at Mystic (82).

And with no apparent sense of incongruity, Underhill recounts an Indian ambassador's explanation of Stone's murder. In a fairly common ploy, Dutch traders had taken a sachem hostage for a wampum ransom; upon payment the Dutch had returned the sachem—dead. When Stone—banished for piracy from Plymouth on pain of death—shortly thereafter sailed up the same river, the natives took their revenge on him and his crew. The Pequot ambassador pleads to the Puritan soldiers, "Could ye blame us for revenging so cruel a murder? for we distinguish not between the Dutch and English, but took them to be one nation, and therefore we do not conceive that we wronged you, for they slew our king" (58). Either the Pequot ambassador or Underhill apparently fails to recount a crucial aspect of Stone's death: these "murderous" Niantics gained passage to Stone's ship only because *he*, *too*, plotted to hold the Niantics for wampum ransom (see Jennings, 189–90). To the ambassador's plea, the Puritans replied that the Pequots "were able to distinguish between the Dutch and English, having had sufficient experience of both nations" (Underhill, 58). Sufficient experience, indeed.[25]

Newes from America makes surprisingly little effort to document the "official" reasons for the war: Pequot savagery. Instead, Underhill so much assumes the positional superiority of the white as ultimate justification for their actions, that the Indians he depicts are ineffectual buffoons and laughingstocks. Underhill indeed seems very intent on proving the superior potency of the Puritans: they aim to kill, whereas the impotent Indians resort to ridiculous warring practices, hiding among the trees rather than coming out to fight like men. Ironically, it is an Indian interpreter voyaging with the Puritans who offers the most pointed example of English virility. Dressed in English clothes, and supplied with an English weapon, this Anglicized Indian provides a "pretty passage worthy observation." When one of the Pequots questions him, "What are you, an Indian or an Englishman?" the Indian translator replies, "Come hither, and I will tell you," and as Underhill recounts: "He pulls up his cock and let fly at one of them, and without question was the death of him" (54).

By contrast, in his scoffing reflection on Indian warfare practice Underhill asserts,

> I boldly affirm they might fight seven years and not kill seven men. They came not near one another, but shot remote, and not point-blank, as we often do with our bullets, but at rovers, and then they gase up in the sky to see where the arrow falls, and not until it is fallen do they shoot again. This fight is more for pastime, than to conquer and subdue enemies. (82)[26]

Yet he generously commends the warriors who are scorched to death defending their flaming village:

Many courageous fellows were unwilling to come out, and fought most desperately through the palisadoes, so as they were scorched and burnt with the flame, and were deprived of their arms—in regard the fire burnt their very bowstrings—and so perished valiantly. Mercy did they deserve for their valor, could we have had but opportunity to have bestowed it. (80)

The Puritans, on the other hand, exercise consistent physical and spiritual superiority, which accumulates in Underhill's *Newes from America* as textual authority. Underhill describes the admiration of the horrified Narragansetts: "Our Indians came to us, and much rejoiced at our victories, and greatly, admired the manner of Englishmen's fight, but cried Mach it, mach it; that is, It is naught, it is naught, because it is too furious, and slays too many men" (84).

Catherine Belsey argues that "the work of ideology is to present the position of the subject as fixed and unchangeable, an element in a given system of differences which is human nature and the world of human experience, and to show possible action as an endless repetition of 'normal,' familiar action" (90). One of the important social functions of *Newes from America* is to normalize the action that might be contested as unjustified: the slaughter of four to six-hundred sleeping Pequots, most of whom were old people, women and children. Underhill dances around this by recounting the charges made against the Indians on behalf of Stone and Oldham; also, he alludes briefly to an abduction of two English girls by the Pequots. Only once does he explicitly confront the issue in an extended passage worth quoting in full:

Down fell men, women and children; those that scaped us, fell into the hands of the Indians that were in the rear of us. It is reported by themselves, that there were about four hundred souls in this fort, and not above five of them escaped out of our hands. Great and doleful was the bloody sight to the view of young soldiers that never had been in war, to see so many souls lie gasping on the ground, so thick, in some places, that you could hardly pass along. It may be demanded, Why should you be so furious? (as some have said). Should not Christians have more mercy and compassion? But I would refer you to David's war. When a people is grown to such a height of blood, and sin against God and man, and all confederates in the action, there he hath no respect to persons, but harrows them, and saws them, and puts them to the sword, and the most terriblest death that may be. Sometimes the Scripture declareth women and children must perish with their parents. Sometimes the case alters; but we will not dispute it now. We had sufficient light from the word of God for our proceedings. (81)

Like promotionalist texts written before passage of America, Underhill's text seeks confirmation in (strategically Old Testament) biblical precedent, thereby normalizing, or making "ordinary" what might alternately be read as extraordinarily brutal action.[27]

The Puritan's divine mission against the Pequots, like that of the angry Indian god portrayed by William Byrd a century later, was to "have blotted every living Soul of them out of the World" (Byrd, 292). After the massacre of the village inhabitants, the Puritans, out of ammunition, returned to their ships. The main body of Pequot warriors, who were camped some ten miles away preparing for battle, arrived just in time to be useless in defending their village, but to make themselves completely vulnerable to the reloaded Puritans. Two hundred surrendered, and were sold into slavery in the Indies. Others fled to join the Mohicans and Niantics. The Puritans returned home, appropriating Pequot land as they erased their name.[28] John Underhill's text not only reflects this, but actively and materially participates in the appropriation: as much as being an account of a war, *Newes from America* is a promotional tract, with Underhill as Indian breaker/land broker.

What *Newes from America* offers is at once containment (of savage Indians) and expansion (of possible action in available land). Precisely, it is description and prescription, telling of past action, and forecasting future acts. Kenneth Burke argues forcefully that literature is "equipment for living," that it functions socially as proverbs do in that it offers "*strategies* for dealing with *situations*" (*Philosophy*, 296; Burke's emphasis). Underhill's text (and literature in general as Burke argues), develops strategies as it establishes a perspective on its object (Pequots and their land). Such perspectives are not innocent but actively formational. As Frank Lentricchia pointedly observes, "to write is to know is to dominate" (*Social Change*, 146). Thus, *Newes from America* suggests an effective means of domination (Underhill in fact includes an illustrated mapping of the attack, depicting the relative positions of the village, its inhabitants, the Puritan soldiers and Narragansett reinforcements[29]) as it *enacts* a textual domination. The text thereby offers advice on controlling a situation, while at the same time providing (and mapping) a means of, as Burke would have it, "encompassment."

Underhill's text functioned most generally to validate the rightness of the Anglo-colonial mission, the centrality of the European's political role and physical place on the new continent. In this regard *Newes from America*, as we will see of *Notes on the State of Virginia*, is colonial literature par excellence, engaging as it does in the demarcation and normalization of what we might call the "right of white." Both texts inscribed the central role of the Anglo-Saxon Europeans in the world. Challenged by their encounters with new lands and new peoples, "white" Europeans worked to incorporate these phenomena into the story of Euro-centricity, writing their (white) right to dominate as they crossed the continent and circumnavigated the globe.

A Difference Fixed in Nature

One of the most pervasively influential considerations of slavery and Africans in American history is Thomas Jefferson's *Notes on the State of Virginia*. According to Winthrop Jordan, "against the backdrop of changing attitudes and actions concerning Negroes and Negro slavery, the writings of one man became a fixed and central point of reference and influence. In the years after the Revolution the speculations of Thomas Jefferson were of great importance because so many people read and reacted to them" (429). In two famous passages, Query XIV ("Laws") and XVIII ("Manners"), Jefferson attempted a rational approach to the explosive issue, developing an argument *and* an aesthetic based on 'right-reason' and 'common-sense.' Yet hidden in the empiricist rhetoric is a real perceptual/positional dilemma. Critics often cite Jefferson's profound ambivalence over racism and slavery as evidence of his laudably moral intentions; many point to passage XVIII as its manifestation. Yet, as Abdul JanMohamed has observed, ambivalence is not necessarily dynamic: it can be a privileged stasis, self-consciously displayed as evidence for moral recognition, yet valued precisely in that the ambivalence does not promote acting on that recognition ("Economy," 60). Thus the ambivalence manifest in *Notes on the State of Virginia* over the issue of slavery is finally less relevant to an analysis of Jefferson's ethical stance than the way his text creates a space for "white" subjectivity, and a perspective on his "black" object.

Donald Robinson, noting Jefferson's empiricist stance in Query XIV, has suggested that "where the categories of analysis [in Query XIV] are relatively static and scientific, those [in Query XVIII] are dynamic and moral" (92). Taking his cue, perhaps, from the regretful, even apocalyptic tone of the passage, which culminates in Jefferson's exclamation:

> I tremble for my country when I reflect that God is just: that his justice cannot sleep for ever: that considering numbers, nature and natural means only, a revolution of the wheel of fortune, an exchange of situations, is among possible events: that it may become probable by supernatural interference! The Almighty has no attribute which can take side with us in such a contest.[30]

Robinson is able to make a fair case. But a careful reading might equally suggest the opposite. Regret does not replace moral action; Jefferson's concern in Query XVIII is, as many have noticed, for "our people" precisely as opposed to the slave. While he observes the moral degradation suffered by the slave ("he must lock up the faculties of his nature, contribute as far as depends on his individual endeavours to the evanishment of the human race, or entail his own miserable condition on the endless generations proceeding from him"), he is much more concerned for the moral and physical threat produced by the slave system for "our people" and "our children"—his white compatriots. The abrupt break in the text which follows his apocalyptic forecast is indicative of his refusal to pursue the moral consequences of his pronouncements, displacing them brusquely with a "back to business" summary: "—But it is impossible to be temperate and to pursue this subject through the various considerations of policy, of morals, of history natural and civil. We must be content to hope they will force their way into every one's mind." The train of thought here is evasive, not dynamic, his morality—like his prose—equivocal and tentative.

By contrast, the permutations that occur in the passage on "Laws" (XIV) provide much more insight into the depth of Jefferson's real perceptual/conceptual dilemmas and ethical evasions on the subject of race, and racial slavery. Jefferson's initial empiric observations on the profound differences between the black and white races come in response to his proposal for a law providing for slave emancipation and distant colonization, and indeed, as Robert Ferguson convincingly demonstrates, "Law" in Query XIV is the "central rationale" of this text ordered on the philosophy of natural law (401). Its consequent failure (here, as elsewhere) at "rational management" of the issue of slavery is a signpost to the Enlightenment philosophers's profound inability to master the incongruity between slave system and legal contract, between arbitrary power and "natural" authority. We see this most clearly in Jefferson's lengthy discussion of thievish slaves:

> That disposition to theft with which they have been branded, must be ascribed to their situation, and not to any depravity of the moral sense. The man, in whose favor no laws of property exists, probably feels himself less bound to respect those made in favour of others. When arguing for ourselves, we lay it down as fundamental, that laws, to be just, must give a reciprocation of right: that, without this, they are mere rules of conduct, founded in force, and not in conscience: and it is a problem which I give to the master to solve, whether the religious precepts against the violation of property were not framed for him as well as his slave? And whether the slave may not as justifiably take a little from one, who has taken all from him, as he may slay one who would slay him? (142)

Jefferson here confronts the Enlightenment colonist's dilemma, for he cannot reconcile the "social contract" basis for law and authority with the slave institution, which, as Ferguson underscores, "exists outside the law," becoming, as a consequence, "a structural incongruity in *Notes*" (491).[31]

This passage, in fact, abstracted from its context, seems much more coherent and liberal than it actually is in place. Indeed, it is not at all clear if this passage is intended to refer to the black American slave. When, prior to this passage, Jefferson attempts to document the inherent inferiority of the black race, signal in their inability to produce poetry, he turns to the Augustan age of slavery to garner support for his position. Roman slaves were much more harshly treated, argues Jefferson, and yet these slaves "were often the rarest artists." But, he emphasizes, "they were of the race of the whites," which leads him directly to conclude: "It is not their condition then, but nature, which has produced the distinction" (142). He at no point here or subsequently clarifies to which group of slaves his pronouns refer—to white or black—as he proceeds: "Whether further observation will or will not verify the conjecture, that nature has been less bountiful to them in the endowments of the head, I believe that in those of the heart she will be found to have done them justice." Here proceeds the above-quoted passage on thievery and laws, followed immediately by a quote from Homer on the shifting moral imperatives of a slave, to which Jefferson appends, as if to remind himself, "But the slaves of which Homer speaks were whites" (142).

I wish to suggest that Jefferson dodges the inevitable conflict of his arguments, alternating between declarations of inherent or environmentally determined racial difference. While he comes very near in this passage to an explicit repudiation of his previous affirmation of essential, rather than socially constructed, inferiority ("The improvement of the blacks in body and mind, in the first instance of their mixture with whites . . . proves that their inferiority is not the effect merely of their condition in life" [141]), he masks it, perhaps even for himself, in a tangle of pronouns and an increasingly vacillatory train of thought.[32]

John Diggins argues persuasively that Jefferson was caught in the contradictions of the Enlightenment principle of equality:

> The problem . . . is not only that equality was, and continues to be, a harsh doctrine that could be used against the Negro as much as in support of him—a *conservative* doctrine that demanded that the Negro compete in a white culture and be rewarded only for capacities and talents esteemed by that culture. . . . The crucial problem is that the Negro's "fundamental equality"—and the white man's for that matter—could not be confirmed by the empirical criteria of the Enlightenment. (225)

Jefferson was trapped in the empiricist tautology of equality: Man's equality is "self-evident" because we can see it to be so in nature. As a matter of fact, "blacks" were not empirically equal; Jefferson and other Enlightenment philosophers became trapped in supposing equality to be an empirical proposition when it was instead a moral imperative.[33]

In this "radical disjunction of ethical sentiment and empirical science" Diggins locates Jefferson's inability to confront the contradictions of slavery. Yet in his reflections on morality elsewhere, Diggins notes, Jefferson was able to become "conspicuously subjective," and in his various correspondence, the Virginian statesman represents the quality of morality in a radically different way: "It is not *what* one believes [according to Jefferson], but *how* one honestly avows and acts upon a belief that is held less for its objective truthfulness than for its emotional rightness." Despite this principle, Diggins continues, "Jefferson could not bring himself to extend his own dictum to the slavery question." Instead, in confronting the slave question, Jefferson, as we have seen, turns doggedly to empiric observations, "becomes an empiricist *par excellence*" (227–28). By this, he inscribes for himself, and prescribes for his audience (white, European, male), a position of static ambivalence, appealing to the authority of "objective" observation to disguise his subjective unwillingness to relinquish his social superiority and its psychological advantages.[34]

Jefferson grounds his empiricism in the universal criterion of Beauty. Thomas Metscher observes that "certain 'knowledge,' certain contents of consciousness, a certain view of the world, certain attitudes, values and norms— whatever they are, however 'right' and 'wrong'—are articulated in and mediated by art" (21). The aesthetic function is, above all, a social dynamic, as Jan Mukarovsky has established, which grows from cultural dialogue. Yet while aesthetic cognition arises as a result of contesting cultural "voices," it is the drive of the aesthetic to monologize, to make itself "universal," "commonsensical," in short, to conceal the social process which sustains it. In fact, it is "common sense" to which Thomas Jefferson refers in his empirical observations in Query XIV on the "beauty in the two races." Jefferson argues:

The first difference which strikes us is that of color. Whether the black of the negro resides in the reticular membrane between the skin and scarf-skin, or in the scarf-skin itself; whether it proceeds from the colour of the blood, the colour of the bile, or from that of some other secretion, *the difference is fixed in nature* and is as real as if its seats and causes were better known to us. *And is this difference of no importance?* Is it not the foundation of a greater or less share of beauty in the two races? (138; my emphasis)[35]

By establishing "Beauty" and "Nature" as his ultimate authorities, Jefferson grounds his aesthetic conclusions in a "difference fixed in nature and as real as if its seats and causes were better known to us" (138). His subsequent catalog of the inferior beauties of black slaves confirms his mastery over "them" aesthetically, as well as morally and economically.

As Susanne Kappeler observes, "the claim to universality stems from the fact of the disinterestedness with which the subject regards the represented object" (54). The subject of representation is objectified, its qualities abstracted; "beauty" in fact becomes a sanctuary apart from political struggle. But in fact "beauty" can never be understood outside of its political/social context.[36] When pained by the contradictions in his own thinking (all men are created (un)equal), Thomas Jefferson turned to the panacea of "beauty"—a universal norm located outside of himself, but which he was happily possessed of—for reassurance, and moral and intellectual confirmation. But Jefferson's natural law, that which he holds "self-evident," finally traces its own contradiction: his "common sense" is at last an ethical dodge.

Toward a Sociological Criticism of Literature

Representation, then, is the (concealed) intersection of the aesthetic and the social. Its mission, argues Kappeler, is "not so much the means of representing an object through imitation (matching contents) as a means of self representation through authorship: the expression of subjectivity" (53). The foundation of Underhill's and Jefferson's enterprise is self-reflecting: as authors depicting and dominating the Other, they inscribe and confirm their own (superior) identity. It is this intrinsic connection between literature and social action that Kenneth Burke explores in his essay "Literature as Equipment for Living." In it, he casts literature in a proverbial role, as an active mediator of social reality, offering "*strategies* for dealing with *situations*." He here makes an explicit, even avowedly sinister, connection between the strategic value of literature and militaristic "strategy": "One 'maneuvers,' and the maneuvering is an 'art'. . . . One tries, as far as possible, to develop a strategy whereby one 'can't lose.' One tries to change the rules of the game until they fit his own necessities" (*Philosophy*, 298). Conceived as such, colonial ideology and its manifestations in literature may be viewed as forwarding various strategies for "winning" in the "New World," a maneuver on the part of "white" Europeans to reclaim and affirm a central role in the order of things. Intrinsic to this maneuver is a process of positioning, of naming situations so that they fit

European conceptual necessity. "Race" was a name that evolved into precisely such a winning strategy for Anglo colonialists. Yet as a discontinuous and heterogeneous apparatus, there were always challenges to, and ruptures within colonial discourse on "race."

Critical apprehension of the dynamics and tensions of "race" in colonial texts calls for a sociological criticism of literature. Kenneth Burke suggests broad outlines for such an endeavor. Sociological criticism, he proposes, "would seek to codify the various strategies which artists have developed with relation to the naming of situations." While the names themselves may occasionally vary, he speculates, "beneath the change in particulars, we may often discern the naming of one situation." This strategy for literary analysis, as Burke points out, "automatically breaks down the barriers erected about literature as a specialized pursuit. . . . Sociological classification . . . should apply both to works of art and to social situations outside of art (*Philosophy*, 303). Rather than abstracting literature from its site of origin, supposing that it somehow transcends social reality, sociological criticism assumes that literature is always already implicated and interfering in the social.

I contend in this study that while "race" as a concretized idea was not fully realized until after the latest of these texts were composed (i.e., the late nineteenth to early twentieth century), the *situation* named by these various texts deals with what we now categorize as "race": the arbitrary enforcement and institutionalization of Anglo superiority in United States history. The literary task, then, is to interpret the processes by which our (always multiple) understandings of "race," and concomitantly "white" privilege, are deployed. In what follows, I test the plausibility of such a sociological criticism as it applies to the representation of "race." Subsequent chapters examine a diverse selection of writing and writers from a variety of perspectives, concentrating on a single text or on a grouping of texts. Throughout, these questions will unify the range of analyses: How do these texts frame the representation of the racial Self and Other? How do they position themselves in the social dialogue on "race," and what social action do they mediate? In short, how do these texts read "race"?

2

Economies of Morality and Power: Reading "Race" in Two Colonial Texts

Colonial Discourse and the Colonizer Who Refuses

In order to remind us of the heteroglossia of early American attitudes on "race," scholars like Roger Bruns have amply documented a segment—however small at times—of the Anglo-European community who dissented from the various and more prominent racist theorizing of other American colonists. These "colonizers who refused," or at least *resisted*, complicated American colonial discourse on "race" by countering the growing power of the dominative and justificatory social fictions which would arbitrarily subjugate one "kind" of people in order to maintain the privilege of another. Retrieving these voices, then, works at the most immediate level to refute simplistic assumptions that the Anglo-Europeans entered into racial oppression against Africans and Native Americans "unthinkingly" or because they somehow didn't know better. Such voices highlight that the American colonialists did not slip into a practice already provided for by preexisting social, political, and economic institutions as much as they invented and structured an ideological formation that would allow it to seem so—for themselves and others.[1]

Just as important, these voices of dissent can be valuable, in terms of contemporary discussions of "race," for their intrinsic as well as extrinsic manifestation of cultural dialogue. While some colonialists voiced powerful objections to oppressive social practices based on distinctions of "race," Albert Memmi's portrait of the "colonizer who refuses" reminds us that we still must consider that all colonists, acquiescent or otherwise, were on the receiving end of a system predicated on racial privilege. The central experience of the colonizer is structured around a privilege that is at once economic and psychological. Memmi details how the colonizer cannot avoid realizing that his or her benefit comes at a high cost to others: "This easy profit is so great only because it is wrested from others. In short, he [*sic*] finds two things in one: he discovers the existence of the colonizer as he discovers his own privilege" (7). In other words, acknowledging the profit is a simultaneous acknowledgment of the dominative, colonizing Self.

For the dissenting colonial then, the structure of his or her experience becomes contradiction: "It is not easy to escape mentally from a concrete situation, to refuse its ideology while continuing to live with its actual relationships. . . . [The colonizer who refuses] lives his [sic] life under the sign of contradiction which looms at every step, depriving him of all coherence and all tranquility" (20). The resistance grows out of a conscious awareness of some level of exploitation against the colonized. Yet simultaneously, the structure of colonialist praxis (exploitation) infiltrates and co-opts the colonialist's sense of self. Accordingly, we might assume that the colonialist discursive system will obliquely shape from *within* any attempt of a colonialist to differ from its arbitrary dispensation of privilege and oppression. Most immediately, we can see this operating in the fact that it is the colonialist system that authorizes the voice of the colonizer to speak in behalf of the colonized.

Recently Abdul JanMohamed has argued, along lines similar to Memmi, that we must take into account the actual workings and effects of colonial legal and social institutions in order fully to understand colonialist discourse: "The dominant pattern of relations that controls the text within the colonialist context is determined by economic and political imperatives and changes, such as the development of slavery, that are external to the discursive field itself" ("Economy," 63). To put this another way, we must read in colonial discourse the patterns of power which sustain and justify it. This carefully constructed situation of power of the colonizer in relation to the colonized — what Said calls "flexible positional authority" — structures any utterance within the colonial context. Colonial privilege compromises the "colonizer who resists" at the same time it authorizes him or her to speak. Thus, those who would speak against the system from their place *within* are faced with a dilemma which critical readers must examine closely.

For the colonial dissenter, as Homi Bhabha has argued, contradiction becomes a structural ambivalence. The question becomes: How do we read "ambivalence," and what value can we attach to it? Ambivalence for the colonizer who refuses can be an agonizing moral position. But it can also be, as both Memmi and JanMohamed observe, a privileged stasis, a position which replaces real confrontation with moral outrage. As Memmi puts it, "indignation is not always accompanied by a desire for a policy of action. It is rather a position of principle" (20) — principle which does not clearly challenge the actual balance of power between colonizer and colonized (for instance, in the case of Thomas Jefferson, whose clearly agonized reflections on slavery in *Notes on the State of Virginia* did not lead him to free his slaves during his lifetime).[2] Yet this recognition should not lead us to indict these writers out of hand. Just as these dissenting voices could offer a generative challenge to their larger culture, so too can the difference inscribed *within* any particular text be productive, opening new discursive valences for alternative social models. Edward Said puts it this way:

To believe that politics in the form of imperialism bears upon the production of literature, scholarship, social theory, and history writing is by no means equivalent to saying that culture is therefore a demeaned or denigrated thing. Quite to the contrary: we can better understand the persistence and the durability of saturating hegemonic systems . . . when we realize that their internal constraints upon writers and thinkers were productive, not unilaterally inhibiting. (14)

All of this signals a need to carefully reassess colonial writings that dissent from more widely accepted colonialist formulations of "race." The key question here might be: Given that the colonial author can never write outside the power motives of colonial discourse, what are the results of the interplay between resistance and consent? Two colonial texts, Cotton Mather's "The Negro Christianized" (1706) and William Byrd's *Histories of the Dividing Line Betwixt Virginia and North Carolina* (written between 1728 and 1730), provide a useful site for such an analysis. Both writers are often cited as progressive and open-minded on the racial issues they address. This is certainly so, yet it seems important to press the questioning further. The discussion that follows will examine the underlying motivations of each text and will focus particularly on the economy of racial representation in each.

An Essay to Do Good

In 1706 Cotton Mather published a small pamphlet entitled "The Negro Christianized." The theme of the essay, "as we have opportunity let us Do Good unto all men" (6), anticipates in many ways a lengthier pamphlet Mather would publish four years later, *Bonifacius: An Essay to Do Good*. Both tracts function as an "essay" at two levels: as a written text exhorting its audience to "Do Good," the text prescribes social action; as a performance, it becomes a good deed in itself that provides models for those seeking to "Do Good." In this capacity, the essays are social action.

The concept "Do Good," which links both texts, was one that had long impressed the Puritan minister. As he explains in his preface to *Bonifacius*, there was a "passage, in a Speech from an Envoy from His Britanick Majesty, to the Duke of Brandenburgh Twenty years ago; A Capacity to Do Good, not only gives a Title to it, but also makes the doing of it a Duty. . . . To be brief, Reader, the Book now in thy Hands, is nothing but an Illustration, and a Prosecution of that Memorable Sentence." It would seem from the subtitle of "The Negro Christianized" that this earlier work was similarly motivated: "An Essay, to excite and assist that Good Work; the Information of the Negroes in Christianity." Mather's good intentions extended beyond the mere writing of his text, as he recounts in his *Diary* (May 13, 1706): "My Design is; not only to lodge one of the Books, in every Family of New England, which has a Negro in it, but also to send Numbers of them into the Indies; and write such Letters to the principal Inhabitants of the Islands, as may be proper to accompany them" (565).

The argument of "The Negro Christianized" is fairly straightforward. "It is a Golden Sentence," Mather begins, "that has been sometimes quoted from Chrisodem, That for a man to know the Art of Alms, is more than for a man to be Crowned with the Diadem of Kings. But to Convert one Soul unto God, is more than to pour out Ten Thousand Talents into the Baskets of the Poor" (1). Running against popular sentiment, Mather proposes in his tract that it is every Christian slaveholder's duty to Christianize his slave. To make his case, he appeals to the reasonableness of his audience: "Show yourselves Men, and let Rational Arguments have their Force upon you, to make you treat, not as Bruits but as Men, those Rational Creatures whom God has made your Servants" (4). Mather enumerates his reasons for such a proposal. First, God requires that any man's servants also be His. Second, a man does not deserve the title "Christian" unless he does everything in his power to ensure that all in his household are Christian, too. Third, Christian compassion requires that the owner do something for the improvement of his suffering and sinful slaves. Fourth, the compassionate owner will see the "incomparable benefit" of Christian consolation for his efforts. "A Good Man," observes Mather, "is One who does all the Good that he can. The greatest Good that we can do for any, is to bring them unto the fullest Acquaintance with Christianity" (9).

Mather overtly works to break down racial tropes, which he perceives as a barrier to slaveholders' willingness to Christianize their slaves. After presenting his arguments for Christianizing the Negro as each slave owner's duty, Mather asks, "And now, what Objection can any Man Living Have?" Anticipating and answering to the "idle and silly cavils" of his audience, Mather tackles two major arguments of the day, that blacks do not have rational capacity, and that dark skin color was an external manifestation of moral degradation.[3] He responds to both charges simply by asserting their irrelevance:

> It has been cavilled, by some, that it is questionable Whether the Negroes have Rational Souls, or no. But let that Brutish insinuation be never Whispered any more. Certainly, their Discourse, will abundantly prove, that they have Reason. Reason shows it self in the Design which they daily act upon. The vast improvement that Education has made upon some of them, argues that there is a Reasonable Soul in all of them. (23)

As for their color, which is also made an objection, Mather scoffs: "A Gay sort of Argument! As if the great God went by the Complexion of Men, in His Favours to them!" (24). In contrast to the dominative hierarchy that frames their social relationship, Mather argues for a *horizontal* space for Christian relations between slaveholders and slaves.

Despite Mather's good intentions and assertions contradicting the increasingly determinist racial sentiment of his contemporaries, the text is more complicated and in the end much more conservative than it seems at first glance. While establishing what seems to be a common ground between black and white men, Mather places their capacity for reason in opposition. Mather's

address privileges "white" sensibility, basing itself from the outset on the rea-
sonable persuasion of his white reader. Yet he markedly does not expect the
same from the black slaves. Shortly after affirming their rational soul, Mather
says of them:

> Indeed, their stupidity is a discouragement. But the greater their stupidity, the
> greater must be our Application. If we can't learn them as much as we could, let us
> learn them as much as we can. . . . And the more Difficult it is, to fetch such
> forlorn things up out of the perdition whereinto they are fallen, the more Laudable
> is the undertaking: There will be more of a Triumph, if we Prosper in the undertak-
> ing. (25)

The Negro may have a rational soul, but it is certainly not qualitatively the
same soul as that of the white. In fact it is fixed firmly in a relation inferior to
the "white" soul. This position, coming later in the essay, begins to undermine
his initial assertions. Winthrop Jordan concludes that "Mather was completely
decided [favorably] on the Negro's essential nature . . . despite his dreadful
punning on the Negro's color" (201). Yet if, as JanMohamed urges, "any
evident 'ambivalence' is in fact a product of deliberate, if at times subcon-
scious, imperialist duplicity," we should analyze these apparent contradictions, rather than discarding them as irrelevant, since colonialist discourse on
"race" often operates by such contradictory means ("Economy," 61).

The color imagery—what Jordan characterizes as "dreadful punning"—
subverts Mather's explicit intentions to discard categorization of Christians by
color. The rhetorical device rife through this text—in fact the only trope
seemingly available to Mather in distinguishing good from bad, saved from
damned—is dark and light imagery. He may affirm that the issue of the African's color is a "trifle," but the figure of speech he uses immediately after this
discussion in considering the difficulties of educating the black is loaded: "It
may seem, unto as little purpose to Teach, as to wash an Aetheopian" (25).[4]
Like Barthes's analysis of a Negro in French uniform saluting a French flag on
the cover of *Paris Match*, with its seemingly benign signification of patriotism
masking a more insidious apology for imperialism, Mather's text explicitly
sponsors a liberal, humane reading of "blackness" while implicitly proposing
a very conservative, commodified figuration (109–59; esp. 116–31).

In fact, Mather's figurative language develops a covert text that works
against the overt text throughout. He introduces slaves as "the Blackest Instances of Blindness and Baseness," associating these qualities by alliteration.
While he reminds his readers parenthetically that it is not yet proved that the
slaves are not descendants of the biblical Ham, he leaves room for doubt,
which reinforces rather than undermines a persistent conceptual link in the
text between skin color and moral degradation. He continues, "Let us make a
Trial, Whether they that have been Scorched and Blacken'd by the sun of
Africa, may not come to have their Minds Healed by the more Benign Beams
of the Sun of Righteousness," figuratively linking physical to moral condition
(1–3). Later in the text, Mather further blurs distinctions between physical

and moral condition, suggesting a conflation: "We read of, People destroy'd for lack of knowledge. If you withhold Knowledge from your Black People, they will be Destroy'd. But their Destruction must very much ly at your door; You must answer for it. It was a Black charge of old brought in against the Jewish Nation; Jer. 2.34. . . . Surely, Things look very Black upon us" (16). We see here the full range of passion that the color imagery is intended to evoke, and its confusing, even counterproductive effects for Mather's argument. It is at this point especially that Mather seems entirely trapped in what JanMohamed describes as Manichaean allegory, as his color imagery of light and dark acquires a momentum of its own which begins to displace Mather's initial arguments.[5]

This subtext of "The Negro Christianized" further works against the overt one by displacing the ostensible subject of the piece—the black—with his or her white owner as the recipient of benefit. In other words, it is the "white" Christian who clearly becomes the subject *and* object of the text, the "black" heathen/African only a means by which the Christian can advance himself on a cosmic scale. The act of Christianizing the heathen is "the noblest Work, that was undertaken among the Children of men" (2)—"children of men" clearly excluding the African slave. The "black" slave is an "opportunity," a "trial," a "creature." "Who can tell," queries Mather, "but that God may have sent this Poor Creature into my hands, so that One of the Elect may by my means be Called; and by my Instruction be made Wife unto Salvation! The glorious God will put unspeakable Glory upon me, if it may be so!" (3). The "white" Christian accrues eternal benefits through his acting on black slaves—by making them "objects for the Nobles of Heaven to take Notice of!" (20). Important in this process, this material "object"—the Christianized slave—will in fact serve to reflect the Anglo master, says Mather: "It cannot but be a vast accession unto your Joy in Heaven, to meet your Servants there and hear them forever blessing the gracious God, for the Day when He first made them your Servants" (20). Like the saluting African on the cover of *Paris Match*, Mather's slaves have no meaning in themselves but are rather an eternal index to "white" superiority; they will both literally (in this life) and figuratively (in heaven) stand for their Christianizing master.[6]

Mather's interest in the benefits of "doing good" highlights the economic dynamic that structures colonial discourse. Virginia Bernhard, in her essay, "Cotton Mather and the Doing of Good: A Puritan Gospel of Wealth," observes that Mather's *Bonifacius*, unlike more somber English tracts which focus on the thanklessness of Doing Good, "abounds with optimism and constantly stresses both spiritual and temporal benefits which accrue to the individual who does good" (232). A similar optimism frames the argument of "The Negro Christianized." "Benefits," "revenues," "accounts," "inheritances," "shares," and "recompense" are metaphors for the heavenly profits available to the Christianizing master. Even more emphatically, Mather underscores the temporal, specifically monetary rewards the plan will garner the reluctant slave owner: "Yea, the pious Masters, that have instituted their Servants in Christian Piety, will even in this life have Recompense" (20). The

slaves will be more tractable, more dutiful and faithful, hence, more profitable. He observes that slaves "are to enjoy no Earthly Goods, but the small
Allowance that your Justice and Bounty shall see proper for them" (19), clearly
indicating that by contrast the white man's privilege is the accumulation of
worldly goods.

It is curious, then, when Mather departs from this theme of Anglo economic
entitlement in order to chastise those who would object to his plan on the
grounds that it will entail economic penalties. Mather at this point acknowledges the prevalent argument that baptism will entitle slaves to freedom, which
can mean only pecuniary *loss* for the owner, and his response is frankly scornful of such "base" concerns: "Man, if this were true; that a Slave bought with
thy Money, were by thy means brought unto the Things that accompany
Salvation, and thou shouldest from this tie have no more service from him,
yet thy Money were not thrown away" (26). He continues to reprimand the
selfish owner/reader severely for several more lines. Then comes a remarkable
shift in tone and argumentation: "But it is all a Mistake. There is no such
thing. What Law is it, that Sets the Baptized Slave at Liberty? Not the law of
Christianity, that allows of Slavery; Only it wonderfully Dulcifies and Molli-
fies and Moderates the Circumstances of it" (26). Here Mather considers the
possible laws that might interfere and concludes, "The Baptised then are not
thereby entitled to their Liberty" (27). Since the charm of Mather's proposal is
the financial reward that owners will gain by their benevolent action, Mather's
reassurance that such action will result neither in loss of money nor property
is powerful, and only barely disguised by the admonitory lecture.

Mather's plan for the actual process of Christianizing the African slaves
also revolves around economic considerations. He proposes that the busy
owner, who may not have time to devote to schooling his slaves in creeds and
catechism, should "employ and reward" (29) white children and servants to
perform the task for him.[7] Further, as incentive for the slaves to learn, Mather
proposes the owner offer *them* some small, "agreeable recompenses" as well.
Throughout "The Negro Christianized," Christianity and the condition of
whiteness are linked to financial gain—not only will the owner recognize a
metaphysical acquisition, he will see a physical, tangible benefit as well. Mather's plan is, in short, a scheme of cosmic capitalism. Money becomes the
metaphor *and* the message. The black slave becomes a figurative as well as
literal commodity, becomes commodified in the act of purchase as well as
Christianization.

As we have seen, Mather's linguistic choices—racial tropes, loaded figures
of speech, and a cost-effective logic—undergird the racialist economy of "The
Negro Christianized." But larger, extratextual economies are not irrelevant to
the racist subtext of his pamphlet. In fact Mather's motivation for writing
"The Negro Christianized" may have been neither self-effacing nor self-
sacrificing. For the date 1706, March 1, Mather records in his *Diary*:

I am exercised, in my Family, with the want of good Servants. . . . I plead, that my
Glorious CHRIST appeared in the Form of a Servant; and therefore the Lord would

grant good Servants unto those that were alwayes at work for Him, and wanted the Assistences of such living Instruments. I resolve, that if God bless me with Good Servants, I will serve him with more Fidelity and Activity; and I will do something that not only my own Servants, but other Servants in this Land, and abroad in the world, May come to glorify Him. I have Thoughts, to write an Essay, about, the Christianity of our Negro and other Slaves. (554)

With curious irony, God apparently did fulfill His end of the bargain. On December 13 of the same year Mather records:

This Day, a surprising Thing befel me. Some Gentlemen of our Church, understanding (without any Application of mine to them for such a Thing,) that I wanted a good Servant at the expence of between forty and fifty Pounds, purchased for me, a very likely Slave; a young man, who is a Negro of promising Aspect and Temper and this Day they presented him unto me. It seems to be a mighty Smile of Heaven upon my Family; and it arrives at an observable Time unto me. (579)

Mather named his slave Onesimus;[8] in subsequent entries, he dutifully notes his children's successful completion of catechizing the slave. As David Levin has recently reminded us, we must remember that the *Diary* was not strictly a diary but a retrospective rendering of Mather's life, a "collection of annual glosses upon discarded diaries" (201). So any attempt to read Mather's intentions for "The Negro Christianized" from the *Diary* is problematic at best. Yet we can see how his text and his actions are situated in a certain temporal economy of exchange even as Mather outlines a providential model.

I do not mean to discredit either Mather or his goodwill toward the slaves of New England. I do mean this as an example that points up the inevitably political and economic motivation of any racial characterization in colonial America (in *any* colonial situation). Mather sets out to undermine racial tropes; that his own text is overwhelmed by the language available to him in color imagery and by his own pecuniary interest should alert us to the ways in which discourse and institutions—as Michel Foucault points out—shape the author as much as vice versa. The compelling tension in "The Negro Christianized" results from Mather's attempt to resist colonialist discourse and from his perhaps unconscious acquiescence to its financial motivations. His resulting complicity should not obfuscate the difficulty of his gesture: "The Negro Christianized" should be recognized for the social good it proposes and enacts, *along with* its fundamental prejudice and self-interest.

Dividing Lines

While Cotton Mather's text illustrates the imaginative bondage of the manichean allegory, William Byrd's public and secret *Histories of the Dividing Line Betwixt Virginia and North Carolina* exemplify the covert economy of power implicit in colonial discourse. Together, the two *Histories* provide an interesting insight into Byrd's attitudes toward racial issues—one version was intended for a selected circulation, and one was composed for a more general, public audience. As Donald T. Siebert, Jr., cautions, "It is well to note . . . that neither account is purely public or private, that there is no neat contrast in tone or intention between [the two *Histories*], as is often assumed" (537). Both texts provide an account of Byrd's struggle for self-definition among his fellows and among the continent's natives; both serve to define new territory for the colonies, and new possibilities for action in those lands. Thus both the *Secret History* and public *History* function in a proverbial capacity. They model strategies for social relations in the colonies and offer seasoned advice to men setting out to conquer the wilderness. Despite Byrd's apparently liberal attitudes and jocular narrative style, both texts subtly urge a more rigid social hierarchy, one which finally works not to modify but to codify racial and social distinctions.

At the most immediate level, the *Histories* operate as a scouting guide. Especially in the public version, Byrd provides a detailed account of how to prepare for such an undertaking in the wilderness, how to negotiate the terrain, how to deal with dietary problems inherent to a backwoods diet, and how to cope with soggy campgrounds. Byrd actually goes to great lengths in the public *History* to equip his reader, even offering recipes for such "Portable Provisions" that will best outfit the aspiring woodsman/explorer. He gives trapping advice, hunting tips, and, to improve the vigor of the backwoodsman, urges eating plenty of bear meat. The importance of promoting and preparing such hardy adventurers is almost inestimable in terms of the economic advantage they can provide the burgeoning settlement. As Byrd observes: "Such [continued] Discovery would certainly prove an unspeakable Advantage to this Colony, by facilitating a Trade with so considerable a nation of Indians [i.e., the Cherokees]" (246). The bear diet, Byrd underlines, will not only facilitate the physical vigor of those establishing dominion, it will invigorate the project in another way: 'I am able to say, besides, for the Reputation of the Bear Dyet, that all the Marryed men of our Company were joyful Fathers within forty weeks after they got Home, and most of the Single men had children sworn to them within the same time" (252).

Perhaps more important, though less explicit, both *Histories* are guides to the maintenance of social order in the wilderness. As David Smith has noted, the *Histories* carefully delineate a social and political hierarchy. Previous scholars, presumably drawing on Byrd's request to the legislature, have estimated the travel party at about twenty men. Smith, however, has more carefully established a figure of around fifty. The basis for such a large complement was social rather than technical or physical: "The hierarchy, in all its divisions, was not to deteriorate in the Great Woods. Gentlemen were still gentlemen, and needed to be served, and others below that rank needed to see them being served" (303). As the "Dividing Line" contingent physically opened up new land for settlement, it also delineated and maintained social order.

It is not surprising that both texts—though the public does so more extensively—address the issue of colonialist relations with indigenous populations. Contemporary colonialist rhetoric often referred to the "failure" of Indians to assimilate into Anglo-European culture as a justification for policies of intrusion and removal. Responding to this sentiment, Byrd asserts, on the contrary, that the English settlers are at fault for their absurd aesthetic scruples and even for their immoral lack of Christian honor. Byrd speculates that the early settlers might have found a better way to establish harmonious relations with the Indians than by offering gifts of beads and cloth, and a more honorable means of gaining native lands: "The poor Indians would have had less reason to Complain that the English took away their Land, if they had received it by way of Portion with their Daughters" (4). He indicates that it would have greatly dignified the legacy of the original settlers to have shared their enlightening influence socially *and* racially. Although this alternative seems to have repelled those settlers, Byrd insists that the natives are not as repugnant as generally depicted, and makes an audacious comparison between the morality of the natives and the first settlers who exploited Indian hospitality: "Morals and all considered, I cant think the Indians were much greater Heathens than the first Adventurers, who, had they been good Christians, would have had the charity to take this only method of converting the Natives to Christianity" (3).

His comments here and again later in the *History* (see 120) dismantle popularly accepted oppositions between Anglo-Europeans and "Indians" at two levels: physical and moral. This line of argument explicitly contests the view of the day that miscegenation would lead inevitably to the deterioration of the superior race (a view which, as Alden Vaughan notes, justified segregationist and increasingly exploitive colonial policy; see "White Man," 919; 934–35). Racial characteristics, Byrd asserts, are not fixed in a hierarchical relationship. Rather, such differences are a factor of material and cultural circumstance: "The principal Difference between one People and another proceeds only from the Different Opportunities of Improvement" (120).

The public *History* counters popular colonial rhetoric in other ways. It historicizes Indian savagery, laying the blame for the mythologized Indian Menace at the feet of the colonists.[9] The "false delicacy" shown by the early colonists to the natives triggered what Byrd portrays as an appropriate response among the Indians. The resulting alienation between the groups, which led to a certain amount of suffering for the early colonists ("many of them were cut off, and the rest Exposed to various Distresses"), is depicted as the fault of the settlers not of the Indians (4). Casting farther back into the historical record, Byrd takes the same stance toward Indian hostilities against French and Spanish explorers in the Carolinas: they met "such returns from the Indians as their own cruelty deserved" (10). All these groups are contrasted to the Quakers, whom Byrd notes "have observed exact justice with all the Natives that border upon them . . . which has savd them from many Wars and Massacres" (10).

Thus, from its outset the public *History* establishes a critical perspective on the policies of the colonists and more than a modicum of cultural relativity.[10] Byrd adopts a cosmopolitan viewpoint throughout the *History* that goes beyond comparisons between Anglo and Native American cultures. He digresses, for instance, on Chilean pacos to illustrate that while Indian tribes in the

Carolinas were unfamiliar with pack animals, other native cultures were not (266). Here, as well as in his extended observations on various North American tribes, he disrupts the kind of colonialist discourse that depicts a mythologized, monolithic Indian. His comparative commentary also extends to Anglo groups in, for example, a wry but passingly favorable observation of the North Carolinians. Noting a similarity with Rome in the way North Carolina bolstered its population with vagrants and thieves, Byrd concludes: "Considering how Fortune delights in bringing great things out of Small, who knows but Carolina may, one time or other, come to be the Seat of some other great Empire?" (58).

Byrd's initial arguments about Anglo-Europeans and Native Americans emphasize similarity over difference. This is a significant argumentative framework, for the descriptive choice of identity or difference will determine very different possibilities, and a different relationship (horizonal or vertical) of power. Yet like "The Negro Christianized," the subtext of Byrd's *Histories* finally serves to reinforce and essentialize cultural distinctions, reasserting the vertical power structure that Byrd's arguments have overtly questioned. While the cosmopolitan perspective can promote a kind of cultural relativity, this discursive strategy is double-edged. Byrd's narratives join in a long tradition of travel literature. More specifically Byrd's *Histories* (the public in particular, as I will shortly argue) are framed within the ideological project of colonialism and thus function at least in part to normalize that project. Byrd and his Virginian compatriots are prominent shapers of the frontier in the text, but Byrd's narration in the public *History* often prefigures the "effaced narrator" that becomes a predominant feature of nineteenth-century colonial travel literature—particularly in his discussion of local Indians and local landscapes. Colonial travel literature assumes an objective distance from its subject, but by locating it in its historical and political context we can see that such literature can never be separated from the workings of colonialism. In the *Histories*—the public version in particular—Byrd's disinterested worldliness functions to mask his very specific interestedness, and it is possible to discern colonial strategy beneath his supposedly objective discussion of local Indians. What his discussion *omits*, the connections it declines to make, is often the leading indicator of his colonial investment.

Both versions of the *Histories* pay close attention to the Indians encountered in the survey, developing a kind of "portraits of manners" of the natives contacted. For instance, one Sabbath on the excursion, Byrd and his fellows question "our Indian"—a Saponi who used the hunting name Bearskin—about his religion. Byrd relates Bearskin's comments to his public reader, pointing out affinities to Western religions: Bearskin's account "contain'd . . . the three Great Articles of Natural Religion: The Belief of a God; The Moral Distinction betwixt Good and Evil; and the Expectation of Rewards and Punishments in Another World." Yet Byrd's account is more insistent when he finds in the religion a bent that is "a little Gross and Sensual," as much as "cou'd be expected from a meer State of Nature, without one Glimpse of Revelation or Philosophy" (202). Parting from his strategy elsewhere of emphasizing points of commonality between cultures, Byrd's comparativist strategy here takes on a different aspect.

At other points in the *Histories*, Byrd has been willing to consider transatlantic cultural parallels which would dismantle racial oppositions. Even when discussing as sensational a topic as native scalping practices, the public *History* draws a comparison to a similar practice of the ancient Scythians, suggesting a far-European (Byrd himself calls it Asian) origin for the natives (308). But here and later in recounting a native legend that bears striking parallels to Christ's earthly mission, he refrains from drawing any significant connections between Bearskin's story and the specifically Christian beliefs of the colonists (a perspective that is especially ironic because it seems clear that Bearskin's accounts of Saponi cosmology and religious beliefs have been influenced fundamentally by Christian contacts). Rather than using Bearskin's testimony as an opportunity to further his initial tactics of undermining racial distinctions by emphasizing commonalities, his account of Saponi cosmology underscores a moral *deficiency* in the natives. In an account of an enterprise which is often noted for its *own* sensual bent, Byrd's pronouncement on Bearskin's heaven ("a little Gross and Sensual") contains its own irony.

In the public *History* particularly, Byrd expands his portrait of Indian manners in a way that portrays an essential rather than circumstantial opposition between the two groups. For example he comments repeatedly on "lazy Indians," noting that "it must b [*sic*] observ'd, by the way, that Indian Towns, like Religious Houses, are remarkable for a fruitful Situation; for being by Nature not very Industrious, they choose such a Situation as will Subsist them with the least Labour" (208). Later he explains at length:

> I never could learn that the Indians set apart any day of the Week or the Year for the Service of God. They pray, as Philosophers eat, only when they have a stomach, without having any set time for it. Indeed these Idle People have very little occasion for a sabbath to refresh themselves after hard Labour, because very few of them ever Labour at all. Like the wild Irish, they would rather want than Work, and are all men of Pleasure to whom every day is a day of rest. (262)

Unlike the industrious crew of men on the survey, who hazard swamp and storm to stake an imaginary line, "the little Work that is done among the Indians is done by the poor Women, while the men are quite idle" (116).

We see the tendency of Byrd's account to essentialize the Indian no more clearly than in the *Histories'* contradictory portrayal of Bearskin, hired as much to provide fresh game as to navigate the woods. Bearskin's actions serve to repeat and reinforce Byrd's observations of Indians in general. For instance, when Byrd acknowledges in the public *History* the Saponi's hunting prowess, he subtly suggests that Bearskin's success is owing to a savage nature: "Our unmerciful Indian kill'd no less than two Braces of Deer and a large Bear" (260). But when Bearskin fails to round up enough food for the crew, it is attributed to what Byrd has also explained as "Indian nature"—an inborn tendency to avoid work, even if it means going hungry. The *Histories'* mythologized version of "Indian" thus contains and naturalizes contradictions so that Indians can be at once essentially lazy when they fail to provide food and essentially savage when they successfully furnish food—and both ways morally inferior to the Anglo-Americans.

There is a tactical as well as descriptive objective for Byrd's commentary on Indian presence. Throughout his survey of the colonies' boundary, Byrd is attentive to the economic potential of the areas under survey. Mary Louise Pratt has pointed out the economic motives which inevitably underlie colonial travel narratives like Byrd's *Histories*. Nowhere can this be more prominent than in the notion of the "survey"—the fixing of an imaginary political and economic boundary between two Anglo-European colonies. Like a real estate brochure, the public *History* in particular highlights the economic potential of the areas under survey, explicitly as often as tacitly encouraging further Anglo settlement and expansion. Even through the awful Dismal Swamp, the vigilant commissioner speculates at the feasibility of draining the land in order to render it usable.

While he plans for colonial appropriation of the lands he surveys, Byrd strategically refers to the mythologized "Indian Menace." Because of the colonists' aversion to intermarriage, they will have to face Indian resistance. Byrd points to the Carolinians' violent policy toward Indians, and openly sympathizes with the native's revolt against "Tyranny and Injustice," almost applauding their war on "those little Tyrants" (304). In this context, it is striking that his cross-cultural analysis does not extend to Virginia's relations with the local natives—which highlights Byrd's attitudes toward both North Carolinians and Native Americans. He does not seem to regard continued violence from the Indians against Virginians as a serious threat; but given that he repeatedly depicts Indians as a dying breed, there is perhaps little wonder in his nonchalance.

The public *History*'s portrayal of the steadily decreasing numbers of Indians is worth noting. In much the same way that the two texts "fix" Indian nature, depoliticizing and dehistoricizing, the public version also explains the decreasing native population as the inevitable result of Indian savagery and intertribal warring (helped along by white disease and liquor). And, like John Underhill's pamphlet *Newes From America* (1638), which promises bounteous land while narrating coincidentally the (providential) demise of the Pequots, Byrd keeps an eye on the attractive lands which become available through native depopulation. For instance, Byrd notes that the Usherees were formerly

a very Numerous and Powerful People. But the frequent Slaughters made upon them by the Northern Indians, and, what has been still more destructive by far, the Intemperance and Foul Distempers introduc'd amongst them by the Carolina Traders, have now reduc'd their number to little more than 400 Fighting Men, besides Women and Children. It is a charming Place where they live, the Air very Wholesome, the Soil fertile, and the Winters ever mild and Serene. (300)

Innocent and apparently objective observations like this, JanMohamed would argue, reveal the extent of colonial duplicity. Byrd's description minimalizes ("little more") while underscoring the degree of the "Indian Menace" (Fighting Men"), and at the same time indicates the real source of concern that motivates the colonists' conceptual need for an "Indian Menace": the availability of fertile lands. The more the native population is "reduc'd," the more "charming Place[s]" are made available.

At certain points the *History* seems a virtual catalog of the demise of various tribes. It notes the fate of the Meherin Indians (decimated by the Catawbas) and assures the reader that the whole number of Indians in Nottoway is reduced to about two hundred, including women and children. These are, Byrd asserts, "the only Indians of any consequence now remaining within the Limits of Virginia" (116). As for the Carolinian Tuscaroras, though "heretofore very numerous and powerful, making within time of Memory, at least a Thousand Fighting Men . . . [now] there remain so few, that they are in danger of being quite exterminated by the Catawbas, their mortal Enemies" (290).[11]

Byrd's observations on the inevitability of Indian extinction are backed in the public *History* by Indian legend. Although skeptical of Indian religion, Byrd in effect uses it to confirm his own depoliticized observations about the declining Native American populations, citing this "odd legend" that the race will inevitably be killed off by "their God." Byrd passes up the opportunity to draw obvious Christian parallels from this native story of a perfect man sent to model behavior and encourage harmony among a dishonest and impious population. Like Jesus Christ, the messenger is scorned, harassed, and finally impaled on a tree. The text details how the native god becomes enraged at his people's failure to reform as well as at their execution of his messenger. As a result this god will never "leave off punishing, and wasting their People, till he shall have blotted every living Soul of them out of the World" (292). The "odd legend" diverts attention from the Indians' political, physical, and economic interaction with the whites, offering instead a *mythic* explanation for their extinction. As Barthes reminds us, myth is always a "value, never separable from the system that creates it . . . a perpetual alibi" (123). It is interesting that Byrd casually offers the legend as the summation of his story of Indian demise.

While the natives are not then a physical threat to the Virginians, their dangerous influence manifests itself in other ways. Despite his unreserved and even mischievous banter on intermarriage, his discussion of the "slovenly" and "tallow-faced" backwoodsmen who have intermarried among the Indians and have adopted their customs and habits counters his earlier assertions that such practice will "blanche" and socially improve the Indians, not vice versa. Rather, the *History* suggests that backwoods miscegenation has led to traits of slothful sensuality Byrd finds characteristic to the Indians, and implies that the whites who live in the "lubberland" must consciously assert their racial heritage of "Industry and Frugality" as the "two Cardinal Virtues" which will banish such undesirable traits (36).[12] Those who acquire what Byrd regards as affinities to the Indian way of life seem to Byrd degenerate and diseased, and he carefully marks the scabs and facial deformities that some exhibit because of their lack of initiative in growing vegetables and reliance instead on their diet of pork (54).

Richard Slotkin tries to reconcile these comments with Byrd's former, more liberal assertions on racial intermarriage by suggesting that he had an agenda for a "proper" sort of intermarriage, as opposed to that which had taken place in the backwoods among the frontiersmen (*Regeneration*, 222). It seems, however, that Byrd's arguments for the moral integrity that the whites would gain and the physiognomical advantages that the Indians would gain by intermarriage are subtly but completely countered by the cumulative message of the public *History* in particular. We can briefly rehearse here the profoundly conservative undertone of Byrd's initial comments on racial union. The scheme for intermarriage includes no recognition of Indian culture or racial characteristics but rather a desire to "bleach" them—wash them of color—while at the same time civilizing them so that they disappear into European appearance and manner. Hand in hand with this suggestion is the real motivation: assimilation is a means to peaceful and relatively cost-free procurement of land title. Byrd's stake in colonial acquisition thus underwrites his interest in racial fraternity. Like Cotton Mather's admonition against placing pecuniary concerns over Christian duty, Byrd's advice on racial integration remains philosophical at best.

We can push Byrd's stance on racial union one step further. Byrd notes that the white men never could bring themselves to intermarry with the native women. Nor do the members of Byrd's company find any marriageable native women in their venture. Yet as the company men take frequent and even violent advantage of local "tawnies" (an activity portrayed more prominently in the secret than in the public version), it becomes clear that *sexual* union is not what is repugnant to the colonizer. Rather, what are portrayed as the laughable antics of Byrd's cohorts counter his remarks on interracial union; instead they reaffirm the actual historical practice of the colonists: the right of might.

While Siebert's caution about making overly simplistic distinctions between the two *Histories* is a good one, it seems plausible to point out that the public version participates much more overtly in the project of colonialism than does the secret one. In this sense the contrast between the two is instructive, for it is in the public version alone that Byrd outlines his feelings on interracial union, *and* it is in the public version alone that Byrd develops his portraits of Indian manners. While the *Secret History* provides an ever jovial if often rebarbative reading of relations between the colonies, the public *History* offers a well-developed, if often highly contradictory, perspective on relations between the colonies and the Native Americans. It is the contradictory trend of that project that renders it so interesting. Ultimately, the interplay between the two texts, as well as the ways in which the public *History* differs within itself, offers a revealing commentary on the dynamic politics of resistance in colonial representation of the Other.

As we have seen, Mather and Byrd attack racial tropes of difference, yet both their texts are finally compromised by the economy of privilege which structures colonial discourse. The most generous and resistive impulses of "The Negro Christianized" and the *Histories* must thus be read *against* as well as *within* the power context of colonial discourse and its economic interests. Kenneth Burke's formulation of the "bureaucratization of the imaginative" may speak to the common dynamic we have seen in these two very different texts:

> All imaginative possibility (usually at the start Utopian) is bureaucratized when it is embodied in the realities of a social texture, in all the complexities of language and habits, in the property relationships, the methods of government, production and distribution, and in the development of rituals that re-enforce the same emphasis. (*Attitudes*, 225)

Acknowledging this dynamic between individual and institution, text and discourse, leads us not only to temper our idealism about the real-world efficacy of literary "resistance" (and concomitantly it should help us be more realistic in our expectations of those who attempt to *work* resistance from within dominant culture), but it reminds us always to question the institutional forces that shape any utterance—the contesting dialogue over the uses of power that we see inscribed in texts like Mather's and Byrd's.

3

Romancing the Border: Bird, Cooper, Simms, and the Frontier Novel

Reality Versus Romance

"The business of a writer of fiction," states Cooper unequivocally in his 1831 introduction to *The Last of the Mohicans*, "is to approach, as near as his powers will allow, to poetry" (7). There is an unresolved tension in Cooper's introduction between his commitment to realism—giving an accurate account of "the Aborigines of the American continent" (5)—and his attraction to romance—"poetically to furnish a witness to the truth" (7). To achieve the latter, Cooper acknowledges, one must fudge a bit on realism: Cooper's Natty isn't quite so vulgar as he might have justifiably been portrayed by a more realistic pen.[1]

Two other frontier novelists, William Simms and Robert Montgomery Bird, wrestled with the opposing demands of romance and realism. Simms's advocacy of romance in his preface to *The Yemassee* is still a touchstone for modern critics. Romance, he urges, is the modern substitute for the epic, with loftier aims than the mundane realism of the British novel. And *The Yemassee* is an "*American* romance . . . styled as much of the material could have been furnished by no other country" (6). But while Simms advances romance as his strategy for *The Yemassee*, he also claims his share of realism. As he explains, his novel purports to deliver a "correction" of erroneously "vulgar opinions" the reader might have had concerning "red men" (4). His project here, as he delineates it in his preface, will run counter to the goals of romance, which are to exceed the possible, or even the probable (see 6). Rather, his efforts are to "remove much of that air of mystery" surrounding Indians and to restore historical veracity to their portrayal in his novel (4).

While Simms rejects as unrealistic the depiction of Native Americans "in degrading attitude only, and in humiliating relations with the whites," Robert Montgomery Bird counters that these are *precisely* the "*real* Indians" (32; my emphasis). Bird's fictional aims here were also avowedly the opposite of

Cooper's, whose noble Indians he abhorred. He rejects his colleagues' depictions as romanticized: "In his natural barbaric state, [the Indian] is a barbarian—and it is not possible he could be anything else" (32). He further rejects Simms's historicization, contending that his own version draws Indians "as they appeared, and still appear" (32). Bird advances realism as a novelistic strategy somewhat more rigorously than does Cooper or Simms. Although he claims a strict realism for his Indians, he confesses that his Nick, while based in fact, is "sustained" by "poetical possibility" (34–35).

Many critics have discussed the formalistic, psychologic, or mythologic implications of the dual impulse toward realism and romance in *The Last of the Mohicans, The Yemassee*, and *Nick of the Woods*. Fewer, however, have examined the specifically sociopolitical significance of this narratorial ambivalence.[2] In the case of the frontier novel, "realism" and "romance" might be said to mirror the two countervailing drives of the frontier itself—one arising from and ostensibly committed to depicting real, historical/material conflict, the other an ideological apparatus which serves to displace the historical culpability of the culture of the writer. It is not coincidence, of course, that Cooper, Simms, and Bird all declare a commitment to a realistic depiction of "Indians" and apply their romantic urges to compatriots in cause and country.[3] Of course the breakdown between romance and realism is not so simple as even this formulation would indicate: we might also note that their Indians are probably less realistic in all than their more complicated and "romanticized" Anglo characters.[4] The ambivalence of purpose, application, and result that we see in this tension can lead us to an interesting question, then: What are the cultural implications of the "romance" imposed by members of the dominant culture on the "reality" of the American frontier?

The Significance of History

Following the lead of Charles Brockden Brown, who "gothicized" the American landscape in *Edgar Huntly* and found (despite popular sentiment of the day) *ample* materials for fiction in America, Cooper, Bird, and Simms also turned to American subjects and landscapes. Responding to the *North American Review*'s call for a national literature as well as to British skeptics like Sydney Smith, these authors deployed an American past to prove that there was *indeed* such a thing as an American book. Cooper drew on the French and Indian wars of 1757, Simms on the Yemassee uprising of 1715, and Bird on the exigencies of the Kentucky frontier of 1782. All three strove to create a sense of historical depth and of national tradition for a young and self-conscious America.

Critics of these works have treated the novels predominantly as chronicles of America's epic past, sagas of the confrontation of civilization and savagery or primitivism in a world that was, by the time the novels were written, under the sway of what Richard Slotkin calls the "metropolis."[5] The frontier novel's exploration of social problems has interested critics mainly in a historical sense, as Richard Chase explains of Cooper's fiction: "Such a culture was momentarily possible in eighteenth-century America. But since it had become all but impossible in the time of Cooper, the myth that enhances and justifies it has perforce to be nostalgic, ironic, and self-contradictory . . . its ultimate meaning is anti-cultural" (*American Novel*, 54). The three novels explore social problems, the solutions of which are forgone, their legacy a matter of historical record. As such, the novels' "larger meanings" are read most typically as attempts to mythologize and symbolize (*Mohicans, Yemassee*) or psychologize (*Nick*) the American frontier experience which in turn embody larger, eternal conflicts in human nature or within the individual.[6]

Recent interest in historicist and cultural–materialist approaches to literature have led to a reexamination of the ideological function of frontier novels. In *The Fatal Environment* Richard Slotkin brings to his earlier mythological thesis of the frontier a poststructural and Marxist frame of reference that sees myth in a more socially mediative light. Viewed through this critical framework, frontier novels can be seen to function as more than an account of the past that simply mediates "eternal" conflicts and values. As they work to formulate a cultural tradition, they simultaneously frame specific, contemporary social action: "These myths [of the frontier] not only define a situation for us, they prescribe our response to that situation" (*Fatal Environment*, 19). Slotkin deftly argues that frontier novels create a myth that is ideologically loaded: they "aim at affecting not only our perceptions but our behavior—by 'enlisting' us, morally or physically, in the ideological program" (19).

These novels have great socially mediative potential, and their contemporary significance cannot be overlooked. Granted that New York, the Carolinas, and Kentucky no longer bordered "wilderness" at the time the novels were published, but the frontier experience did continue farther west. Moreover, the Native Americans were an ongoing "problem" for Anglo Americans in areas that were now considered "civilized." These novels deal with historical situations but concomitantly suggest attitudes toward the frontier that had immediate and possibly even formative relevance to the period in which they were first read.[7]

Slotkin argues the importance of recognizing cultural prevalence of the frontier ethos during the period that these novels became popular, but he argues that the frontier myth was tempered as settlers reached the Rockies, and that for this reason the contemporary relevance of frontier novels published during the twenties and thirties was diminished. The formidable range of mountains was perceived, he suggests, as a "permanent barrier" and America believed, albeit prematurely, that it had reached its "last frontier" (*Fatal Environment*, 110–11). Yet as Reginald Horsman documents, while the frontier reached a physical barrier, the frontier *spirit* did not reach an *imaginative* impasse during this period. Instead it continued to strengthen. Horsman points out that in the years just before these novels were written, statesmen, journalists, and other public figures were predicting the nation's progress *past* the Rockies. For instance, as early as 1811 John Quincy Adams prophesied that "the whole continent of North America appears to be *destined by Divine Providence* to be peopled by one *nation*, speaking one language, professing one general system of religious and political principles, and accustomed to one general tenor of social usages and customs" (qtd. in Horsman, 87). Henry Clay made similar predictions in 1820 (see Horsman, 93). And we cannot overlook the fact that the 1830s were the definitive era of "Indian Removal."[8] Although the frontier may have slackened its forward march during the period when these novels were written, its ambitions were not thereby limited. In fact Americans in these two decades were giving voice to a powerful new chapter in their superiority narrative which both justified and fueled their progress across the continent: Manifest Destiny.

William Dowling suggests that "the world comes to us in the shape of stories," underscoring narrative not simply as a literary form but as an "epistemological category":

> Like the Kantian concepts of space and time . . . narrative may be taken not as a feature of our experience but as one of the abstract or 'empty' coordinates within which we come to know the world, a contentless form that our perception imposes on the raw flux of reality, giving it, even as we perceive, the comprehensible order we call experience. (95–96)

Clearly, we should not underestimate the role of frontier literature—stories which order that experience, suggesting strategies of ideological containment—in shaping social realities. Edwin Fussell has rightly observed that "the West was won by American literature" (11). This conquest functions on two levels. Symbolically, the West was won in history by selectively replaying past victories and claiming them as a continuous national tradition. More immediately, these stories offered a certain perspective and encouraged reader identification with the characters, who embodied a particular kind of "successful" national tradition. Whether, as with Natty Bumppo, the death of Indians was inevitable and regrettable or, as with Nathan Slaughter, their death was necessary and laudable, the end result was an acceptance of a historical *and* ongoing policy toward living Native Americans, as though it were "natural" and already graven in (tomb)stone.

Story and Identity in *Nick of the Woods*

One of the ways in which we can most clearly see the contemporary, mediative function of these frontier histories is by examining their common denominators. Each novel contains an awareness of its role in portraying for its civilized audience the brutal exigencies of frontier reality. In fact, each novel features a subplot that highlights the constant and strategic necessity for the "metropolis" or the "civilized" sector of the colony to *accept* what are portrayed as the actualities of the frontier, including the inevitable 'removal' of Indians.[9] In this respect we might take *Nick of the Woods* as paradigmatic. This text foregrounds frontier storytelling as the means by which a nation coalesces its attitudes about Indians. This important aspect of *Nick of the Woods* delineates *how* narrative can operate as social medicine—how in fact the West *might* be won by American literature—and establishes the importance of frontier literature to the shaping of contemporary attitudes.

Nick of the Woods devolves around several convoluted plots. The aristocratic mainstays, Virginian cousins Roland and Edith Forrester, are deprived of their inheritance and come to Kentucky to seek their fortune. Roland, the city boy who comes to the wilderness to nurse his wrongs, is sulky and imperious and he has foolishly led himself and Edith into a compromising situation. Earlier scornful of the frontiersmen's bloodlust for the Indians, Roland is now in a fix that tests his haughty attitudes. He personally encounters the villainous and drunken Indians he has heard tell of—in fact, his life is temporarily in the keeping of three bloodthirsty Shawnees and might quickly have been extinguished but for the Quaker Nathan Slaughter.

Until this point in the narrative, Nathan has been portrayed as a pacifist who steadfastly refuses to lift his weapon against a human target—this despite the extensive and persistent castigation of his fellow backwoodsmen. Now, however, he must explain to Roland how the three Indians guarding him are (viciously) killed and Roland set free. At first he adopts a regretful pose of "border necessity," in response to which the excessively relieved Roland proclaims Nathan an international hero. But shortly after, as the two set off together to rescue Edith from the Shawnee chief, Wenonga, Nathan becomes so exasperated with Roland's citified foolishness and vain scruples that he sits him down to educate him properly. He tells him a story. Representing the deeper motive behind the backwoodsman's curious behavior, Nathan's story is a lesson in realism on the frontier.

Slaughter's tale begins on the Pennsylvanian frontier, in Bradford, when he was married and supporting his mother, wife, and five children. One day the famous Shawnee chief (of whom Roland has not heard, a key indicator of his city ignorance) came onto Slaughter's property with a band of warriors. To show Wenonga that he was a man of peace, Nathan handed the chief his gun and knife. Wenonga proceeded to slay and scalp, with Nathan's own weapons, all of the family. He in fact scalped Nathan, as Nathan dramatically reveals to Roland by pulling off his hat.

Enacting the story, reliving it in the telling, sends Nathan into an epileptic seizure. Its effects are nearly as powerful for Roland. When he recovers Nathan questions Roland: "Had they done so by *thee*, what would thee have done to them?" Roland, "greatly excited by the story," replies: "Declared eternal war upon them and their accursed race!" "Thee is right," affirms Nathan and elevates the lesson to the level of (Quakeresque) incantation: "Thee would kill, friend, thee would kill, thee would kill!" (236). This episode marks the true beginning of Roland's education. He now perceives Nathan as heroic and models his own behavior after the Indian-hater's. As he declares in the end, "A braver heart, a truer friend, never served man in time of need" (346). Roland never becomes adept in the woods of the frontier, but he learns to accept frontier "necessity," and to participate in and eventually to condone Indian slaughter. Moreover, when he returns to civilization, he returns equipped with Nathan's story and perspective.

Nathan provides a frame of reference for Roland's subsequent experience of the Kentucky frontier. It is important to remember (as we will see in the following discussion of Sedgwick's *Hope Leslie*) that Nathan's vindictive perspective was not the *only* alternative. But Nathan's story becomes Roland's interpretive grid through the rhetorical function of identification. Roland immediately associates his own experience with Nathan's—he, too, is in danger of losing his beloved to evil Indians. Kenneth Burke discusses the rhetorical function of identification as a means of persuasion, an analysis which is relevant to the rhetorical function of Nathan's story. Nathan's experience has transformed his own life, and his narrative transforms Roland's estimation of Nathan as he tells it—from cowardly pacifist to righteous and heroic Indianhater. Further, Roland models his own vow—eternal enmity—on Nathan's if Edith cannot be rescued. In short, Nathan's story transforms Roland too. Roland now shares Nathan's perspective of undying hatred against the Indians. Even if Roland does not personally enact violence, he participates vicariously by condoning and encouraging Nathan.

At another level the *reader* is encouraged to identify with Nathan and to consider him heroic. The narrator functions as Roland's twin, bringing the frontier lesson back to civilization and forward in time. Like Roland *we* have heard Nathan's tale, "what the Shawnees have done to me—they have killed them all, all that was of my blood!" Nathan's question is put to the reader as well: "Had they done so by *thee*, what would thee have done?" The question encourages that the reader as well as Roland identify him or herself with the narrator, in fact presupposes that alignment, as the rest of *Nick of the Woods* is oriented around that approval. "Identification" embodies rhetoric's (or narrative's) highest goal, that of "perfect understanding and community" (Lentricchia, *Social Change*, 148). Thus, this powerful rhetorical device marks the character of the frontier story as socially mediative in a contemporary sense, offering a political positioning to the reader in the metropolis of the 1830s.

Frontier myth, as Slotkin argues, links past heroic achievement with "another in the future of which the reader is the potential hero" (*Fatal Environment*, 19). Deploying the rhetorical function of identification, frontier novels invoke "tradition" as a unifying force, an essential grouping of experiences, perspectives, and strategies particular to a certain group of people. As many critics have observed, these early frontier novels self-consciously strove to frame a distinctly American tradition. What has often been overlooked is how these novels can serve to mediate contemporary situations by invoking a distinctly American tradition or history.

Tradition, observes Frank Lentricchia, is "always already a present and a future." It must never be understood, therefore, as an "entity, a static thing, a completed process," but must be seen as a dynamic and political formation, an ongoing formulation: "'the tradition' should be seen as techniques of psychic defense against our own complicity," techniques that have further a "marked disposition to suppress . . . material conditions" (*Social Change*, 124–25). Nathan Slaughter's story seeks to implicate its readers in its drive for revenge precisely by absolving them of complicity in political and historical circumstance. Instead, it offers them a reason to hate Indians that arises from a sense of innocent personal loss. After all, Nathan was a Quaker, living peacefully with his family on the frontier. His story, however, elides the historical, material circumstances that placed Nathan in Bradford on the frontier, and omits any historical consideration of why the Shawnees were in the area marauding local inhabitants.

Nathan's story is situated within a framework of historical events that, though not explicitly mentioned, would indicate that Bird was aware of Shawnee history within the Pennsylvania region and the Ohio valley.[10] Briefly, in order to enjoy a peaceful life under the benevolent auspices of Quaker William Penn, a band of Shawnees had joined the Delawares in the Susquehanna valley of Pennsylvania in the early eighteenth century. By mid-century, however, as Gary Nash documents, frontier families, eager to acquire and cultivate the fertile lands of the region, were becoming increasingly hostile and aggressive toward the native population. Finally, to clear the land completely for agrarian expansion, Pennsylvanian statesmen coerced Iroquois leaders to force the Delawares and Shawnees to leave the valley (Nash, *Red, White, and Black*, 98–100). This dispossession would have taken place twenty to thirty years before the action of the story in 1782. Bradford, located in north–central Pennsylvania and in the Susquehanna valley, may well have been vulnerable to the attacks of angry Shawnees who felt again betrayed and increasingly frustrated by white incursion. Nathan's story, however, invites us to overlook these factors, focusing instead on the innocence of Nathan, who hands over his weapons, and the other helpless victims. This rhetorical pattern recurs throughout much frontier literature: historical consciousness of any cultural dialectic is elided and replaced with a mythologized Other. The "Indian" is fixed timelessly in his role as enemy; the author, the reader, and their shared (dominant) culture are relieved of responsibility and guilt.

The Timeless Present

We should examine this process of Othering more closely. At a basic level, *The Last of the Mohicans, The Yemassee*, and *Nick of the Woods* serve to inform their white audiences about the Indians that the stories dominate. Much as Thomas Jefferson assiduously collected relics from the dying tribes, these novels eternalize the Indians while they sing their funeral anthem. All three novels feature sections that memorialize the manners and customs of the various Indians under discussion. As Mary Louise Pratt notes, such descriptions are a common feature of frontier literature and seldom occur as discrete texts, but they are most usually contained within a "superordinate genre." The manners and custom portrait is, she observes, a "normalizing discourse, whose work is to codify difference, to fix the Other in a timeless present where all 'his' actions are repetitions of 'his' normal habits" (121).

This notion of a timeless and fixed Indian essence was highly strategic to a society that prided itself on its "march of progress," and it is important to consider how it is deployed in each novel. In rendering Indian life-styles, each author abstracts his portrait from immediate interaction or conflict with Anglo intruders. Pratt helpfully summarizes this dehistoricizing narrative mechanism:

> The people to be othered are homogenized into a collective "they" which is distilled even further into an iconic "he" (the standard adult male specimen). The abstracted "he"/"they" is the subject of verbs in a timeless present tense, which characterizes anything "he" is or does not as a particular historical event but as an instance of a pregiven custom or trait. . . . Through this discourse, encounters with an Other can be textualized or processed as enumerations of such traits. (120)

As we begin to see, the root motive of manners and customs is not curiosity but domination. As a communication or social exchange, they establish a point of intersubjectivity between (in this case) Anglo-American authors and Anglo-American readers who seek to "know" the native, not for humanistic purposes, but instead as a means to power. Literature can be seen this way as *elemental* to the material process of society. As Lentricchia reminds us, "To write is to know is to dominate" (*Social Change*, 147). Examining the novels, then, from this perspective helps to illuminate their contemporary usefulness.

The Last of the Mohicans is not straightforward romance, but combines the genres of frontier romance, travelogue, and novel of manners. In fact, the opening pages of the story introduce all three within as many chapters. In the third chapter begin the sketches of Indian manners and customs that will recur throughout the novel. As that chapter opens, Leatherstocking and Chingachgook are engaged in a discussion, apparently over the legitimacy of the Anglo colonial presence in America. The narrator introduces and describes the physical appearance of each character, immediately establishing himself as an authority on Indians and the frontier life by footnoting for additional detail exceptional and curious items of dress and habit of the two characters — Chingachgook's scalp-lock, Leatherstocking's hunting-shirt.

Indian (or, more precisely, Delaware) tradition is the subject of discussion at the point that the reader "enters" the scene, and notably, Leatherstocking is summarizing it. From this early point the narrator apparently defers to Natty Bumppo's expertise on "Indians." The footnotes continue and are reserved mostly for what we might term "frontier knowledge" — asides on mockingbirds, historical events, the nature of the forest. The Indian asides are left to Natty, who is forever clarifying to his Anglo audience "Indian nature," "Indian skill," "Indian ways," and "Indian gifts." Natty's demonstration of his expertise begins immediately, when Chingachgook subtly questions Natty's use of Delaware tradition to make a point in his (white) favor. Natty comments, "There is reason in an Indian, though nature has made him with a red skin!" (30).

Chingachgook is allowed to speak for his tradition and in his telling, the reader "glimpses" native history and cosmology. But here, as in depictions of native life and religious belief in the second volume of the novel, native tradition is insistently called into question, either by a reference to "white" knowledge or even by the native characters themselves. In this passage Chingachgook is explaining why the delta area of the river alternates between fresh and salt water. In Delaware cosmology the explanation is fluid dynamics. The river runs out to the ocean until an equilibrium is reached. Then the ocean water mingles with the fresh water until the balance is again offset, to the point where the river must run again. A feasible explanation by itself, Chingachgook's theory is called into question by Natty's more authoritative (biblically documented — "the truest thing in nature," 31–32) tidal theory.[11]

Through a similar process of narratorial filtering, Indian behavior, like Indian knowledge/intellectuality, is cast in an inferior light. Although the actions and motivations of Uncas and Chingachgook are clearly intended to be seen as noble, they are always characterized by Natty as representative, not exceptional, Indian action. For instance, when Uncas makes what is presented as an exceedingly difficult shot with his bow and arrow, Natty (in a comment reminiscent of William Byrd's regarding Bearskin) does not congratulate him for unusual prowess, but comments, "twas done with Indian skill" (35). The cumulative effect of such comments makes it clear that there is nothing really *exceptional* about Chingachgook and Uncas. Whether the Indian is "good" or "bad," his "gifts" are essentially the same.

Lacking space to catalog or even survey the countless expositions of the narrative on "Indian nature," I will proceed directly to the most developed one. In it is an excellent example of how the "timeless present" is constructed and how it mediates a political agenda.[12] Richard Slotkin notes the "mythic" qualities of the second volume or section of *The Last of the Mohicans*, where Natty and company have pursued the evil Magua to a Huron settlement. Slotkin argues in his introduction that here the novel leaves all pretense of historicity, entering instead an "unchanging and archetypal wilderness" for a fictional purpose ("Introduction," *Mohicans*, xx–xxxiii). That purpose, he proposes, is to allegorize the course of (Anglo) civilization: "Cooper's Indians are a metaphorical rendering of our own civilization" (xxxiii). While admitting the plausibility of Slotkin's reading, I would like to propose an equally meaningful social and intercultural (as opposed to intellectual and monocultural) function for the mythic tone of volume 2. Slotkin himself notes Cooper's dependence for information here on John Heckwelder's *History, Manners and Customs of the Indian Nations* (1818). Seen as a portrait of manners, this section so effectively mythologizes the Indian as a means of Othering that it distracts readers from seeing how its timelessness served (and perhaps continues to serve) the Anglo political agenda.

Volume 2 of the book takes place in Indian encampments. In short order the reader is presented with accounts of Indian village life, tribal government, and social practice — gauntlet-running, executions, exorcism rituals, and burial practice. Prominent in this section is what Pratt characterizes as "the very familiar, widespread and stable form of othering." We see this clearly in the first paragraph of chapter 23, which is worth quoting in full:

It is unusual to find an encampment of the natives, like those of the more instructed whites, guarded by the presence of armed men. Well informed of the approach of every danger, while it is yet at a distance, the Indian generally rests secure under his knowledge of the signs of the forest, and the long and difficult paths that separate him from those he has most reason to dread. But the enemy who, by any lucky concurrence of accidents, has found means to elude the vigilance of the scouts, will seldom meet with sentinels nearer home to sound the alarm. In addition to this general usage, the tribes friendly to the French knew too well the weight of the blow that had just been struck, to apprehend any immediate danger from the hostile nations that were tributary to the crown of Britain. (232)

Recall Pratt's definition of the Othering process: "The iconic 'he'/'they' is the subject of verbs in a timeless present tense, which characterizes anything 'he' is or does not as a particular historical event but as an instance of a pregiven custom or trait." Here the narrator presents unchallengeable authority in an apparently objective, fully knowledgeable, and empiric description. The time-less "general usage" is that the "Indian generally rests secure," due to his "knowledge" (albeit less "instructed") and position. We should recall at this point that Indian knowledge according to the narrative is not structured upon empiricism. Rather, it is an inherent feature of Indian nature, as Natty ex-claims of Chingachgook in the opening pages: "These Indians know the nature of the woods, as it might be by instinct!" (34).

The Indians Heyward encounters and the narrator describes are clearly "homogenized into a collective 'they'" whose actions are often sudden and—curiously for all the authority the narrator assumes—inexplicable. Heyward sees native children as he approaches the village. But suddenly "the whole of the juvenile pack raised, by common consent, a shrill and warning whoop; and then sank, as it were, by magic, from before the sight of their visitors" (232). This collective and unexplained action prefigures a more frightening and unanimous action to come, as Heyward's negotiations with tribal mem-bers are interrupted by a "sudden and terrible" cry. "At the same moment, the warriors glided in a common body from the lodge" and shortly, "the whole encampment, in a moment, became a scene of the most violent bustle and commotion" (235). Unified by their "nature," the Hurons' actions here can only be described, not explained in any way that makes sense to the "white" reader. In the same manner, Natty had earlier excused Chingachgook's appar-ently unmotivated murder of the French guard (137). And we should note the strategic cultural value of the fact that any action that threatens Anglo-colonials is presented as being inexplicable, attributable only to some mysteri-ous imperative of Indian "instinct."

But other, less physically threatening aspects of native life are perfectly explicable. Whereas earlier Chingachgook lent some authority to Indian cos-mology by preferring it to white accounts, the credibility of native spiritual medicine is undermined by the natives themselves. Heyward is called on to express the goodwill of his "Great Father" by healing the daughter of an elder warrior. Heyward, who after all has taken no Hippocratic oath, consents to perform an exorcism of the evil spirit in order to further his chances of finding the captive Alice. The description of native belief is given an odd twist, to be performed by a "white," and described through his perspective:

> The impatient Heyward, inwardly execrating the cold customs of the savages, which required such sacrifices to appearance, was fain to assume an air of indifference, equal to that maintained by the chief, who was, in truth, a near relative of the afflicted woman. The minutes lingered, and the delay seemed an hour to the adventurer in empiricism. (246)

Duncan's white, scientific perspective casts the ensuing ritual as a fraud from the start; unlike Chingachgook's earlier account of river and ocean currents, there is no doubt left to the white reader that Indian medicine is sheer "self-delusion" (264). The sham is amplified when Natty appears, doubly disguised as a Huron medicine man in the costume of a bear. According to superstitious Indian custom, the medicine-man-*cum*-bear is accorded the respect and fear of a real bear. The two whites are easily able to turn Indian beliefs against their "weak-minded" believers in order to accomplish their own ends.

Of course, not *all* Indians are fooled so easily. The wily Magua scorns Indian "superstition." He, the readers are told, "is far above the more vulgar superstitions of his tribe" (261) and disdains to humor the conjuror, whom he associates with "women and children." And Natty, so far successful in his disguise, realizes as well its limitations: "At the same time that he had presumed so far on the nature of the Indian superstitions, [Natty] was not ignorant that they were rather tolerated than relied on by the wisest of chiefs" (264). The integrity of native tradition is hereby subverted since the "wisest of chiefs," whether good or bad, understands its fraudulent essence. It is striking, too, that this strategy leaves the honor of superior knowledge on the side of the Anglo author and reader: The "wisest" of Indians manages to know what the white author, characters and readers all *already* know.

As in *The Last of the Mohicans, The Yemassee* attests to its own authority on Indian life and manners even before its opening pages. In his 1853 preface Simms explains that "when I wrote, there was little understood, by readers, generally, in respect to the character of red men; and, of the opinions entertained on the subject, many, according to my own experience, I knew to be incorrect" (4). Accordingly Simms sets out to correct these misconceptions, to "remove that air of mystery which was supposed to disguise their most ordinary actions" (4).

Among the most important to Simms was to correct the "rude portraits of the red man, as given by those who see him in degrading attitudes only, and in humiliating relations with the whites." These, Simms insists, "must not be taken as a just delineation of the same being in his native woods, unsubdued, a fearless hunter, and without any degrading habits, to make him wretched and ashamed" (4). Simms's strategy for depicting the manners and customs of his Yemassee Indians makes a curious departure from Cooper, whose Indians were relatively unchanging in their behavior. This is not to say, however, that

Simms's Indians had a changeable *nature*; they didn't. But their *behavior* was much more flexible and was influenced completely (for the worse) by the superior Anglo settlers.

The opening pages of *The Yemassee* provide readers with a historical sketch of the Yemassee tribe. This passage is marked with frequent footnotes, the first of which sets an undeniable tone of authority: "We are speaking now of authentic history only" (9n). Subsequent notes document the narrator's extensive knowledge of Yemassee language. (This authority, however, is somewhat undermined, as Richard C. Shaner observes, when the narrator characterizes the Yemassee tribe as being indigenous to the Carolinas, since they were originally from what is now Georgia and Florida.) Comparable in political savvy to the Romans, the mighty Yemassees had strengthened their own power "by a wise incorporation of the conquered with the conquerors" (10). "Politic . . . generous and gallant" were the Yemassee when the whites first set foot on the continent (11).

The Yemassees' astute political dealings with other tribes could not—and this seems to be Simms's sense of the tragedy—extend to its relations with the whites. Sharing the land with the new settlers was "improvident" (10), and they remained for too long blind to their "inferiority to a power of which they, at length, grew jealous" (11). This jealousy, which arises as they realize their thoroughly subordinate nature, marks a change in Yemassee behavior. No longer noble and brave, "their chiefs began to show signs of discontent, if not of disaffection" toward the whites, and worse, "the great mass of their people assumed a sullenness of habit and demeanor, which had never marked their conduct before" (11).

The narrator is remarkably explicit in affixing some share of blame to the white settlers. Characterized as "bold and incursive" (11), the white backwoodsmen "removed from the surveillance of society, committed numberless petty injuries upon the property, and sometimes upon the person of his wandering neighbor" (20). Further, like William Byrd, the narrator questions the religious ideals of the early settlers:

> An abstract standard of justice, independent of appetite or circumstance, has not often marked the progress of Christian (so-called) civilization, in its proffer of its great good to the naked savage. The confident reformer, who takes sword in one hand and sacrament in the other, has always found it in the surest way to rely chiefly on the former. (20)

"To sum it all up in a little," the narrator later comments, "our European ancestors were, in many respects, monstrous great rascals" (221). But even though the narrator may question some of the actions of those European ancestors, what he never questions is the absolute value of civilization which places the white settlers in a relationship of superiority to the natives. It is the natives' own consciousness of this that brings out the worst in their ultimately inferior nature.

Nearly every characterization of Indians in *The Yemassee*, then, is made in reference to Anglo colonial incursion, for the debased Indian is in some sense a product of his contact with the "white." For instance, the narrator describes Sanutee (the chief of the Yemassee who yet retains strains of nobility though those are increasingly corrupted by jealousy): "The warrior was armed after Indian fashion." He carries a bow and a tomahawk. Suggestively (and reminiscent of the "cock" sported by Underhill's Anglicized Indian), the latter weapon is *not* "after the Indian fashion." Rather, as the narrator reveals, the "light weapon . . . introduced by the colonists," is a "substitute for the stone hatchet" the Indians had formerly carried. Similarly Sanutee's dress "indicated a frequent intercourse with the whites. . . . The warrior before us had been among the first to avail himself of the arts of the whites in the improvement of costume; nay, he had taken other lessons, of even greater value, from the superior race" (15). The Indian's recognition of "white" superiority is indicated in the manner that he clothes and defends himself. Thus, Simms's native is dominated (and possibly emasculated) both by his own recognition and unconscious consent.

Historical dialectic is traced in Sanutee's attire. But relations within the tribe are portrayed in the timeless present. A dominative and instinctive (as opposed to rationally organized) hierarchy structures Yemassee life. As we see in Sanutee's domestic relations with his wife, Matiwan, the husband expects complete subservience. Matiwan is characterized as a "fawn" who is afraid even to touch or speak to her husband uninvited (72), and Sanutee loves her "as a child rather than a wife" (70). (Presumably the contrast here is to how a "white" would love his wife.) Just as rigid, but less effectual, is the tribal structure. The tribe's government is superficially democratic, as the narrator details:

> The Yemassees were ruled by the joint authority of several chiefs—each controlling a special section with arbitrary authority, yet, when national measures were to be determined upon, it required a majority for action. These chiefs were elective, and from these the superior, or presiding chief, was duly chosen; all of these, without exception, were accountable to the nation. (74)

Lest the reader gather too much admiration, the narrator adds, "such accountability was rather the result of popular impulse than of any other more legitimate or customary regulation" (75). And in fact the government, now under the sway of the settlers, is completely ineffectual. The natural aristocracy which formerly predominated with good effect among the Yemassee has given way to the influences of lower Indian nature. For example, when the settlers try to drive a bargain with the tribal government, purposely avoiding the more powerful chiefs whom they know will oppose further land sales, the Indians have a meeting to discuss the deal. Unlike the orderly and ceremonious tribal councils Cooper depicts, this meeting verges on mayhem, with the chiefs who are corrupted by the "whites" opposing the chiefs who are jealous of the "whites." In the end the issue is resolved not rationally but by resort to what is portrayed as Indian habit: superstition and brute force.

As is typical in frontier novels, and indispensable to the process of Other-ing, few Indians are individually delineated. As the narrative progresses, we see an actual diminishment in the individual portrayal of Indian characters. Rather, the narrator more and more focuses on the nature of the Indian mob which is characterized as a degraded and dangerous force which can as easily turn on itself as on the white settlers. The mob is quickly aroused to wreak vengeance on the corrupted chiefs who signed a deal with the colonists. To carry the point home, the narrative portrays how, when the Indian mob rushes out to punish the colonists, in their enthusiasm they mistakenly attack one of their own: "they dashed him to the earth, trampled and nearly tore him into pieces before discovering the mistake" (92). Increasingly through the narrative, the Yemassee are characterized as an iconic "they" who can easily be classified, if not rationally understood. The narrator summarizes the essential point: "the elements of all uncultivated people are the same" (241).

Harrison, the gentleman hero of the action, has the opportunity personally to experience the Yemassee mob. Like Natty, Harrison has an especially ex-pert knowledge of the "true nature" (98) of the natives, a familiarity so com-plete that when he is in their presence his caution is characterized as "Indian instinct" (223). Discovered by the Yemassee mob during their preparations for attacking the Anglo settlement, Harrison notices "a generous degree of forbearance . . . on the part of the better-looking among the spectators." This comes as no surprise to Harrison, who knows that "the insolent portion of the rabble formed a class especially for such purposes as the present [i.e., his torture]" (246). This emphasis on visible manifestation of inner character is important in establishing the continuity of hierarchy among the natives, as well as between Indians and the Anglo colonists. Just as the uglier Indians are inferior to the better-looking ones like Sanutee (see 16), so are the "irritably red features" (223) of the Indians generally an index to the superiority of the "whites." In the end, while *The Yemassee* directs some guilt for the denigrated Indian on the colonists, the guilt is of the most innocent kind. The whites "do" nothing more than be naturally superior, a crime of nothing more than coincidence or fate.

Robert Montgomery Bird's Indians are much less complex than Cooper's and less dynamic than Simms's. Perhaps for this reason *Nick of the Woods* devotes comparatively little space to developing portraits of native manners and customs. Rather, from the outset Bird assumes a universalized and un-changing Indian, one who is thoroughly debased and completely savage. At only two points in the narrative is the reader offered a closer look. In the first, Roland, Edith, and Stackpole are surprised by the troop of Indians they thought they had escaped. Like the irrational Yemassees, these Shawnees are a bloodthirsty mob. Angered at their own losses, the Indians rehearse their vengeance on the already dead bodies of the "whites" by mutilating their corpses, "striking the senseless clay repeatedly with their knives and hatchets, each seeking to surpass his fellow in the savage work of mutilation" (201). "Such is the red-man of America," the narrator comments. Generalizing what is even in this narrative a specific and motivated action (the Shawnees have just defeated the Kentuckians in a skirmish, but have lost several Shawnee lives) to an abstract and eternal Indian nature, the narrator underscores its unchangeability, insisting that the Indians are a "barbarous race, which contact with a civilized one cannot civilize" (202).

Although the narrative plays up the grotesqueness of these actions, they are at least set in a context that makes them attributable to grief and rage. Like Cooper's Indians, though, Bird's Shawnees often act from simple, irrational, and inexplicable bloodthirstiness. An old Piankeshaw warrior to whom Roland is given in the division of spoils alternately threatens the captive with death and cajoles him as a "brudder," with apparently no intervening motivation (202–3). Indian religion, as when the Piankeshaw spreads out the scruffy contents of his medicine bag while performing some unaccountable ritual, is equally ludicrous and unexplainable. The torment of victims is capricious and unpredictable. The narrator summarizes: "It is only among children (we mean, of course, *bad* ones) and savages, who are but grown children, after all, that we find malice and mirth go hand in hand—the will to create misery and the power to see it invested in ludicrous colors" (209).[13] The bad, childlike Indian is sure to do only two things: drink himself into a drunken stupor whenever possible, and kill "white" people at every opportunity.

We might here posit a continuum of Indian statesmanship among the three novels. The Indians in *The Last of the Mohicans* gather to debate political issues. In *The Yemassee*, the Indians gather at least in an attempt to do so. However, in *Nick of the Woods* the Indians gather only to form warring parties, to divide plunder, and to boast. Predictably, Bird's depiction of Indian rhetoric differs significantly from that in the other two novels. No matter how antagonistic Magua was to Anglo colonial interests, his oratorical skills were undeniably admirable even to the colonialists. In *The Yemassee* the power of Indian rhetoric affects only the natives and functions only to incite the mob, as the narrator notes of Sanutee's impassioned speech to prevent further sale of Yemassee lands: "The rash, the thoughtless, the ignorant—all were aroused by his eloquence" (84). In *Nick*, however, Indian speeches are only absurdly garrulous performances. Those who have perceived the Indian as taciturn should be better informed, observes the narrator. Silence on the part of an Indian in the presence of whites comes only from his wish to "cover the nakedness of his own inferiority" (264).[14] Among his own people he gives himself over to "wild indulgence." The chief delivers a speech to the victorious war band and their hostages, very little of which Roland is able to understand as the chief does not know much English:

His oration . . . consisted chiefly in informing him that he was a very great chief, who had killed abundance of white people, men, women and children, whose scalps had, for thirty years and more, been hanging in the smoke of his Shawnee lodge,— that he was very brave and loved a white man's blood better than whiskey, and that he never spared it out of pity . . . the whole speech consisted, like most other Indian speeches, of the same things said over and over again, those same things being scarce worth the trouble of utterance. (204–5)

Like their speeches, the Indians themselves are in *Nick of the Woods* "scarce worth the trouble of utterance," even while their presence in the novel is what fuels its narrative economy.

The reader's closest view of Indian life in *Nick of the Woods* comes when Nathan enters the Shawnee village to rescue Edith. We see in the narrator's observations a process of Othering similar to that in volume 2 of *The Last of the Mohicans*. As Nathan scouts the village, the reader is told of the "oppressed and degraded women" who water the cornfields in their keeping with tears (264). Nathan manages to avoid the Indian dogs by shaking a string of bells at them. The dogs, expecting to be killed "in the usual summary Indian way" run off immediately (268). When Stackpole gives his compatriots away, and he along with Roland and Nathan are captured, the reader learns that "we know of no instance where an Indian, torturing a prisoner at the stake, the torture once begun, has ever been moved to compassionate, to regard any feelings but those of exultation and joy, the agonies of the thrice-wretched victim" (329). The Indian is rendered monodimensional. To know one Indian is to know them all, and by the same token to have reason to kill one is ample rationale for genocide.

Despite (or precisely because of) the authority established by each of these narratives on their Indian objects, such accounts are always dominative and, as Abdul JanMohamed argues, always suspect. "Since the object of representation—the native—does not have access to these texts (because of linguistic barriers) and since the [white] audience has no direct contact with the native, imperialist fiction tends to be unconcerned with the truth-value of its representation" ("Economy," 63). Indeed, Simms's elaborate and extended renditions of Yemassee mythology are complete fakeries, as he passingly admits in his 1853 preface: "That portion of the story, which the reverend critics, with one exception, recognised as sober history, must be admitted to be a pure invention—one, however, based on such facts and analogies as, I venture to think, will not discredit the proprieties of the invention" (4). Simms, amused at pulling one over on his critics, can at once admit that he made it all up while still claiming a definite authority therein.

In all three novels these accounts of Indian life are devoted to developing a perspective on Indian extermination that obscures Anglo colonialist involvement. Dorothy Hammond and Alto Jablow rightly point to a "unifying theme of confrontation" between the "white" colonialist and the racial Other in frontier literature (17). Yet it is important to note that in each of the three novels the dynamics of that confrontation are never the *directly* determining factor in the demise of the racial Other. Rather, responsibility is consistently displaced onto the natives. Here again we can posit a continuum in the three novels, with the most vauntedly "realistic" of the depictions being the one that comes nearest to implicating "white" colonists in the genocide of the Indians, the most "romanticized" most effectively evading that association. In *Nick of the Woods* the Indians' savage quest to kill "whites" demands their death through self-defense and revenge of those "whites." While it is not technically their fault (Nick the pacifist Quaker must go crazy before he is able to participate here), the narrative does let us see Anglo settlers killing Indians. In *The Yemassee* the Indians, besides being completely inferior and therefore subject to the "relentless . . . onward progress" of civilization (69), are by nature so "capricious" that it is "doubtful whether they can, for any length of time, continue in peace and friendship" (158). Even while the narrative manages to locate some of the guilt of the frontier violence on the part of the colonists, the ultimate reason for Indian wars rests with the natives themselves. When we do see a "white" killing an Indian, the action switches curiously into a passive voice. Harrison's role as the "Coosah-moray-te," or Coosaw-killer (he has, apparently almost single-handedly, caused the extermination of the majority of the tribe) is invoked only to explain the surviving Coosaws' unwavering resolution to kill him, but is hardly accounted for otherwise. When Harrison gets the best of the last Coosaw chief in the struggle, the Indian, lying at Harrison's feet, urges him to strike. Apparently the governor does: "The knife was in his heart. Vainly the eyes rolled in a fruitless anger—the teeth fixed for ever . . . a short groan . . . and the race of the Coosaw was for ever ended. Harrison rose and looked around" (338). In this curious passage, the reader sees the end of an Indian race without actually seeing the agency of the white hand in the death.[15]

Similarly, in *The Last of the Mohicans*, the Indians are guilty of their own demise but, significantly, here *not at the hand of the white*. We learn that the Chingachgook's lineage is threatened not by contact with civilization but by the constant enmity of the Delawares against other Indian nations. As Natty recounts, "'tis not often that books are made, and narratives written, of such a scrimmage as was here fou't atween the Mohicans and Mohawks, in a war of their own waging" (126). The Hurons are similarly ferocious; those taken on by the French commander Montcalm care very little who they fight, so long as they can fight. They are a (presumably inhuman) "engine which . . . exceeds human power to control" (171). Again we see how Indian actions that physically threaten "whites" are dehistoricized, depoliticized, and are therefore inexplicable and mysterious, attributable only to "Indian nature." It is nothing less than strategic that the end of the Mohican race in the narrative comes at the hands of a Mingo and is lamented by every "white" person present—including the French aid of Montcalm. Thus, in Dowling's terms, these stories provide "strategies of containment," defensive psychic maneuvers that guard the colonialist/reader against his or her own sense of (continuing) complicity.

A National Identity

Fixing the identity of the Indians in frontier novels was prerequisite to another, equally important enterprise: consolidating a "white" national identity. Roy Harvey Pearce observes that "the American before 1850—a new man [*sic*], as he felt, making a new world—was obsessed to know who and what he was and where he was going, to evaluate the special society in which he lived and to know its past and its future" (135). Anglo Americans were simultaneously expanding their borders *and* trying to limit them. While superficially contra-dictory, the motive underlying the simultaneous drive to expand and codify was the same. As Frank Lentricchia argues, "we purchase and preserve our identity beyond all change with the currency of a will to power rooted in an ethnocentric idea of community (the 'European mind' . . .) that would ex-clude and silence the voices in conflict with it" (130). Overcoming (without eliminating) class boundaries to conquer and silence the Indians was a funda-mental aspect of creating a national identity and, along with it, a national culture and literature—in short, an American book.

As Perry Miller argues in his essay "The Shaping of the American Charac-ter," the problem of the new nation "was to bring order out of chaos, to set up a government, to do it efficiently and quickly" (8). Like Miller, many scholars have sensed the importance of literature to the project of coalescing a national identity, its role in establishing an ideal through which very diverse Anglo American readers could recognize themselves together—hence the pro-fusion of studies of "the American novel." Burke's comments on identification pertain directly to the Anglo American identity quest in frontier novels. He argues that "identification is affirmed with earnestness precisely because there is a division. Identification is compensatory to division. If men were not apart from one another, there would be no need for the rhetorician to proclaim their unity" (*Rhetoric*, 22). The three frontier novels discussed here, while superficially acknowledging the profound socioeconomic differences within the Anglo-colonial system, work to repress class and social discrepancies under the rubric of a larger and fundamentally "white" American identity. White Americans become a unified front whose internal social and material conflicts are displaced onto a conflict fictionalized as Progress versus Nature, or White versus Red.

In *Virgin Land* Henry Nash Smith has discussed the implications of Natty's inferior socioeconomic status. He argues that although the issue is shunted aside in favor of action in *The Last of the Mohicans*, it created a "predicament for the novelist by revealing to him that his most vital character occupied a technically inferior position both in the social system and in the form of the sentimental novel" (*Virgin Land*, 70).[16] Cooper's own affinity to the aristo-cratic way of life has been immortalized (and perhaps overdrawn) by D. H. Lawrence, and certainly all of the Leatherstocking tales contain explorations of social hierarchy—the ultimate meaning of which are still up for debate. It is possible, however, to see Natty as a *resolver* of Anglo social tensions, rather than as a nagging reminder. Natty's firm insistence on "white gifts," for in-stance, delineates a universally "white" reaction to every frontier situation, usually fixed in firm opposition to a "red" one. Slotkin persuasively argues this position:

> Natty Bumppo is a commoner by birth who is lifted beyond the limitations of class by his apprenticeship to the Indians and the wilderness. But unlike the squatters, he never presumes on his special status, or on the peculiar freedom from restraint

provided by the wilderness . . . he symbolically renounces property . . . hence he will never become a competitor with his social superiors. . . . Instead, he . . . facilitates the resolution of social tensions. (*Fatal Environment*, 105)

The lowly born Natty is able to help the obviously more genteel Monro daughters, as well as the more cultured and slightly more capable men like Duncan Heyward and Monro himself. Colonialist men of different social and economic backgrounds close ranks against the Indian Menace, as Natty educates Heyward and they work together for "white" social and political interests.

My reading of "white unity" is obviously complicated by Natty's relationship with Chingachgook and Uncas, affirmed at the opening and closing of the novel. Without ignoring the ambivalence this creates for the novel's stance, we should also note how that ambivalence is qualified. In a key scene we understand more clearly how Natty is not compromised by his affiliation with the two Mohicans. The obverse does not fully apply. We see Uncas nearly executed for treason against his own Delaware people for consorting with the "Yengees." The sage chief Tamenund pronounces: "My people have not seen a bright sun in many winters; and the warrior who deserts his tribe when hid in clouds, is doubly a traitor" (308). Uncas is saved only by the revelation of his royal lineage. Natty, on the other hand, while consorting with the Mohicans, steadfastly refuses to betray Anglo colonial interest, even while he shuns its effects. His identity revolves around strictly delineated, specifically white "gifts." Even though he occasionally expresses reservations about his racial brothers' uses of those gifts, he insists on the importance of the distinction, more firmly than any other character in the novel. When Monro, overcome with grief, wishes Natty to express his sentiment that racial differences will be overcome in the next life, Natty categorically refuses to translate Monro's hope. "To tell them this," insists Natty, "would be to tell them that the snows come not in the winter" (347). "White" skin, like white snow, must retain its integrity. Natty's remarks hold the white line on the frontier.

In *The Yemassee*, the message of Anglo unity is the same, but Simms cannot be charged with sidestepping the political aspects of the issue as Henry Nash Smith accuses Cooper of doing. Rather, *The Yemassee* contains an explicit lesson on the Anglo project of civilization which will be realized through lower-class acquiescence to the leadership of the gentry. This lesson is emblematized in the dashing and gentlemanly Governor Craven, who is "disguised" during most of the novel's action as the mysterious (and gentlemanly) Gabriel Harrison. Craven has taken on a more humble persona to discover any plotting of the local Indians, and to avert their potentially devastating effects. In this guise he falls in love with (and is reciprocated by) the pastor's daughter, Bess Matthews. Although her father is upset at Harrison's inability to document his lineage, Bess and her mother need no material evidence to see that Harrison is "born and bred a gentleman" (199).

Bess is also unknowingly the beloved of a lowly born, backwoods boy named Hugh Grayson. Hugh hates Harrison and reacts vehemently against Harrison's noble bearing, as he relates to his brother:

> I cannot like that man for many reasons, and not the least of these is, that I cannot so readily as yourself acknowledge his superiority, while, perhaps, not less than yourself, I cannot help but feel it. My pride is to feel my independence — it is for you to desire control, were it only for the connexion and the sympathy which it brings to you. You are one of the millions who make tyrants. Go — worship him yourself, but do not call upon me to do likewise. (45)

Hugh is in fact clearly linked to the revolutionary figure Thomas Paine when he later explains, "my own mind is my teacher." (Simms cleanly tips his hand on the political context of that association when Grayson adds, "and perhaps my tyrant" [210].) It is clear from the ensuing action that the problem is not Grayson's concept of freedom — Harrison also confesses that "freedom is my infirmity" (48). Rather, the real problem is Grayson's prideful insubordination against his social betters. Literally deranged by grief after he witnesses a romantic interlude between Harrison and Bess, Grayson attempts to kill Harrison. Harrison, who can imagine no fellow "white" harboring enmity against him, adamantly refuses to believe that Grayson "has the right man." He saves Grayson from himself, as it were, and enlists him in the aid of the settlement (215–19). When the threat of the Yemassee uprising is realized, Grayson's better nature asserts itself. As the narrator relates, Grayson,

> with all his faults, and they were many, was in reality a noble fellow. Full of high ambition — a craving for the unknown and the vast, which spread itself vaguely and perhaps unattainably before his imagination — his disappointments very naturally vexed him somewhat beyond prudence, and now and then beyond the restraint of right reason. He usually came to a knowledge of his error before it had led too far. (304)

Grayson sets aside his social pretensions as he discovers his duty to be a "man and a citizen" (305). He unites with Harrison's cause against the Yemassee and, later, chastised and purified by battle with the Indians, learns further to submit to the wisdom of "that air of conscious superiority . . . that tone of command . . . of a power unquestionable" (347) that Harrison exudes through his gentlemanly bearing. Grayson becomes a happier and better "man" by playing his part as a "citizen" — recognizing and submitting to the authority of his social betters. This purification comes about, significantly, through the (white) civic project of Indian-killing. It is worth note that James Hall's "The Pioneers," published the same year as The Yemassee, recounts the Indian-hater William Robinson's boast in terms strikingly similar to Grayson's: "I believe that in killing the savage I performed my duty as a man and served my country as a citizen" (86). From this we can begin to see how class/social tensions are displaced onto a unified national identity (citizen) that is coalesced through the project of Indian killing.[17]

For Robert Montgomery Bird, the project of Indian-killing is the same, but the thrust of the social lesson is quite different. Unlike Simms' glorification of the natural aristocracy through his hero, Hugh Craven, Bird forwards the commoner–backwoodsman as the hero of the frontier. *Nick of the Woods* was conceived, as Bird promises in his preface to the first edition, to portray

> the character of men by whom — in the midst of difficulties and dangers as numerous and urgent, — perhaps more so than ever attended the establishing of a colony in North America, — were laid, upon a basis as firm as if planted by the subtlest and wisest spirits of the age, the foundations of a great and powerful State . . . drawn from what, in our vanity, we call the humbler spheres of life, — farmers and hunters, the mountaineers of Virginia and the Carolinas. (27)

These men, indigent and ignorant, have been the shaping force in American civilization: "Without the influence of any great and experienced mind to impel, direct or counsel, [they] succeeded in their vast enterprise . . . and secured to their conquest all the benefits of civil government and laws" (27). Robert Winston points out that Bird's proclaimed interest in the common man wanes after the preface (76), but a clear message about their importance is yet a significant aspect of the novel.

Bird is obviously more attracted to the narrative possibilities of his "gentlemanly" character, Roland Forrest, than to his Kentucky backwoodsmen, but he qualifies his endorsement of Roland on all counts. Roland is certainly "entitled to superior attention" (43) but he is also sulky, judgmental, and foolhardy. At first he scorns the backwoodsmen as "but one degree elevated above the Indians" (45), but his experiences in the woods under the guidance of Nathan chasten Roland and give him a healthy respect for the hardy Kentuckians who make it their life to fight off the Indians he cannot begin to cope with. In the end, though Roland is sent back to Virginia to populate civilization with his gentlewoman cousin Edith, Bird provides an equally valuable marriage in the Kentucky settlement, between the renegade's daughter, Telie Doe, and the son of the Colonel, Dick Bruce. Presumably they will provide the frontiersmen that pave the way for the children of Roland and Edith.

While *Nick of the Woods* emphasizes the value of *both* classes to the American vision, it also provides an explicit message on the cost of colonialist disunity at any level, for any reason. Nathan Slaughter is shunned by the Kentucky woodsmen for his pacifist declarations. In another tale that he relates to Roland (before his later revelation), Nathan explains about a time when he encountered the tracks of an Indian party as he was out hunting. Following them, he discovered they were heading toward his "own little wigwam," and fearing for the safety of his neighbors, the Ashtons, he went to warn them. "But verily," he relates to Roland, "they held my story light, and laughed at and derided me; for, in them days, the people hardened their hearts and closed their ears against me, because I held it not according to conscience to kill Injuns as they did" (148). Turned away by the Ashtons, Nathan goes to the Colonel Bruce, hoping to persuade him to dispatch a force to save the

Ashtons, whom he is sure the bloodthirsty Indians will harm. Bruce not only scoffs at Nathan but takes away his rifle saying, as Nathan relates it, "as I was not man enough to use it, I should not be allowed to carry it" (150). Nathan rushes back to the Ashtons only to see them massacred, as we later learn his family had been. The dynamics of this scene become particularly complex in light of the later revelation—for instance, if Nathan has been killing Indians all along (and we should assume that his chancing across the trail was no more fortuitous than his choosing to settle in Wenonga's territory), then why didn't *he* attempt to stop the Indians instead of going to warn the Ashtons and Colonel Bruce? Even so, one lesson is driven clearly and with particular force: "whites" must stand united on the frontier. As the narrator of *The Yemassee* notes, the "generally exposed situation on the whole frontier occupied by the whites, with the delay and difficulty of warlike preparation, rendered every precautionary measure essential" (158). The cost of Anglo colonial discord will be measured in "white" blood.

Although the three novels differ widely in means, the end is the same. Not only are "whites" on the frontier identified through a common cause, but both the cause and identity are carried back into, and sustained by, civilization. Each novel features some transaction between characters on the frontier and characters from civilization. In *The Last of the Mohicans*, Alice Monro and Duncan Heyward, neither of whom proved particularly adept (or adaptable) on the frontier, will marry and return to civilization. Similarly Roland and Edith Forrest, rescued from the Shawnees and restored to their inheritance, return to the now cultivated Virginia. Gabriel Harrison/Charles Craven, in his role as governor and by right of his noble birth, can move from civilization to frontier and back with authority and ease. In these transactions it is important that each group of whites is informed by the mission of the other. The ideal, as Harrison puts it in *The Yemassee*, is to form "one community" (125). The project of that community is, as Bird affirms in his preface, to "wrest . . . from the savage the garden-land of his domain," and to "secure . . . to their conquest all the benefits of civil government and laws" (27).

In *The Fatal Environment* Slotkin argues that frontier ideology succeeded by displacing white class conflict onto an archetypal formulation that figures whites unified against the forces of Nature. "Instead of interpreting history as a competition for power and resources by classes of fellow citizens, the Myth projects competition outward, and imagines the strife as that between a fully human entity—'civilization'—and an entity that is primarily inhuman" (*Fatal Environment*, 79). Yet the "engine which . . . exceeds human power to control" is presumably *not* beyond white "human power" and *must* be controlled to guarantee the success of the white civilizing mission. In order to accomplish this, whites on the frontier and in the metropolis must think in concert and must sustain the "white" mission on all fronts.

Each novel establishes a communicative link between the expanding geographical border and the cultural border that will allow identification between Anglo Americans and will provide for the establishing of a common perspective regarding both the frontier as potential Anglo settlement and the Native

Americans who currently inhabit it. Portraying an already successful history, these stories pave the way for *contemporary* readers to identify with the action of the novel, encouraging them to endorse the novel's outcome. Thus, these novels are social and cultural agents in a specifically material sense because they could shape attitudes toward current situations that readers encountered during the continued expansion of imaginative and physical frontiers during the 1820s and 1830s.

Tradition and the Novel

If, however, as Lentricchia argues, "tradition-making functions precisely to hide class conflict by eliding the text's involvement in social struggle," this task is compromised by the demands of the novel, which Mikhail M. Bakhtin has so fruitfully explored as a form that is constructed heteroglossically. As the frontier novel waffles between realism and romance, the frontier tradition also contains two contradictory urges: it is at once a project of containment and a project of continuance. It is interesting to speculate how these two impulses transmute into narrative. Bakhtin argues that the epic as a genre is the embodiment of containment; it speaks to an absolute past of national tradition. "Everything incorporated into this past was simultaneously incorporated into a condition of authentic essence and significance, but therefore also took on conclusiveness and finality, depriving itself, so to speak of all rights and potential for real continuation" (16). If, as this chapter has argued, one of the fundamental social roles of frontier novels was to *create* a sense of frontier tradition and white unity for their *contemporary* significance during the period these novels were written, then the epic genre could not be suitable to their rhetorical purposes. Rather, the *novel* could, in Bakhtin's words, provide a "zone of maximal contact with the present," even in a historical novel, which is characterized by "a positively weighted modernizing, an erasing of temporal boundaries, the recognition of an eternal present" (11, 365). The novel could do this because of its "folklore roots" (21), which subvert the hegemonic drive of authority and the containment of other, idealized genres like the epic. The novel is, as Bakhtin persuasively argues, "associated with the eternally living element of unofficial language and unofficial thought" (20), the discourse of which is rooted in heteroglossia—a "social diversity of speech types" (263)— and is therefore inevitably sedimented with the very social history frontier *tradition* seeks to repress.

It might be argued, then, that the frontier novel narrativizes the contradictory urges of frontier ideology, which were geographically and temporally centrifugal and culturally centripetal. Bakhtin argues that the same forces that operate ideologically are also manifest in the "life of language":

> At any given moment of its evolution, language is stratified not only into linguistic dialects . . . but also—and for us this is the essential point—into languages that are socio-ideological. . . . This stratification and heteroglossia, once realized, is not only a static invariant of linguistic life, but also what insures its dynamics. (271–72)

Alongside this expanding drive work the 'centripetal" forces of language—those that seek to unify and normalize. These forces, suggest Bakhtin, "develop in vital connection with the processes of sociopolitical and cultural centralization" (270–71). The novel, unlike other genres, embodies this struggle between the two antithetical trends in both ideology and language.

Bakhtin proposes that the "languages of heteroglossia . . . encounter one another and co-exist in the consciousness of real people—first and foremost, in the creative imagination of people who write novels" (291–92). In outlining what he perceives to be the novel's (and novelist's) "dialogic imagination," Bakhtin argues that unlike a poet, who seeks to eliminate the chaos of heteroglossia and language diversity, the novelist welcomes them, "not only not weakening them, but even intensifying them" precisely in order to interact with them (298). The novelist forms his or her own artistic vision from heteroglossia itself. "The prose writer makes use of words that are already populated with the social intentions of others and compels them to serve his own new intentions, to serve a second master" (300).

But the author can never remove the traces of social and ideological struggle from the words he or she appropriates. Thus, sedimented in the artistic rendering of heteroglossia in the novel is always a history of prior intentions. Bakhtin summarizes: "Heteroglossia, once incorporated into the novel (whatever the forms for its incorporation) is *another's speech in another's language*, serving to express authorial intentions but in a refracted way." This results in what Bakhtin terms "double-voiced discourse," which "serves two speakers at the same time and expresses simultaneously two different intentions: the direct intention of the character who is speaking, and the refracted intention of the author" (324; Bakhtin's emphasis).

The language of any character, then, despite the author's intentions, contains the history of its material contexts. Thus, *The Yemassee*'s caricature of the language of the black slave Hector at once serves the narrator's parodic and political intentions while it contains its own history. In the novel's action, Hector is the ever-faithful, obsequious slave. When Harrison notifies Hector that he is being liberated for saving Harrison's life, Hector comically and categorically refuses:

> I d——n to h——ll, maussa, ef I guine to be free! . . . I can't loss you company, and who de debble Dugdale [Harrison's Indian-eating dog] guine let feed him like Hector? 'Tis onpossible, maussa, and dere's no use for talk 'bout it. De ting aint right; and enty I know wha' kind of ting is freedom wid de black man? Ha! You make Hector free, he turn wuss more nor poor buckrah—he tief out of de shop—he git drunk and lie in de ditch—den, if sick come, he roll, he toss in de wet grass of de stable. You come in de morning, Hector dead—and, who know—he no take physic, he no hab parson—who know I say, maussa, but de debble fine em 'fore anybody else? No, maussa—you and Dugdale berry good company for Hector. I tank God he so good—I no want any better. (355–56)

Charles S. Watson observes of this passage that "Simms is skillful in having the black himself present the argument [of white proslavery advocates] in his own picturesque Gullah dialect" (341). Yet, however rhetorically effective Simms's strategy may be for the proslavery stance, he cannot obscure the historical and material circumstances that populate the Gullah dialect—the history of enslavement and exploitation that are sedimented in Hector's language. Simms can neither parody nor exploit Hector's speech without the help of the Gullah dialect itself, which is precisely what constitutes the "double-voicedness" of his use of it. The two languages—Gullah dialect, and Simms's intentional rendering of it—interact dialogically: "It is as if they actually hold a conversation with each other" (324). *The Yemassee* presents Hector's speech to refute charges of "white" oppression of "black" slaves; Gullah dialect contains the history of that very oppression.

In the same manner, Bird's representation of Wenonga's barely intelligible pidgin English portrays the novel's desire to depict the Indian as debased, ignorant, and degraded. At the same time Wenonga's pidgin details the history of Native American/white relations. As the narrator reveals, Roland could understand the Shawnee warrior only when he made some attempt to speak in English. The fact that the Wenonga could speak English at all chronicles the trail of Indian concessions to the European colonialists, who for their part rarely reciprocated the favor. "The human being in the novel," argues Bakhtin, "is first, foremost and always a speaking human being; the novel requires speaking persons bringing with them their own unique ideological discourse, their own language" (332). As we have seen, the novelist may shape that language according to his or her artistic/political purposes, but the heteroglossic nature of the novel always "relativizes" the author's intentions (316).

Thus the novel is *inevitably* ambivalent, a "tension-filled unity" (272). Each frontier novel considered here manifests this ambivalence—between romance and realism, between the monologic drives of American tradition-making, and the heteroglossic nature of their medium—in a different way. In *The Last of the Mohicans*, Natty himself embodies what Frank Collins calls a "faltering synthesis" (79). Natty enacts his political role as a British scout and his social role as a resolver of social tensions, but at the same time he manifests a profound aversion to the political and social system he espouses.[18] In *The Yemassee* the ambivalence is centered on the logical contradiction contained in the novel's portrayal of Indians. The novel depicts a formerly noble and now debased savage as it seeks to locate the responsibility for white violence against the Yemassee in "nature" and, specifically, the inherently inferior "Indian nature." Yet Simms cannot have it both ways. No matter how *The Yemassee* attempts to displace white responsibility onto Indian nature, the narrative outlines historical Anglo-colonial guilt in its historicized reading of Indian life before and after "white" contact.

Finally, in *Nick of the Woods* Nathan Slaughter seeks to expunge violence from America's forests by exterminating the Indians entirely. Yet he cannot do so without implicating himself in that very Indian violence. More and more Nathan takes on an "Indian" way of life precisely as he tries to eliminate it, as we saw in his characterization of his house as "my own little wigwam." By the end of the novel he is transformed into a striking image of Wenonga, wielding an axe, covered in blood, carrying a string of scalps, and whooping in the spirit of "never-dying revenge" that parallels Wenonga's own characterization (see 323–24, 344). Ultimately none of the three novels is able to sustain a consistent vision of "white" American tradition and history. The heteroglossic nature of the novel inevitably compromises the ideological/rhetorical drive of frontier literature to establish a monologic American ideal.

The Social Value of Frontier Literature

When Chingachgook questions Natty on the accuracy of white accounts of border conflicts, Natty obliquely acknowledges the monologic drive of "white" history books: "My people have many ways, of which, as an honest man, I can't approve. It is one of their customs to write in books what they have done and seen, instead of telling them in their villages where the lie can be given to the face of a cowardly boaster and the brave soldier can call on his comrades to witness for the truth of his words" (31). Natty's concern with white bookishness is not so much that the truth value of the book will diminish, but that the reader will be withdrawn from social action in his scholarly pursuits: "In consequence of this bad fashion, a man who is too conscientious to misspend his days among the women, in learning the names of black marks, may never hear of the deeds of his father, *nor feel a pride in striving to outdo them* (31; my emphasis). That Natty speaks precisely from the medium of the novel he excoriates allows Cooper a double-voiced message purposefully turned to the motives of frontier fiction. Cooper presents Natty as a *figurative* frontier father — a pathfinder who paves the way for America's civilized progeny. At the same time, Natty's voice reminds Cooper's reader that the job is not done, that sons of the frontier should not merely read of border exploits, but should "striv[e] . . . to outdo them."

It is important to recognize the ways in which these frontier novels presented a history that would shape contemporary Anglo American values, policy, and action while disguising the very basis for the same. Although the novel's characteristic multivoicedness may have subverted the possibility for frontier literature to accomplish an undiluted message, the monologized vision of "white" Americans versus Indian savages (however compromised) became relevant to contemporary readers paradoxically through the novelistic medium. That is to say, the novel at once prevented a monolithic tradition from being fully realized while it facilitated the impact of that fictionalized tradition by providing a "zone of maximal contact with the present" for the reader. And one reader, at least, was able to find continued (and transatlantic) social relevance in these fictive works. The British colonist and writer W. Winslow Reade provided this assessment of Africa in his travel account:

> This vast continent will finally be divided almost equally between France and England. . . . Africa shall be redeemed. . . . In this amiable task they [the Africans] may possibly become exterminated. We must learn to look upon this result with composure. It illustrates the beneficent law of Nature, that the weak must be de-

voured by the strong. . . . When the cockneys of Timbuctoo have their tea-gardens on the Oases of the Sahara; when the hotels and guide books are established at the Sources of the Nile; when it becomes fashionable to go yachting on the lakes of the great Plateau; when noblemen building seats in Central Africa, will have their elephant parks and their hippopotami waters, young ladies on camp-stools, under palm trees will read with tears, *The Last of the Negroes*. (*Savage Africa* [1864]; qtd. in Hammond and Jablow, 73)

4

W/Righting History:
Sympathy as Strategy in *Hope Leslie*
and *A Romance of the Republic*

The Politics of Sentiment

In her 1860 article "How Women Should Write?" Mary Bryan traces women's growing involvement in literary fields. It is in response to men's demand "for intellectual food through the length and breadth of the land . . . they want books for every year, for every month—mirrors to 'catch the manners living as they rise,' lenses to concentrate the rays of the new stars that dawn upon them" (Freibert and White, 369). Woman, responding as always to man's call, "steps forward to take her part in the intellectual labor," but then is strangely hindered by the qualms of the male establishment. Bryan incisively chronicles the dilemma of women writers in nineteenth-century America:

> Thus is apparent what has gradually been admitted, that it is woman's duty to write—but how and what? This is yet a mooted question. Men, after much demur and hesitation, have given women liberty to write; but they cannot yet consent to allow them full freedom. . . . With metaphysics [women] have nothing to do; it is too deep a sea for their lead to sound; nor must they grapple with those great social and moral problems with which every strong soul is now wrestling. . . . Having prescribed these bounds to the female pen, men are the first to condemn her efforts as tame and commonplace, because they lack earnestness and strength. (370)

Bryan argues forcefully in behalf of women writers who have begun to confront the "earnest age we live in." These women recognize that "there are active influences at work, all tending to one grand object—moral, social and physical advancement." These are women who have come to understand that "the pen is the compass-needle that points to this pole" of social change (371).

Bryan presents an admittedly utopian hope that women writers will become "God's chosen instrument in this work of gradual reformation, this reconciling of the harsh contrasts in society that jar so upon our sense of harmony, this righting of the grievous wrongs and evils over which we weep and pray, this final uniting of men into one common brotherhood by the bonds of sympathy and affection" (373). She perceives literature as a powerful agent of "gradual reform" that might resolve the awful contradictions of antebellum America. Her essay at once acknowledges and projects the social mission of nineteenth-century women's fiction.

A little more than thirty years before Bryan's complaints, Catherine Maria Sedgwick was mounting her own effort against the male-dominated publishing and cultural industry through her historical frontier novel *Hope Leslie; Or, Early Times in Massachusetts* (1827). As Lucy Freibert and Barbara White observe, Sedgwick, among several other women authors, "played an important role in the development of the [frontier novel] . . . and authored one-quarter of the examples published before 1828, when the frontier romance had become a clearly recognizable genre" (103). Frontier novels explicitly took as their subject one of the "awful contradictions" in America, in both a historical and a contemporary sense: the Anglo-American conquest of the Native Americans and assimilation of their lands. Some of the women who wrote early frontier novels, Sedgwick and Lydia Maria Child in particular, presented a clear challenge to Anglo-American policy toward the Native Americans, dealing explicitly with issues of miscegenation and presenting more generally favorable and sympathetic versions of Indian-ness than did male colleagues such as James Fenimore Cooper, Robert Montgomery Bird and William Gilmore Simms.

At the same time, Lydia Maria Child was taking on another "awful contradiction" in U.S. society: slavery. Particularly after the 1830s, as the abolition effort mounted in the United States, Anglo-American fiction writers attempted to move their audiences to a recognition of the horrors of slavery. Women were major contributors to the effort. But, as Carolyn L. Karcher has established, a publishing industry and reading public largely hostile to abolitionist agitation put serious constraints on what women writers could address. Although abolitionist tracts and slave narratives provided a compelling, more authentic view of slavery, the public could not be induced to buy them. Such material was considered indecent by most, unscrupulous and dishonest by many. So, while abolitionist fiction became central to the abolitionist enterprise, it was, as Karcher observes,

> fraught with contradictions: the conventions of romance must serve to dispel the readers' romantic illusions about slavery; a language shorn of ugly details must convey the violence of flogging to an audience convinced that abolitionists exaggerated the cruelty of slavery; a code of gentility that did not protect slave women against rape or white women against their husbands' philandering must govern fictional treatment of sexuality. ("Censorship," 12)

Child is one of the best examples of a woman writer who tested the limits of the genre—often to her own financial detriment.[1] Child's 1867 publication of her fourth novel, *A Romance of the Republic*, exemplifies her career-long opposition to slavery and racial discrimination, confronting a bitter historical legacy and mapping an alternative.

Labeled pejoratively and dismissed as "sentimental" in the past, the works of many U.S. women writers of the nineteenth century are now being reconsidered. Growing interest in these writers has led to a reassessment of the role their constructions of sympathy played in the cultural dialogue of the 1800s. Formerly derided as intellectual fluff and artistic trash, sentiment is now being studied on its own terms, critically and carefully.[2] Scholars like Gregg Camfield, who in a careful study of sentimentality and *Uncle Tom's Cabin* has convincingly traced the sentimentalists' subscription to a credible philosophy of realism, have brought the debate to a new level: scholars need no longer apologize or rationalize their interest in sentimental novels. In this context, then, we can reexamine the sympathetic frame of reference employed by writers like Sedgwick and ask how it provided a more positive cultural vision, proposing likenesses between cultures and developing affinities and relationships between characters of different "racial" groups.

But despite the manifest sympathy in texts like *Hope Leslie* and *A Romance of the Republic* toward Native and African Americans, we should not, as Annette Kolodny cautions, uncritically conclude that these women writers were in fact advocating radical social change. Kolodny's insight is important: sentimental portrayals which manipulated the emotions of a reader "represented a genuine political tool for writers otherwise disenfranchised." Through the sentimental development of a scene, these women writers did hope to influence their male compatriots and family to an increased awareness and responsiveness. Yet, Kolodny argues, women writers of domestic fictions tended more toward *amelioration* of social contradictions than toward the *solutions* that Mary Bryan imagined taking place through women's powerful visions (*Land Before Her*, 163).[3] The situation is delicate, for women's authorial position was a crucial component of their social vision. Without some kind of credibility, they had no voice with which to advocate for alternative social models. The question, then, more properly should address *how* Sedgwick and Child use sentiment in *Hope Leslie* and *A Romance of the Republic*. Do they utilize it simply as an effective strategy to gain authorial advantage in Anglo-American culture or do they also employ it to proffer an alternative social vision? What are the implications of their sympathetic readings of "race"?

Lady Writer, Lady Historian

Hope Leslie was published in two volumes in 1827. As Sister Mary Michael Welsh and Mary Kelley document, the work was well received and was compared favorably by critics to Cooper's *Last of the Mohicans* (see Welsh, 25; Kelley, "Introduction," *Hope Leslie*, x–xi). Sedgwick claimed to be somewhat abashed by the overwhelmingly favorable reviews published in women's magazines and in the *North Atlantic Review*.[4] She was apparently not disconcerted, though, at the controversy which arose over her depiction of Indians, the defense for which she had already prepared in her original preface:

> In our histories, it was perhaps natural that [the Indians] should be represented as "surly dogs," who preferred to die rather than live, from no other motive than a stupid or malignant obstinacy. Their own historians or poets, if they had such, would as naturally, and with more justice, have extolled their high-souled courage and patriotism. The writer is aware that it may be thought that the character of Magawisca has no prototype . . . it may be sufficient to remark, that . . . we are confined not to the actual, but to the possible. (6)

Nor was she surprised by criticism of her less than hagiographic view of the Puritans, which she carefully qualified but refused to back down from in a private letter. Insisting that she bore only "filial reverence" to the Puritans, Sedgwick yet avers that "their bigotry, their superstition, and above all their intolerance, were too apparent on the pages of history to be forgotten."[5]

Clearly, and despite the numerous textual apologies regarding her humble inadequacies as historian and author, Sedgwick had set out to redefine opinion regarding both race *and* gender conventions. Sedgwick's refusal to accord Puritan historians de facto authority over her subject is basic to her fictional design, and her critique of Puritan racism is inextricable from her insistent attention to the debilitating effects of patriarchy in early America. Sedgwick was not alone. Numerous critics—among them Lillian Schlissel, Susan Armitage, Glenda Riley, Annette Kolodny, and Leland Person—have now documented at length how the frontier vision of Sedgwick and other female frontier novelists and diarists specifically counters the "Adamic myth" and its valorization of white-male conquest—conquest over nonwhite males and women of any color. But *Hope Leslie* is remarkable for its valorization and foregrounding of feminine heroics: a woman who actively resists her male superiors in order to act on the good impulses of her heart.

Indeed, the enterprise of racial revisioning is inseparable from a confrontation of patriarchal authority in *Hope Leslie*, as the narrator's asides attest.[6] Nor is her critique simply historical, as her narrator's repeated disclaimers of authority begin to reveal. For instance, as she offers her readers a "formal introduction to the government-mansion" (143), the narrator pauses to clarify her unpretentious, lackeylike relation to the "mighty master of fiction." Rather than attempting to "imitate the miracles wrought by the rod of the prophet," the narrator promises to rely for her description on quotations from "an authentic record of the times" (143).[7] Here, as in her preface, Sedgwick has her narrator assure male authorities (and those who are invested in upholding them) that she does not presume upon their position. In the preface the narrator confirms in the first and final sentences: "The following volumes are not offered to the public as being in any degree an historical narrative, or a relation of real events. . . . These volumes are . . . far from being intended as a substitute for genuine history" (5–6). Her repeated insistence, however, combined with the content of comments sandwiched between these apologies, might suggest that the apologies themselves are less sincere than calculatingly rhetorical, designed to assuage those who, as Mary Bryan insists, refuse to grant women writers any "metaphysical" or political authority. Furthermore, as we can see in her flattering reference to James Fenimore Cooper's *Last of the Mohicans* (81), such deferral actually highlights Sedgwick's own authority (by means of her good judgment) at the same time as it calls attention to her *alternative* (and differently authoritative) account.[8]

A closer examination in this vein illuminates Sedgwick's subversive political commentary on the patriarchal assumptions of the Puritans *and* her contemporary male audience. Sedgwick promises the same kind of deference and submission to male authority that she models in her novel through Mrs. Fletcher, Esther Downing, and Mrs. Winthrop. But *Hope Leslie* cagily qualifies the value of their meek subservience, suggesting that such behavior breeds an unthinking temper and frank servility. The novel presents a paragon of Puritan girlhood in Esther Downing, who, the narrator at one point reflects, "could not have disputed the nice points of faith, sanctification and justification, with certain celebrated contemporary female theologians" (135). Sandwiched within her honorific depiction of Mrs. Winthrop is a comparison of the Puritan first lady to a horse on a bit, "guided by the slightest intimation from him who held the rein" (145).

These narrative asides make clear that for the narrator, the more admirable course is the more independent, and we see that what Sedgwick actually *does* as the author of *Hope Leslie* is more in the spirit of the title character. Hope, following the guide of her own heart and genius, often defies patriarchal authority, secretly moving to assert a humane justice toward people whom the Puritans would trample, like the unfairly harassed Nelema.[9] "It may be seen that Hope Leslie," the narrator notes, "was superior to some of the prejudices of the age" (123). Sedgwick snubs historical authority more directly, as Sandra Zagarell points out, by having Hope Leslie reject a possible marriage to Puritan historian William Hubbard ("Expanding America," 240). So, while Sedgwick frequently has her narrator claim a reverent distance from any actually historical enterprise, she in fact broadly tackles it, beginning in her prefatorial comments on the "Indians of North America," and the (ad)vantage of historical perspective (quoted above).

From the beginning of chapter 4—which is central to this analysis—Sedgwick indicates her willingness to confront authorized history. She takes as her epigraph a modified version of one of the most censorial comments of early Anglo-American historical legacy: "It would have been happy if they had converted some before they had killed any."[10] In the chapter that follows, Sedgwick delivers two versions of the Pequot war, one based on actual Puritan accounts and the other fictionalized from a sympathetic stance and wary rereading of the same Puritan accounts. While Natty Bumppo can acknowledge that "every story has its two sides" (*The Last of the Mohicans*), Cooper refuses to follow through on his implied challenge to Anglo historical authority. Instead, Chingachgook's side of the story supports the Anglo-American version in its refusal to confront it, as Chingachgook tells only of the good days before white contact, and how his tribe is coming to an elegiac end—carefully avoiding any attribution of direct blame for this to the European invaders. *Hope Leslie*'s two-sided history is decidedly more confrontational.

The Wand of Feeling

One method Sedgwick uses to explore racial configurations is to stage debates between various characters on precisely this subject. For example, Digby, a veteran of the Pequot "war," is thoroughly suspicious of any Indian: "They are a treacherous race . . . a kind of beast we don't comprehend" (41–42). He maintains a staunch party line represented in the historical accounts of the Pequot massacre by Hubbard, Trumbull, and Winthrop. In contrast, Everell (who is decidedly attracted to Magawisca) is skeptical and doggedly questions Digby's defensive assertions. When Digby insists that "we know these Pequods were famed above all the Indian tribes for their cunning," Everell counters: "And what is superior cunning among savages but superior sense?" (43). Their exchange points toward the power of representation, the way the same incident can be interpreted differently depending on the prejudices or sympathies the interpreter brings to it. The narrator underscores this by commenting on the authority of the combined accounts: When Everell bests Digby, the narrator observes that Digby felt "the impatience that a man feels when he is sure he is right, without being able to make it appear" (43).

By a similar process of narratorial intervention, Magawisca's account of the Pequot "war" is lent important authority. Her side of the story focuses on the cruelty of the Puritans' planned attack on sleeping women, old people, and children by sneaking up and setting fire to the village—fire "taken from our hearth-stone, where the English had been so often warmed and cherished" (49). Magawisca's story, supported by the narrator's consequent expansion, thoroughly subverts the command of the male Puritans' versions. First, it insistently historicizes and contextualizes the situation, emphasizing the causal, reactive quality of "Pequod treachery" and subtly revealing *white* treachery. Further, it recognizes the Indian foe as human, not "beast," emphasizing Pequot families, hearths, and homes. Magawisca's account challenges the unexamined politics of historical representation embedded in authorized histories, focusing particularly on the persuasive power of narrative and narrator. In fact, Magawisca exploits the power Everell grants to her as narrator in the telling of her story, as Shirley Samuels observes: her tale serves to defer an explanation of her recent actions, which would confirm Digby's suspicions of imminent danger.[11]

Magawisca prefaces her story with a warning for Everell, which doubles as a metahistorical commentary for the reader: "Then listen to me: and when the hour of vengeance comes, if it should come, remember it was provoked" (47). Like Fredric Jameson's caveat to "always historicize," Magawisca's words offer a reply to Digby's dehistoricized observations on Indian "nature." The Indians are not by "nature" vengeful but are so in this situation because of the wrongs they suffered at the hands of the Puritans. In this manner *Hope Leslie* again responds to Cooper's *Last of the Mohicans*. As Zagarell observes, "The acts of Cooper's Indian have nothing to do with the whites' policies; he is intrinsically malevolent, and the murder he commits touches off a wanton massacre of the English. *Hope Leslie*'s narrative structure, however, situates its analogous and undeniably horrifying act as part of a chain of white initiated historical events" ("Expanding America," 235).

Magawisca recounts the burning of Mystic and the ensuing massacre of surviving women and children: "All about sat women and children in family clusters, awaiting unmoved their fate. The English had penetrated. . . . Death was dealt freely. None resisted" (53). Everell is so moved by this account that he weeps. Thus the narrator highlights the power accrued simply by being *able* to tell the story. Magawisca's alternative version of the Pequot war is in fact persuasive enough to transform Everell, whose imagination,

> touched by the wand of feeling, presented a very different picture of those defense-less families of savages, pent in the recesses of their native forests, and there extermi-nated, not by superior natural force, but by the adventitious circumstances of arms, skill and knowledge; from that offered by those who "then living and worthy of credit did affirm, that in the morning entering into the swamp, they saw several heaps of them [the Pequods (CMS)] sitting close together, upon whom they dis-charged their pieces, laden with ten or twelve pistol bullets at a time, putting the muzzles of their pieces under the boughs, within a few yards of them." (54)

Everell is sympathetic to Magawisca initially through what seems to be an adolescent crush. In this scene, however, we see his sympathy raised to a more intellectual level. Having earlier accepted that "our people had all the honour of the fight" (48), Everell's historical understanding is complicated by Maga-wisca's story. This happens precisely through his emotional openness toward Magawisca. Sedgwick's point here is unmistakable, offering as it does both a new historical method and a vision of cross-cultural relations.

When Magawisca finishes, the narrator smoothly picks up the threads of the story to fill in the "factual" and most gruesome background from Puritan records, quoting Winthrop and Hubbard. Although the narrator had protested earlier that she merely followed the histories of the Puritan fathers, here she does not hesitate to direct the intentions of those accounts to a different purpose:

> In the relations of their enemies, the courage of the Pequods was distorted into ferocity, and their fortitude, in their last extremity, thus set forth: "many were killed in the swamp, like sullen dogs, that would rather in their self-willed madness, sit still to be shot or cut in pieces than receive their lives for asking, at the hands of those into whose power they had now fallen." (54)

The narrator highlights the unfeelingly prejudiced nature of the histories avail-able and the apparent contradictions between the Puritan mission and Christian humaneness.[12] Her comments point up the fact that once one is conscious of the political aspect of historical representation, quite different versions can be constructed—versions both more balanced and hence more accurate. It is precisely her sympathetic frame of reference which leads her to this point.

The text thereby underscores what Susanne Kappeler has insightfully analyzed, the dominative structure of representation. Magawisca's story not only affirms the *possibility* of dialogized history, but insists on the inherent *necessity* of it, as the narrator recounts Everell's thoughts: "Here it was not merely changing sculptors to give the advantage to one or the other of the artist's subjects; but it was putting the chisel into the hands of truth, and giving it to whom it belonged" (53).[13] The Father of Puritan History, who in his story represents his own political ends and thereby dominates the Pequots not one but three ways (materially, textually, and historically), is not possessed of the "hands of truth." Rather, the narrator suggests, it is the silenced object of Puritan representation—the Indians, and by inference white women—whose story speaks both emotively and truly.[14]

Having issued a challenge to the authorized white versions of the Pequot war, the narrator combines forces with Magawisca through an acute analysis of the Pequot dilemma. Significantly, the focus here is on the more dangerous and less pitiable Pequot chief, Mononotto. Magawisca's tale, sentimental though its tone may be, has paved the way for the narrator's radical and unsentimentalized commentary on Mononotto's dilemma. The narrator notes that "Magawisca had said truly to Everell, that her father's nature had been changed by the wrongs he had received" (56), hereby historicizing Mononotto's behavior and refuting the received Puritan version of Indians as "naturally" savage. While a rival chief, Sassacus, manifested "a jealousy of [the English] encroachments" and "employed all his art and influence and authority, to unite the tribes for the extirpation of the dangerous invaders," Mononotto, "foreseeing no danger from them, was the advocate of a hospitable reception, and pacific conduct" (50).

Ironically it was Sassacus, as the narrator is at pains to indicate, who was right about the "dangerous invaders" ("invaders" is doubly emphasized when repeated as the last word of the chapter). Mononotto is betrayed by his own generous impulses: "He had seen his people slaughtered, or driven from their homes and hunting-grounds, into shameful exile; his wife had died in captivity, and his children lived in servile dependency in the house of his enemies" (51). Only "in this extremity," and not at all unreasonably the narrator implies, is Mononotto driven to revenge. Apart from establishing sympathy for Mononotto at a personal level, the narrator also uses his story as a trenchant comment on the broader predicament of the various Indian nations which, divided between those who counseled war and those who advocated hospitality, were finally unable to forestall English treachery. Thus through a sympathetic frame of reference, Sedgwick is able to establish a historical dialogue that had been suppressed from the Puritan accounts.

The Sweet Sacrifice of History

Sedgwick's sympathetic construction of the racial Other has important implications at the semiotic level. In his study of the Spanish conquest of America,
Tzvetan Todorov develops a useful semiotic model of analysis for both "positive" and "negative" colonial depictions of the racial Other.[15] Examining the
underlying characteristics of colonial discourse, Todorov differentiates between two "touchstones of alterity," one of which is structured around "a
present and immediate second person" (i.e., me vs. you), the other which
revolves on "the absent or distant third person" (i.e., me [us] vs. them). He
argues that it is at this point, where the Other is designated as either present
or absent, "that we can see how the theme of perception of the other and that
of symbolic (or semiotic) behavior intersect" (*Conquest*, 157). Whether one
regards the racial Other as a second person, immediate presence, or a third
person, absence can profoundly affect the possible actions conceptually available toward that Other.

This frame is illuminating in a careful analysis of Sedgwick's radically conceived fourth chapter, which by enacting dialogue between English and Pequot
characters, places the relationship in a "me/you" semiotic frame. Within this
second-person symbolic relation, the narrator speaks to the cruelty of Puritan
policy toward the Pequots, acted out in the semiotic perspective of a third-
person frame. From the "us/them" vantage, the Puritans can act viciously
and record with no sense of irony the very passage the narrator quotes from
Bradford: "It was a fearful sight to see them thus frying in the fire, and
the streams of blood quenching the same, and the horrible scent thereof; but
the victory seemed a sweet sacrifice, and they gave the praise thereof to
God" (54). Such a perspective is impossible when one recognizes the Other
as an immediate presence, indeed, talks and listens to the Other as Everell
does.

Todorov's frame is also helpful to explain a curious passage that follows
only two chapters later. The passage is a patriotic paean to "the noble pilgrims" which also serves to counter the powerfully dialogized version of
history constructed earlier. After the scene in which the Fletcher family is
ruthlessly slaughtered by Mononotto and his accomplices, the narrator
pauses to address the reader directly. "We hope our readers will not think
we have wantonly sported with their feelings." The narrator continues to explain that such events, "feebly related," were common in early Puritan
life. "Not only families," the narrator elaborates, "but villages, were cut
off by the most dreaded of all foes—the ruthless, vengeful savage" (72). The
semiotic structure here—the "touchstone of alterity"—is suddenly not second
but third person. In the passage that ensues, we witness the representational
implications of this switch, the violence now permitted, easily effaced, and
rationalized.

"In the quiet possession of blessings transmitted," the narrator elaborates,
"we are, perhaps, in danger of forgetting, or undervaluing the sufferings by

which they were obtained. We forget that the noble pilgrims lived and endured for us" (72). Chronicling the sacrifices made, the narrator then outlines their mission: "to open the forests to the sun-beam and to the light of the Sun of Righteousness." As a reward, the Puritans "saw, with sublime joy, a multitude of people where the solitary savage roamed the forest—the forest vanished, and the pleasant villages and busy cities appeared—the tangled foot-path expanded to the thronged high-way—the consecrated church planted on the rock of heathen sacrifice" (73). The implications of this passage's semiotic structure are a stunning contrast to those of chapter 4. Here the women, children, and *families* of Indians are transmuted (by means of the third-person frame of reference) to a "single, solitary savage." The historical context of the colonial conquest is effaced—the Puritans are "rewarded" for sacrificing "the land of their birth . . . their homes . . . all delights of the sense" (72). And the historical struggle, textually elided, is sanctioned by the merit of the Puritan's religion, their metaphorically and literally "enlightening" influence on the land itself. The narrator continues to make an oblique reference to the colonists' actions against America's original population:

> And that we might realize this vision—enter into this promised land of faith—they endured hardship, and braved death—deeming, as said one of their company, that "he is not worthy to live at all, who, for fear or danger of death, shunneth his country's service, or his own honour—since death is inevitable and the fame of virtue is immortal."
>
> If these were the fervors of enthusiasm, it was an enthusiasm kindled and fed by the holy flame that glows on the alter of God. (73)

Here we have a holy mission, not white treachery. We see the traces of deleted historical content when we begin to ask questions about this passage. What magnitude of service could "the country" require against that "single, solitary savage"? How much work can it be to build a church on a rock—unless the expression is a metaphor that represses a less pleasant meaning? Rather, this passage, in sharp contrast to that discussed above, uncritically highlights how the representatives of that "consecrated church" built on the "rock of sacrifice" also have the power to choose the terms by which their history will be written.

It is perhaps impossible to explain the juxtaposition of these two exceedingly divergent passages. Which one did Sedgwick intend? Maybe both. Cultural hegemony is pervasive and "enlightenment" not always foolproof. Albert Memmi emphasizes the imaginative difficulties of "the colonizer who refuses": "It is not easy to escape mentally from a concrete situation, to refuse its ideology while continuing to live with its actual relationships" (20). Certainly Sedgwick does not abandon her attempt to deal fairly with her Indian characters at this point. As will be discussed briefly below, Sedgwick establishes a modicum of cross-racial understanding, indicating that the most serious racial difficulties arose at the hands of the whites. Further, she offers an alternative behavior model to the received frontier wisdom of her day. Ultimately she does not see clearly any resolution of racial misunderstanding and instead establishes a metaphor that allows the Indians to fade peacefully from the vision of her text.

Rent by a Divided Duty

Tension and ambivalence mark the remainder of *Hope Leslie*. Sedgwick is at many points more successful than other frontier novelists in establishing cultural relativity between whites and Indians. That is, Sedgwick allows her Indians dignity in their *difference*; she highlights similarities between the two groups but she does not try to make Indians "human" by showing them to be *identical* to Anglo-Americans. She reveals the Indians to be governed by cultural and moral principles different from those of the Puritans. Magawisca is the most frequent spokesperson here. For instance, in defending her brother against one of Hope's few racist outbursts, Magawisca affirms the moral integrity of her culture: "Yes, an Indian, in whose veins runs the blood of the strongest . . . who never turned their backs on friends or enemies, and whose souls have returned to the Great Spirit, stainless as they came from him" (188). Magawisca also defends the legitimacy of the Indian life-style. When Hope pleads with her to stay in Boston, insisting that her "noble mind must not be wasted in those hideous solitudes," Magawisca makes it completely clear that such a life—though different from Hope's—is equally valuable to her. Notably, Hope accepts Magawisca's answer.

As Mary Kelley discusses in her valuable introduction to the Rutgers University Press edition of *Hope Leslie*, Sedgwick goes a long way toward suggesting cross-racial equality through her "parallel" portrayals of Hope and Magawisca. Magawisca is, Kelley notes, "the only Indian woman in early American fiction invested with substance and strength" ("Introduction," *Hope Leslie*, xxvi). Her character in many ways corresponds to Hope's and in some ways exceeds it. The respect her character accrues during the narrative is not merely token. As Kelley observes, both Hope and Magawisca challenge their culture's patriarchal order. It is Magawisca who commits the "ultimate act of resistance" when she prevents Everell's execution, sacrificing her arm: "hers is the most heroic act in the entire novel" ("Introduction," *Hope Leslie*, xxvii).[16]

Sedgwick also demonstrates an awareness that, as Todorov puts it, "each of us is the other's barbarian" (*Conquest*, 190). When Magawisca informs Hope of Mary's (Faith) marriage to Oneco, Hope shudders, exclaiming "God forbid! . . . My sister married to an Indian!" (188). The narrator then relates how Magawisca recoiled "with a look of proud contempt, that showed she reciprocated in full measure, the scorn expressed for her race" (188). Magawisca's reciprocal scorn is fully authorized in light of her version of the massacre at Mystic. Such an awareness serves Sedgwick's enterprise here by complicating received history, suggesting an alternative story that is ever-present in the authorized text.

Finally, Sedgwick uses Magawisca to comment on the historical construction of racial difference. At her trial, affirming her enmity toward white colonists, Magawisca queries "can we grasp in friendship the hand raised to strike us?" In this argument, the colonists' relations with the Native Americans are again contextualized. Although Magawisca holds that white and Indian differences are presently ineradicable, those differences arose historically because of white hostility and double-dealing. Through this narrative tack, which serves always to contextualize Indian violence, Sedgwick suggests an alternative to "Indian-hating." In their later summaries of this cultural phenomenon, Robert Montgomery Bird and James Hall would insist that white "Indian-haters" responded "naturally" to the treachery and violence of the Indian foes. Everell in particular and also his father are witnesses to the violent murder of the rest of their family. Yet, unlike Nathan Slaughter in *Nick of the Woods*, the two men in *Hope Leslie* do *not* swear "eternal vengeance." Instead, by relying on their religious faith, and their sensibility, and their recognition of the humanity of their enemies, the two men continue in life without becoming embittered toward the Indian "race." Everell applauds Hope's rescue of Nelema and himself engineers Magawisca's escape from Puritan punishment.[17]

Flowers Wild and Cultivated

In the end, however, while Sedgwick goes far toward suggesting a relative cultural standard and an alternative model for cross-racial relations, she is not able to resolve fully the implications of her critique for her contemporary audience. Instead she adopts a Manichaean allegory aesthetized by a garden metaphor to dispense with the Indians at the end of her narrative. Having earlier associated the Puritans with enlightenment (they "open the forests to the sun-beam, and to the light of the Sun of Righteousness"), Sedgwick has Magawisca herself adopt those abstract and naturalized terms in her own defense: "Take my own word, I am your enemy; the sun-beam and the shadow cannot mingle" (292). Magawisca, however, more frequently emphasizes the incompatibility of the two peoples by means of a flower metaphor. She elaborates on this twice, both in relation to Mary's embrace of the Indian life-style. Mary is a key factor in this formulation. Through her Magawisca is able to emphasize that the differences are not inherent or racial but *cultural*. This qualification, though revolutionary in its own right and starkly opposed to Cooper's formulation of white and red "gifts," ultimately finds no constructive resolution. "The lily of Maqua's valley, [*sic*] will never again make the English garden sweet" Magawisca says, preparing Hope for their meeting (188). Pleasant though this figure may be, Magawisca later reveals its full implications, this time as she warns Hope of Mary's inevitable return to Oneco: "When she flies from you, as she will, mourn not over her, Hope Leslie—the wild flower would perish in your gardens—the forest is like a native home to her—and she will sing as gaily again as the bird that hath found its mate" (331–32).

The Indian's destiny in *Hope Leslie* is made clear, for the Puritan's mission, as the narrator has indicated, is to *cultivate* the forest. Sedgwick's reference to the principle of vacuum domicilium (126) is neither gratuitous nor obsequious.[18] Rather it is the unspoken ideological principle which structures Sedgwick's own vision—a fiction which ignores the evidence of agricultural technology among the Indians and predicates its proprietary right upon an imagined lack in the Indians, an imagined superiority in the Europeans. The guilt latent in this formulation creeps into the narrator's passing reference to the Native American inhabitants of the Housatonick valley. These people were an "agricultural tribe," the narrator admits, elaborating "as far as that epithet could ever be applied to our savages" (85). We must note the stance of authority *over* the Indians which the narrator assumes at this point, a *proprietary* authority which underscores Indian Otherness: "our savages." The text elsewhere declines to speak to Indian husbandry in any significant detail, and like Winthrop's argument in "Reasons to be Considered," focuses only on the domestication of the wilderness effected by the Europeans, contrasting metaphorically domestic flowers (hardy, enduring) with the wild lily (fading toward extinction).[19] The "garden" in *Hope Leslie* is not simply a domestic space but a political and moral space that provides proof of the superiority of and justification for the dominance by the Anglo-Americans. Thus we see how women's visions of gardens in the wilderness may yet have oppressive political implications, tacitly depending as they do on space cleared in violent conquest by their husbands and sons.[20]

Indian destiny will, according to the text, be "lost in the deep, voiceless obscurity of those unknown regions" (339). By "regions" the narrator refers to "far western forests," but in Sedgwick's own lifetime, *those* forests were being cultivated. Thus *Hope Leslie* never successfully challenges the euphemistic Anglo construction of the ultimate "fate" of the Indians. Rather, the text succumbs to the same processes of historical representation that it formerly condemns in the Puritan accounts of the Pequot massacre, in which Indian genocide is something that happens outside the agency of whites, and is left to "deep, voiceless obscurity" of Anglo-American history.

Hope Leslie is finally a mixed bag. While Sedgwick clearly sees the necessity of re-envisioning racial constructs, she is so clearly invested in Anglo-America's historical inheritance that she cannot resolve the "Indian problem" in any meaningful way for her contemporary readers. Her "sentimental" metaphor of wild and domestic flowers allows her to gloss over the horrible results of Anglo policy toward Native Americans that she had confronted earlier. Yet we must not overlook how *Hope Leslie* provides a powerful reading that challenged and revised contemporary historical, racial, and gender formulations most effectively *through* its "sentimental" dimensions. *Hope Leslie* confronts directly the brutal effects of Anglo-American policy toward the Native Americans through its sympathetic employment of Magawisca's alternative history. This "very different picture" provides a model for a dialogic history which realizes practical (through the realization and subsequent actions of Everell) as well as theoretical (meta-historical and textual) implications in the novel. The novel thus establishes a space of authority for Sedgwick as a woman author through its challenges to male cultural authority emblematized in the title character of the story and through Sedgwick's own revisioning of Puritan history. The legacy of sentiment in *Hope Leslie* is mixed and is important precisely because it allows us to analyze the powerful hegemony of racism as well as the redoubled vision of resistance by a woman writer in nineteenth-century America.

Romancing Readers

Lydia Maria Child also wrote a frontier novel, *Hobomok, A Tale of Early Times*, which was published in 1824, three years before *Hope Leslie*. Child later read Sedgwick's novel and enjoyed it, as she indicates in a letter written late in her life to her close friend Sarah Shaw. Her esteem for the book itself was diminished, however, by her regard for its author. The letter to Shaw was to acknowledge the volume of Sedgwick's memoirs that Shaw had sent. Child, while agreeing to read them, also promises to return the volume, "as it is not the kind of book I care to keep" (May 20, 1872; *Selected Letters*, 506). Elaborating, Child insists that "any person who *apologized* for slavery must be deficient in moral sense" and more specifically charges that Sedgwick, while wishing "well to the negroes . . . could not bear to *contend* for them, or for anything else . . . She was very deficient in moral *courage*" (506; Child's emphasis). As she tells Shaw, she had several years earlier contributed her copy of *Hope Leslie* to a library.

Child's charge against Sedgwick was heartfelt. She herself had ruined her literary career to "contend" for slaves in print—both in scholarly treatise and fiction. Time and again she braved public hostility and censure to argue on behalf of emancipation and racial tolerance. *Appeal in Favor of that Class of Americans Called Africans* (1833) was a well-researched and copiously documented study of historical and contemporary slave institutions, including a careful analysis of African history and the slave trade's effects on the continent. As she notes, hers was the "first anti-slavery volume published in this country" to set forth an argument for immediate emancipation (*Selected Letters*, 232). Her well-argued appeal for emancipation and an end to antimiscegenation laws earned her the censure of many fellow citizens, resulting in the Boston Athenaeum revoking her library privileges and in a costly decline in subscriptions to her *Juvenile Miscellany*.[21] Despite the intimidation of what Carolyn Karcher calls "social ostracism, economic boycott, and mob violence" ("Censorship," 285), Child proceeded (unpaid) to edit the *National Anti-Slavery Standard* for two years (1841–43), and published antislavery fiction and tracts like the ironic and incisive *The Patriarchal Institution, As Described by Its Own Family* (1860). It is interesting that her least noted effort on behalf of black and white relations came after the Civil War—an intriguing novel titled *A Romance of the Republic* (1867).[22]

Child wrote *A Romance of the Republic* six years after helping Harriet Ann Jacobs to publish *Incidents in the Life of a Slave Girl*.[23] Her belief—like Mary Bryan's—that the writer is social mediator led her to choose fiction as a vehicle more effective than "the ablest arguments, and the most serious exhortations" (qtd. in Karcher, "Rape," 327). As Child detailed in another letter to Sarah

Shaw in 1865, the end of the Civil War had not occasioned for her an end to work on behalf of the now freed slaves. On the contrary,

> I have been thankful to God for the wondrous change; but, what with the frightful expenditure of blood; and emancipation's being forced on us by *necessity*, instead of preceding from the repentance of the nation; and the shameful want of protection to the freedmen since they have been emancipated; there has been no opportunity for any out-gushing of joy and exultation. (*Selected Letters*, 458)

As she later explains to Robert Purvis, who wrote to compliment her on *A Romance of the Republic* after its publication, "In these days of novel-reading, I thought a Romance would take more hold of the public mind, than the most elaborate arguments; and having fought against Slavery, till the monster is legally dead, I was desirous to do what I could to undermine Prejudice. . . . I have tried to help on this good work . . . and sad as I sometimes am over the present state of affairs, still, on the whole, I feel encouraged" (August 1868; *Selected Letters*, 482–83).

If publishers and the public were antagonistic to abolitionist writing before the Civil War, they gave an equally cool reception to works that rehashed slave issues afterward. Torn apart by the conflict, the nation wanted mostly to rebuild and forget. Child's *Romance of the Republic* steadfastly refused this formulation. To rebuild without remembering was to deny the lessons history had to offer and to ignore the redemptive possibilities of moral growth. Like *Hope Leslie*, Child's *Romance of the Republic* insists on historicizing black and white relations, looking backward in order to look forward.

A Pretty Dilemma

In a recent article on *A Romance of the Republic*, Karcher discusses how the use of the "tragic quadroon" central to the design of this novel in some ways compromises its social vision.[24] As Susan Koppelman was the first to note, Child introduced this figure to American literature and made it a successful vehicle which could at once reveal the sexual plight of women slaves and satisfy the refined tastes of white readers. Koppelman also credits Child for being "the first white writer to grant black and racially mixed women the right to be "ladies." Child portrays the enslaved woman "as partaking with grace and virtue of the life typically reserved for the mistress" (*Other Woman*, 2). But Karcher has long been concerned with the limitations of the figure: "As a vehicle for protesting against racism . . . and as an instrument for probing the connection between white supremacy and male dominance — the archetype of the 'tragic quadroon' proved highly ambiguous" ("Rape," 331). Karcher observes that in the long run the statement that the quadroon makes against the sexual exploitation of women slaves is qualified by "the use of the genteel, near-white heroine," which tends instead to reinforce "the very prejudices antislavery fiction sought to counteract" ("Rape," 331).

Thus, Child's reliance here may have seriously compromised her goals in the novel.

Acknowledging those limitations, however, should not lead us to overlook the sophisticated critique of the patriarchal structure of U.S. society that Child is able to mount by means of her use of the "tragic quadroon." The interracial union that *A Romance of the Republic* urges be legalized in order to end race prejudice is revealed in the novel as the illicit fuel for the sexist and racist construction of Anglo male subjectivity by the novel's trenchant analysis. Through a variety of male characters, *A Romance of the Republic* displays the competitive and commodified construction of this patriarchal Subject in all his gradations.

Through the genealogy of Rosa and Flora, Child chronicles two generations of men who fall in love with enslaved women of African heritage and beget daughters ever lighter in the color of their skin. Both men somehow neglect to manumit their wives and daughters. The grandfather of Rosa and Flora sells their mother—his beloved daughter—to Royal when he faces a financial crunch. And Royal, who becomes the devoted "husband" of Eulalia, is detained from procedures to manumit her by his capital interests and commitments to the business world—as he later feebly explains, "being immersed in business . . . [he] never seemed to find the time" to take his wife abroad to legally marry and manumit her (21).[25] Similarly, business affairs overrule his wish to free his daughters before his death intervenes.

But the text subtly questions Royal's apparently innocent oversight. When we first meet Fitzgerald, it is in Royal's own house, which is described as "the temple of Flora" (4), a paradise secluded from the eyes of the world, a "fairy land" (21), accessible only by the invitation of Royal himself. Here the segregation between the world of men (business) and the feminized (and objectified) domestic space is absolute—absolutely owned by Royal and absolutely enjoyed by him. The adoring daughters attend their father's every whim and perform on command by dancing and singing for him and his male guests. As Royal remarks of Flora, "she is used to being my little plaything, and I can't spare her to be a woman yet" (6). Even the stalwart Alfred King, who is depicted as the model of racial tolerance, is seduced by this panorama of male privilege: "I . . . forget that I am a stranger . . . I forgot it entirely before I had been in the house ten minutes" (6). King's mannerly remark simultaneously clues us to the more sinister implications of the scenario, where Royal's daughters are objectified even by their names (lovely and sensual flowers) for male viewing pleasure—the scenario to which no man in a patriarchal society is a stranger.[26]

It is through the depiction of Gerald Fitzgerald that the text most pointedly suggests that Royal's sins are those of commission rather than omission. Fitzgerald also makes himself "at home" in the Temple of Flora, and his actions as well as his remarks are more vulgarly to the point. He later that evening questions Alfred King on which girl he preferred and comments that "If I were the Grand Bashaw, I would have them both in my harem" (13). His remark reveals his own acquisitive motivations at the same time it underscores how "the Temple of Flora" represents Royal's own pretensions to the Grand Bashaw's harem. When Fitzgerald "rescues" the daughters by taking them to his plantation, his more sinister behavior still mirrors Royal's: in his shammed marriage to Rosa that parallels her mother Eulalia's, in keeping both sisters secluded and veiled in public as had Royal in New Orleans, and even in purchasing many of Royal's effects in order to recreate the atmosphere of his "Temple of Flora."

Child's novel lays bare to reader scrutiny the very gaze of commodification through which Anglo male subjectivity is structured and becomes dominant. In an important passage, where sentimental language conveys a scene almost breathtaking in its frankly sexual tone, *A Romance of the Republic* structures its analysis of the motivations of patriarchy. In this scene Fitzgerald reflects with triumph on his engineered escape for the unfortunate Royal sisters. His pleasant thoughts are interrupted, though, by the alternate specter of what his failure to "save" the two sisters, and Rosa in particular, might have entailed:

> He seemed to see her graceful figure gazed at by a brutal crowd, while the auctioneer assured them that she was warranted to be an entirely new and perfectly sound article, — a moss rosebud from a private royal garden, — a diamond fit for a king's crown. And men, whose upturned faces were like greedy satyrs, were calling upon her to open her ruby lips and show her pearls. He turned restlessly on his pillow and muttered an oath. Then he smiled as he thought to himself that, by saving her from such degradation, he had acquired complete control of her destiny. (66–67)

Here Child makes daring use of romantic images to lay bare the psychological connections between patriarchy and slavery. By "saving" Rosa, even from the "gaze" of other men, Fitzgerald achieves the mastery of complete ownership which allows him more fully to realize his dream of a harem.

Significantly, it is the specter of that *potential* gaze, the envy of those who know they were denied that gaze, that most fully constitutes Fitzgerald's triumph. As Fitzgerald reflects, "it would have been far more convenient to have bought them outright . . . but after Signor repeated to me that disgusting talk of Bruteman's, there could be no mistake that he had *his* eye fixed on them" (67; Child's emphasis). Just as Alfred King's approving gaze on Royal's daughters confirms their worth for him (17–24), so do the admiring gazes of licentious speculators ensure Fitzgerald's male dominance in the patriarchal system of commerce. Thus the right to look is intrinsically connected with the right to purchase, to own, to dominate. The daughters, surveyed by the objective glance of those speculators, are "appraised . . . at six thousand dollars," which, as another commentator knowingly observes, is "much less than they would bring at auction . . . as you all would agree, gentlemen, if you had *seen* them" (69; my emphasis).

As we begin to understand, the gaze is structured through a species of competition — to be a gazing Gazer marks a position of potency and Subjectivity; conversely, to be deprived of that gaze is to impotently envy. In short, controlling the women, sequestering them out of range of the envying gaze of other men, enforces their frustration and, concomitantly, confirms the Subjectivity of the gazing owner. The gaze structures social as well as commercial relations between men, and penetrating the harem is the indubitable sign of manhood. As Bruteman remarks, "I'd rather, a devilish sight, have those girls than the money you owe me" (192). Fitzgerald's fullest defeat is marked by his inability to contain his prize, and he is completely emasculated when, drunk and in debt from his dissipation, he signs away Rosa to Bruteman.

Although the quadroon as a literary device is certainly—in Karcher's words—a "double-edged sword" in that she "has the effect of endorsing an ethnocentric preference for approximations of white beauty" ("*Romance*," 87), the outwardly aimed blade in Child's *Romance of the Republic* is sharp indeed. In Child's critique the slave/mistress quadroon functions as a doubled token of the Subjectivity of the Anglo male in that she simultaneously traces evidence of "white" mastery in her lighter skin and marks the symbolic dominance of her owner over the issue of fellow Anglo males. She is the (visible) site of the competition between men that structures white manhood. At the same time, the light-skinned and gracious quadroon unavoidably mirrors the position of Anglo women in patriarchy, as Karcher has detailed in her analysis of *A Romance of the Republic*. The same motives that underlie laws that reverse patrilineage in the case of slaves underwrite the law of *feme covert* that governs the lives of Anglo women in the United States. As Fitzgerald buys and sells Rosa to Bruteman, so he buys his Northern bride, Lily Bell, "only for her father's money"—in the same way that Lily's father, Mr. Bell, "has sold her for her husband's plantation and his own business prospects in the South" (Karcher, "*Romance*," 91–92). As such, the quadroon serves as the marker of Anglo male Subjectivity—over all the slaves and all the women and, perhaps most important, over less powerful "white" men.

Just as *A Romance of the Republic* employs sentimental language to reveal the exploitively sexual nature of Anglo male Subjectivity, it directly opposes sentimentality to male-structured "business" and "law."[27] In a telltale scene, where speculators meet to discuss the breakup of Royal's property, Flora's future husband, the sensitive Blumenthal, objects to the proposed auctioning of the Royal sisters. Bruteman peremptorily cuts off Blumenthal's protestations, saying "we are not here to talk sentiment, my lad . . . we are here to transact business" (69). Bruteman implies that the young Blumenthal's interest in the women is sexual and indicates he must purchase the right to gaze, in fair competition with the other interested men: "you must buy them at the auction block, if you can. The law is inexorable" (69). In referring to an agency seemingly beyond the scope of his influence—"the law"—Bruteman seeks to veil and sanction the self-interest of patriarchy and slavery. As this scene indicates, law serves as a rhetoric of camouflage. But, as the text makes clear (and as Child has indicated in documentary works like *The Patriarchal Institution*), laws cannot be separated from the motives that occasioned their existence. The novel suggestively associates "the law" with "brute" force as the legal basis for the meeting quickly disintegrates into threatened violence against abolitionists and challenges for dueling among the participants.[28]

The emblem of the quadroon, a visible marker of "mixed blood," also allows *A Romance* to develop a critique of the econometrics of "race," which underscores its perceptual invalidity—the basis on which its distinction rests. Rosa and Flora are so light-skinned as to enable them to "pass" as "white," and while it is their putative (if actually *invisible*) "blackness" that makes them available to be auctioned as part of their father's estate, it is their *visible* "whiteness" that increases their value. And, as the novel elsewhere makes clear, even "whites" can be sold as "blacks" into slavery—for instance when Tulee and the switched Fitzgerald heir, George Faulkner, are kidnapped by slave traders. Although Tulee tells them that the baby belonged to a "white lady," the traders "laughed and said there was a great many white niggers" (372).

The dubious standard of outward appearance is most pointedly satirized by the working-class abolitionist Joe Bright. As he explains to Blumenthal, his conversion occurred when, looking through Southern papers in search of a job, he came across an advertisement describing a runaway slave:

> "'Run away from the subscriber a stout mulatto slave, named Joe, has light sandy hair, blue eyes, and a ruddy complexion; is intelligent and will pass himself for a white man . . . '
> "'By George!' said I, 'that's a description of me.'
> I didn't know before that I was a mulatto." (322)

Bright goes instead to Vermont and, as an experiment, successfully passes himself as that runaway slave, showing the advertisement to confirm his story. This experience is a powerful education for him: "Blue-eyed Joe," as he dubs the man described in the ad, "seemed to bring the matter home" (322). So *A Romance* here makes a provocative suggestion—along with focusing on "blacks" who look "white," the text proposes that "whites" can in fact look "black." In this way the novel underscores the perceptual invalidity of racial tropes and prejudice. It hints of another basis for racist "reasoning" through the merchant Mr. Bell. Informed of Rosa's cradle switch of the two Fitzgerald heirs, the boys' maternal grandfather summarizes it as "a pretty dilemma. . . . My property, it seems, must either go to Gerald, who . . . has negro blood in his veins, or to this other fellow, who is a slave with a negro wife" (394). It is striking that Mr. Bell's most immediate concerns lay bare the economic motives behind racial prejudice in both the northern *and* the southern United States.

Learning to Read History

While *A Romance of the Republic* employs conventions of sentiment to counter racist and patriarchal formations, it also reformulates sentiment to achieve its meta-historical project. The novel revolves around a double message of irony and vision exemplified in the title. It addresses itself overtly to the genre of romance that Simms had described in his 1853 preface to *The Yemassee*, a "substitute which the people of the present day offer for the ancient epic," a genre that "does not confine itself to what is known, or even what is probable" (6). Ironically, while the events of *A Romance of the Republic* do often seem beyond the realm of possibility, Child knew they were grounded mostly in fact. With the exception of the subplot set in Italy, all the other events of the novel are taken from accounts documented in countless newspaper reports and ads for runaways from which Child had drawn in her tract *The Patriarchal Institution*. Quadroon daughters were often unaware of their condition as chattel until their fathers' deaths brought about their sale. Innumerable runaway slaves were described as having "blond hair . . . blue eyes . . . white complexion . . . Roman nose" and were predicted to "pass themselves as whites."[29] And slaves who ran away often met miraculously with family members in the North. As one character comments on Flora's condition, "I have long been aware that the most romantic stories have grown out of the institution of slavery; but this seems stranger than fiction . . . it makes one anxious to conceal he is an American" (157).

Ironically, the poetic qualities promised by a "romance" of the "republic" were the most embarrassing facts of U.S. history. The epic topics of this *Romance* are, no matter how genteelly narrated, the scandals of slavery—lust, dishonesty, and even rape—in the South and weakhearted complicity in the inhumane practice of capitalism in the North. The Republic's historical legacy, by this account, is one of moral bankruptcy. *A Romance of the Republic* was hardly a "romance" at all.

At the same time, however, it suggests the redemptive possibilities of this legacy. The novel ends on a positive note, figuratively—as many of the white characters acknowledge both sympathy and responsibility toward the newly emancipated blacks—and literally—as many of the characters gather in a war's-end celebration, singing both slave spirituals and patriotic tunes.[30] The novel reexamines the most negative facts of the Republic's existence to show how they must be confronted in order to be overcome—that the "color" of "race" lay in the distorted eye of the prejudiced observer, and the way out is to learn to see more clearly, more sympathetically and compassionately. As King observes to the young Fitzgerald: "that is the way I have learned to read history . . . unchanged by looking at it through the deceptive colored glasses of conventional prejudice" (358). Child thus puts "history" and "romance" to specifically confrontative and mediative purposes in order to provide a novel that is at once a revision of America's history, and a re-vision of its future course.

By way of achieving this, the novel turns sentimental expectations to deliver a pointed message. Nina Baym summarizes the paradigmatic sentimental plot, which typically features a young orphan who, through the aid of an older, exemplary mentor, learns womanly, Christian virtues. But in *A Romance of the Republic* the mentors are educated through their experiences with African Americans who have suffered racial persecution from the point of view of the victim. In particular, Mrs. Delano, who helps Flora escape from Fitzgerald, is not at first sympathetic to the abolitionist cause: "It was contrary to Mrs. Delano's usual caution and deliberation to adopt a stranger so hastily; and had she been questioned beforehand, she would have pronounced it impossible for her to enter into such a relation with one allied to the colored race and herself a slave" (147). But her relation with Flora gradually alters her perspective. Concealing Flora's condition compels a quick education in slave resistance, as Mrs. Delano seeks help from prominent abolitionists and for the first time pays serious heed to their arguments.

Mrs. Delano begins a crucial course of moral self-examination which models the meta-historical project of the novel. At one point remembering her youthful romantic acquaintance with Rosa and Flora's father, Alfred Royal, Mrs. Delano reflects, "I ought to do the same for them without that motive . . . but should I?" (222). Shortly she has the opportunity to test herself on this point. During preparations for departure on a steamship after an unsuccessful trip to the South in search of Rosa, another slave of Fitzgerald's, Chloe, appeals to Mrs. Delano to claim her and her two children as Mrs. Delano's own slaves in order to aid their escape. With encouragement from Flora, Mrs. Delano consents to the subterfuge and later describes it to an abolitionist:

> If ever a quiet and peace-loving individual was caught up and whirled about by a tempest of events, I am surely that individual. Before I met this dear little Flora, I had a fair prospect of living and dying a respectable and respected old fogy, as you irreverent reformers call discreet people. But now I find myself drawn into the vortex of abolition to the extent of helping off four fugitive slaves. (266)

Later Mrs. Delano details the revolutionary change in aspect that Flora has provided: "As for my education, I have learned to consider it as, in many respects, false. As for my views, they have been greatly modified by this experience. I have learned to estimate people and things by their real value, not merely according to external accidents" (278).

Mrs. Delano's moral growth conveys an important message to the contemporary readers of *A Romance of the Republic*, predicting the possibility of national progress modeled on self-confrontation and active remediation. As Mrs. Delano at one point meditates, "so one wrong produces another wrong; and thus frightfully may we affect the destiny of others, while blindly following the lead of selfishness. But the past, with all its weaknesses and sins, has gone beyond recall; and I must try to write a better record on the present" (150). This, the narrative underscores, will be effected only through a total commitment to active social reform. Mrs. Delano's social peers gossip about her sponsoring a clerk and allowing him to court her adopted daughter, as well as her attendance at abolitionist meetings. The narrator comments that while Mrs. Delano was becoming "a black sheep in aristocratic circles . . . these indications passed by her almost unnoticed, occupied as she was in earnestly striving to redeem the mistakes of the past by making the best possible use of the present" (283–84). Mrs. Delano in this way becomes a model for post-Civil War America. She provides an example of moral progress expressed through sympathetic social action that suggests the means by which Anglo America can write its own record anew — a *true* romance of the republic.

The novel rejects a view of "history" as a concretized and unreclaimable past. Rather, it turns to historical examination as an active means of confronting and counterbalancing the past. This historically confrontative formulation of sentiment powerfully counters the model described by Philip Fisher in *Hard Facts*. Recounting Rousseau's sympathetic prisoner, Fisher argues that this image of the passive spectator encouraged by the sympathetic model prevents it from forwarding actual social change. Fisher argues:

> The tears that are so important a part of sentimentality are best understood in this context. Weeping is a sign of powerlessness. Tears represent the fact that only a witness who cannot effect action will experience suffering as deeply as the victim. For this reason stories of the long ago past play a central part in sentimentality: their only possible response is that of tears rather than revolt. (108)

A Romance of the Republic strives to write beyond that ending: tears of compassion over the wrongs of the past are the first step; acting to correct the wrongs are the necessary second.

An Imitative Race

That second step, according to the example mapped in the novel, is to be taken by Anglo philanthropists, who make it their business to educate and thereby elevate untutored ex-slaves into respectability, so that they will be on equal footing with their "white" fellow citizens. This is the project that the King family undertakes on behalf of Henriet, the mulatto wife of Gerald Fitzgerald. The description of the results is revealing. After returning from the war, Rosen Blumenthal expresses a desire to check on her progress, and she is summoned for his scrutiny:

> The improvement in her appearance impressed him greatly. Having lived three years with kindly and judicious friends, who never reminded her, directly or indirectly, that she was a black sheep in the social flock, her faculties had developed freely and naturally; and belonging to an imitative race, she readily adopted the language and manners of those around her. Her features were not handsome, with the exception of her dark, liquid-looking eyes; and her black hair was too crisp to make a soft shading for her brown forehead. But there was a winning expression of gentleness in her countenance, and a pleasing degree of modest ease in her demeanor. A map, which she had copied very neatly, was exhibited, and a manuscript book of poems, of her own selection, written very correctly, in a fine flowing hand.
> "Really, this is encouraging," said Mr. Blumenthal. (433)

This passage, offered as the potential result of the novel's project (viz. cultural/racial integration), also encapsulates its imaginative limitations. Most immediately disturbing is the way Henriet is called to stand under the gaze of a white male. She is appraised, albeit to a vastly different end, but just as surely to meet the approval of the arbiter of culture, the white male. The gaze of Blumenthal, one of the most benevolent male characters in the novel, enforces a hierarchical relationship between the gazer and the object of his scrutiny.

The description also highlights the problems that branch out from Child's reliance on the "tragic quadroon." Todorov proposes a three-dimensional analysis of racial relations and representations that will be useful to consider here. He argues that "we must distinguish among at least three axes on which we can locate the problematics of alterity" (*Conquest*, 185). The first, "axiological" level entails value judgment, a statement on whether the Other is good or bad, loved or hated, equal or inferior. At the second, "praxeologic" level, the Subject positions him/herself in relation to the Other. Here the Subject can identify with the Other or can identify the Other with the Subject-self, imposing Subject values on the Other. The third, "epistemic" level, determines whether the Subject knows or remains ignorant of the Other's identity, largely predicted by the results of the first two levels. As Todorov points out, here there are no absolutes, "but an endless gradation between the lower or higher states of knowledge" (*Conquest*, 185).

Todorov's scheme illuminates the limitations of Child's "tragic quadroon" and the ways in which the values that underlie this figure inform her depiction of the other "black" characters in *A Romance of the Republic*. The novel clearly grants all the black characters dignity and humanity. At the axiologic level, then, the novel can be said to value positively the racial Other. In fact it models several levels of loving, cross-racial relationships—between Flora and Mrs. Delano, Rosa and Mr. King, Lily Bell and her "son" Gerald, George Faulkner and Harriet. At the praxeological level, though it can be said that *A Romance of the Republic* "embraces the Other's value," this point must be carefully qualified. The black characters' are embraceable only as (and precisely because) *they* embrace white values of virtue, chastity and republicanism (an imitative race). So Henriet, who cannot achieve real beauty since "features" like her kinky hair don't cover the brown of her skin, can yet succeed in "adopt[ing] the language and manners of those around her." She has succeeded in imitating her "white" mentors, copying and conforming to their standards. Only as such does she become acceptable, her "black sheep" status held in abeyance to her obedience to white middle-class cultural norms.

Although the novel has demonstrated the inherent unfairness of racial categorization, it does not transcend the color line, as is evident in an exchange between Chloe and Tulee when Henriet first enters the King household:

> When black Chloe saw the new-comer learning to play on the piano, she was somewhat jealous because the same privilege had not been offered to her children. "I didn't know Missy Rosy tought thar war sech a mighty difference 'tween black an' brown," said she. "I don't see nothin' so drefful pooty in dat ar molasses color."
>
> "Now ye shut up," rejoined Tulee. "Missy Rosy knows what she's 'bout. Ye see Mr. Fitzgerald was in love with Missy Eulaly; an Henret's husban' took care o' him when he was dying. Mr. King is going to send him 'cross the water on some gran' business, to pay him for 't; and Missy Rosy wants his wife to be 'spectable out there 'mong strangers." (419–20)

Tulee's dialect highlights the precise root of the problem, which is still one of vision: Henriet needs to be rendered "spectable"—pleasing to the gaze of "whites." So the gaze is transferred from the specific agency of the individual Anglo male to Anglo culture in general: either way, the "black" is an appraised object. This is underscored, ironically, when the ever-imitative Flora parodies "the shuffling dances of the negroes" as part of her drawing-room fun, and is greeted by "scream[s of] laughter" (348). Chloe's resentment, though discounted by Tulee and by the narrative itself, comments dialogically and incisively on the novel's ultimate vision. There is too neat a correspondence between the social position and visible color of the novel's "blacks" that finally undermines its critique of "color." From the genteel octoroon Flora, to the socially raised mulatto Henriet, to the "black" Chloe and Tulee, who continue to serve Rosa and Flora, we must heed the uncritical assumptions the novel forwards about color and social rank.

A Romance of the Republic works to eliminate categories of *racial* difference—to show that "blacks" can be like "whites." But what it fails to allow—a positive evaluation of *cultural* or *social* configurations different from those of the white middle class—effectively prevents the novel from establishing any tolerance or understanding of difference at *any* level. As Karcher carefully observes, the novel's black characters are simply not representative of slave experience in the South, where the slaves predominantly worked in the field and lived in the quarter. The characters in *A Romance of the Republic* represent that small proportion of slaves (i.e., house "hands") who lived closest to and as a consequence more often aspired and strove to assimilate to "white" cultural standards. While *A Romance* effectively employs these characters to undermine concepts of "race," the novel is not able to countenance the cultural differences produced by the intersection of African cultural heritages and slave quarter life. Consequently its contributions to cross-racial understanding at the epistemic level are qualified because it fails to imagine cross-*cultural* relationships that would complement the cross-*racial* ones. The "prejudice of equality"—identifying the racial Other with one's own "ego-ideal"—while in many ways more *humane*, is finally no more effective in creating real understanding *between* the Subject and Other than the "prejudice of superiority."

A Romance of the Republic questions adeptly the drives of power and authority in patriarchy, and how they create falsely "prejudiced" social formations. But the novel's projection of an integrated culture formed solely around middle-class Anglo values overlooks alternatives to Anglo middle-class cultural expression—imposing a monologic standard on the dialogic vision of interracial community. It thereby forestalls a fuller questioning of the biases in Anglo-American culture that had permitted slavery and patriarchy and continued to foster "racial" prejudice. In this way we can see how the critical strategy of sympathy in *A Romance of the Republic* confirms Karen Halttunen's reservations about the genre: "Sentimentalism offered an unconscious strategy for middle-class Americans to distinguish themselves as a class while still denying class structure, and to define themselves against the lower classes even as they insisted they were merely distinguishing themselves from vulgar hypocrites"

(195). Child manifests a real concern, both in *A Romance of the Republic* and elsewhere (e.g., in her *Letters from New York*) over the corruptions of capitalism. But while the novel is highly critical of individual misuses of capital in both the North and South, it complacently accepts a system that ultimately guarantees both individual misuses and institutionalized class/race prejudice. We must acknowledge this important limitation.

Still, Child should be recognized for her contribution to a new, if not comprehensive, vision of interracial harmony by proposing cultural strategies that tolerate, assist, and communicate with the Other. Through its deployment of sympathy, the novel provides an important critique of patriarchy; through its reformulation of sentimental plot structure, it provides a new cultural perspective that promotes and models active intercession on behalf of the object of sympathy. Like *Hope Leslie*, therefore, *A Romance of the Republic* speaks practically as well as theoretically to the cultural dialogue on "race."

The reformative "sentimentalism" of both *Hope Leslie* and *A Romance of the Republic* provides powerful alternative readings that challenge and revise contemporary historical formulations of "race." Clearly, Charles Osgood's charge against Child—that she failed to make a useful book out of *A Romance of the Republic*—is untenable (158).[31] As we have seen, these novels argue for cultural change which could offer more humane alternatives to oppressively constructed race relations. Both novels provide important—if very different— critiques of patriarchy and its deployment of history. As such they complicate the debate over "race" by factoring in gender—both at the level of praxis, as women authors, and at the level of theory, by tying the structure of "race" to that of patriarchy. For these reasons, both novels are valuable to an understanding of the social context of American literature. Remarkable for their alternative social vision, if marked by their limitations, the novels are important voices in the literary dialogue on racism and racialism that engrossed nineteenth-century America.

5

Ethnocentrism Decentered: Colonialist Motives in *The Narrative of Arthur Gordon Pym*

"Race" in *Pym* and Poe

In the last thirty years *The Narrative of Arthur Gordon Pym* (1838) has become one of the most popular and controversial texts among Poe scholars. As Douglas Robinson suggests, it would seem that Poe's eccentric narrative is "an interpreter's dream-text . . . a textual vacuum begging to be filled with a reading" ("Reading Poe's Novel," 47). The striking variance of conclusions on The Meaning of *Pym* contributes to current curiosity over the work. Readings of *Pym* range widely, from psychoanalytic exploration to social satire, from self-referential commentary on writing (or reading) to a metacritical demonstration of utter absence of meaning. Those commenting on the text apparently cannot reach any consensus or "thrust toward uniformity" (Robinson, "Reading Poe's Novel," 52), though many seem to concur with J. Gerald Kennedy, who posits *Pym* as "the pivotal text in current discussions" of Poe (*Poe*, 145).[1]

While scholarship through the sixties and seventies frequently attended to issues of race in Poe's narrative, recent analysts have turned more often to the narrative's metatextual suggestiveness, largely abandoning a pursuit of *Pym*'s social or racial dimensions. Strikingly, though, Poe scholars are once again debating Poe's own racial attitudes. The dispute stems largely from one unsigned review in the April 1836 *Southern Literary Messenger* (*SLM*). Published during Poe's tenure as editor, the review favorably cites two proslavery books: *Slavery in the United States* (James Kirke Paulding) and *The South Vindicated from Treason and Fanaticism of Northern Abolition* (probably William Drayton). Early Poe scholars attributed the essay to Poe, who commonly contributed book reviews while editor of this journal. But in 1941 a dissertation by William Doyle Hull challenged this assumption, instead proposing on the basis of an ambiguous but suggestive letter from Poe to Beverly Tucker, that Tucker in fact wrote the review. After several decades of sometimes heated debate,

Bernard Rosenthal published an impressively thorough examination of the issue. In his close reading of the Poe-Tucker letter, his meticulous reconstruction of printing and transportation schedules, and his scrutiny of other *SLM* correspondence, Rosenthal traces the impossibility of attributing the essay to Tucker on the basis of extant evidence.

More important, however, Rosenthal refocuses the discussion of Poe's racist attitudes. Poe's disputed authorship of the review, he insists, is a straw man: "The authorship problem in regard to the Paulding-Drayton review has unnecessarily obscured Poe's pro-slavery views" (30). Whether or not Poe wrote the review, Rosenthal points out, he elsewhere expressed proslavery sympathies—for instance, in his reviews of Robert Montgomery Bird's *Shepperd Lee*, Anne MacVicar Grant's *Memoires of an American Lady*, an unpublished review of John L. Carey's *Domestic Slavery*, and particularly in his stance on works by the noted Southern defender of slavery, Thomas R. Dew (see 30–31). If he did not write the review, Poe elsewhere made clear his sympathy to its views: "His politics in regard to slavery and social structure . . . embodied the kind of mythology about slavery to be found in the Paulding-Drayton review" (31).

Some fifteen years after Rosenthal's important essay, the controversy has again arisen—this time more quietly.[2] Based, it seems, on no new evidence, the issue perhaps speaks more to the critical climate than to any new insight into Poe. G. R. Thompson, for instance, in his essay on "Edgar Allan Poe and the Writers of the Old South" in the *Columbia Literary History of the United States* (1988) asserts parenthetically that "the notorious review of two books defending slavery in the *Messenger* in 1836, upon which some critical interpretations of Poe's *Narrative of Arthur Gordon Pym* have been based, was written not by Poe, but in all likelihood by Beverly Tucker" (269). Thompson minimalizes Poe's concern with slavery, asserting that only in his review of James Russell Lowell's *A Fable for Critics* does Poe take "any kind of stance on slavery" (269). Thompson apparently aims to exonerate Poe from any "regionalist sentiment": "Rarely does he employ Southern locales or character types; he does not embroil himself in the issue of slavery; he does not address matters of Southern autonomy and separatism; he does not confront Southern with Northern personages; he does not cast Southern leaders as knights in the quest of glory" (277). Working to establish Poe as a "major national writer" (262), Thompson argues that Poe, as the "one original voice out of the Old South" deserves continued esteem precisely because he transcended Southern values—including any intellectual involvement with slavery. Herein Thompson most directly voices the recent trend to sweep Poe's politics under the rug. Scholars depict an essentialist Poe, a "true man of letters" who "focuses on the integrity of the work of art in terms of the . . . metaphysical ideal" (Thompson, 277), or a true man of our deconstructionist times, whose works point only to "frustrating indeterminacy . . . or a useless and contrived 'unity'" (Rowe, 94). Without involving myself in arguments about intentionality here, I do want to consider how such a trend toward a depoliticized and dehistoricized reading of the Poe oeuvre concomitantly "saves" Poe for a canon increasingly skeptical of texts that support human oppression. I am *not* suggesting that acknowledging the racist dimension of Poe's work should remove his works from the canon; but I think we must at least consider the cultural work performed *now* by masking that aspect of his work.

My discussion does not attempt to resolve the dispute over Poe's racism. It will possibly make any discussion of Poe's racial views even more problematic by arguing that while on one level *Pym* is a racist text, on another the text provides a reading that counters racist colonial ideology and the racialist, scientific knowledge structure. In this way the two levels of the text exist in a tension, providing examples of the two broad categories which Abdul Jan-Mohamed proposes for colonialist literature: the imaginary and the symbolic, terms which he culls from Lacan's work on the development of the psyche.[3] The imaginary, as Abdul JanMohamed outlines it,

> tends to coalesce the signifier with the signified. In describing the attributes or actions of the native, issues such as intention, causality, extenuating circumstances, and so forth, are completely ignored; in the 'imaginary' colonialist realm, to say "native" is automatically to say "evil" . . . the writer of such texts tends to fetishize a nondialectical, fixed opposition between the self and the native. ("Economy," 65)

The symbolic, on the other hand, is a more conscious, or critical, mode that is somewhat more cognizant of colonial motives. Symbolic texts tend to "thematize the problem of colonialist mentality and its encounter with the racial Other" (66).

This tension between imaginary and symbolic colonialist representation is further illuminated in *Pym* by considering another ambivalence embedded in narrative. As John Limon has recently observed, *Pym* marks the halfway point between "the antiscientific 'Sonnet — To Science' (1829) to the parascientific *Eureka* (1848)" (71). Pym's account appeals to "time and progressing science to verify some of the most important and most improbable . . . statements" (p. 88) and at the same time works as a burlesque of Francis Bacon's *New Atlantis* (see Limon, 71). Thus, the text's (ambivalent) attention to the burgeoning scientific developments of the period and their relation to colonialist epistemology provides another reference point for my analysis.[4]

White Is Right

Between 1800 and 1850 America witnessed a simultaneous surge in scientific professionalization and expansionist fervor which cumulatively resulted in the Anglo-American theory of Manifest Destiny. Limon notes the dynamic transition during this period from Baconian science — "science as generalization and classification" — to dynamic theories of electromagnetism, thermodynamism, and atomic hypothesis — in short, "the beginning of the great era of the unification of force" (72). There was a similarly important paradigm shift in human sciences. Nancy Stepan's *Idea of Race in Science* traces the "move away from an eighteenth-century optimism about man, and faith in the adaptability of man's universal 'nature,' towards a nineteenth century . . . belief in the unchangeability of racial 'natures'" (4). Noting the coincidence of the inception of biological science with racialist emphases, Stepan observes that science in the nineteenth century became simultaneously more "scientific" and also more "racist—in its insistence on the permanency of racial types, and the existence of a scale of racial worth" (5).

Beginning especially in the 1830s, various arguments for Anglo racial superiority gained wide acceptance in England and throughout the United States. Theories such as polygenesis (a theory never widely accepted in the South) and phrenology fueled and were fueled by the arguments of proslavery apologists. In addition to the influence of new, validating scientific theories, other social factors triggered a growing discourse on the "rightness of whiteness." The 1830s marked the powerful onslaught of Northern abolitionist efforts, as well as the Virginia legislative debates over emancipation (1831–32). Together the two events triggered an intensification of the proslavery debate in the South, leading to works, like those of Thomas Dew, which explicitly linked the debased condition of African Americans to their inherent blackness, not to their environment of slavery (see Horsman, 123).

This growing eagerness to substantiate Anglo racial superiority was not particular to the South. As Stepan puts it: "a fundamental question about the history of racism in the first half of the nineteenth century is why it was that, just as the battle against slavery was being won by abolitionists, the war against racism in European thought was being lost" (1). Similarly, in America, as Horsman observes, "northern racial theorists generally agreed with the South that the colored races were unfit to mix with the whites on any equal basis" (125). So science increasingly sanctioned white racial superiority, providing a moral basis for national expansion and racist oppression. The United States continued its march across the American continent. The 1830s were the great decade of Indian removal; by the end of this period most tribes had been relocated west of the Mississippi. Western "exploration" ranged over the seas, among tropical isles, and out toward the poles. As Simeon North summarized in the next decade: Anglo Saxons were the world's enlightening influence, "whose enterprise explores every land, and whose commerce whitens every sea" (qtd. in Horsman, 289). Thus, the increasing confidence of racialist science was wedded to the optimism of colonial expansion, evidencing the direct link between knowledge and power in the colonialist enterprise.

Pym's fictional adventure is situated squarely in this expansionist, Anglo-Saxon ideological context.[5] As Harry Levin notes, *Pym* derives its "imaginative impetus" generally from the abundance of travel literature and fiction of the early 1800s, and particularly from Jeremiah Reynold's *An Address on the Subject of Surveying and Exploring Expedition to the Pacific Ocean and the South Seas*—"a project for discovering the South Pole and claiming the Antarctic continent on behalf of the United States" (109). As Levin suggests, the issue of geographical/scientific exploration was inseparable from that of nationalistic expansion. Less overtly, it was also inseparable from the issue of *capitalistic* expansion, a connection made nearly from the outset of Pym's narrative.

Pym delivers the story of his travels at the urging of a "society of several gentlemen" who "felt deep interest" in Pym's story and urged him, "as a duty," to share his story with the American public. These opening remarks are revealing. Just as colonial exploration was initiated to expand the white/Western capitalist world system, the colonial travel narrative, as Mary Louise Pratt summarizes, joins "the knowledge edifice of natural history" with capitalist expansion (125), thereby documenting a "natural" basis for "white" economic domination. It becomes Pym's "duty" as a citizen of the United States to share his knowledge with his fellow citizens. Pym's account will map white access into regions previously inaccessible, as well as informing the consumer public on lands and materials available for exploitation.

Pym admits resorting to "intense hypocrisy" to "further his project" — deceiving his relatives in order to leave on the *Grampus*. His deception might also be taken as a symbol of his own rhetorical strategy in his narrative and, at a larger level, of a culturally sanctioned policy of colonialist subterfuge. This strategy is reflected in the reasons Pym gives for making the journey and publishing his account. As we have seen, his motive for telling the story is "duty"; his reason for his traveling, however, is "melancholy." As he explains it, after the *Ariel* incident, in which Pym and Augustus capsize in a storm and nearly die, Pym finds his interest in seagoing renewed: "For the bright side of the painting I had a limited sympathy. My visions were of shipwreck and famine; of death or captivity among barbarian hordes; of a lifetime dragged out in sorrow and tears upon some gray and desolate rock in an ocean unapproachable and unknown" (65). No suggestion of fame and fortune enters into his account. But, as Albert Memmi points out in his landmark monograph *The Colonizer and the Colonized* (1957), the material position of a colonist guarantees his "interest" in the economic aspects of the situation. A colonizer is fundamentally aware of his guarantee to superior economic rights in usurped lands based on his exploitation of that land's material and human resources (45–89). Pym's narrative projects the famine and hardships he fears he will suffer among "barbarian hordes." It also documents the "profitable speculation" he hopes for in "discovery," his eagerness to be "the first white" on an island, and his participation in exploitation on Tsalal. His cooperation with the unnamed gentlemen in Virginia in producing the narrative further marks his complicity and profit in the colonial enterprise. Pym's protesting rejection of "the bright side of the painting" should be viewed as legitimizing rhetoric for the real motives of colonial exploration, a rhetorical tactic which, as Pym points out, was a "common" feature of discourse "to the whole numerous race of the melancholy among men" (65).

Pym's record of his travels with the *Jane Guy* reflects colonial ideology and rhetorical strategy. He situates the *Jane*'s mission in the South Seas as part of an international colonialist endeavor of "discovery." The *Jane Guy* was a trade ship of a "peculiar service" — vested with the "powers to cruise the South Seas for any cargo which might come most readily to hand." To this end, Pym notes, "it is absolutely necessary that she should be well armed," although the *Jane* itself was not so well armed and equipped as "a navigator acquainted with the difficulties and dangers of the trade could have desired" (147). Clearly "trade" is a euphemism for the *Jane Guy*'s real mission, which might more accurately be described as *conquest*. The cargo carried also speaks to the real charter of the ship, which "had on board, as usual in such voyages, beads, looking-glasses, tinder-works, axes, hatchets, saws, adzes, planes, chisels, gouges, gimlets, files, spokeshaves, rasps, hammers, nails, knives, scissors, razors, needles, thread, crockery-ware, calico, trinkets and other similar articles" (148)—construction tools (only the nails are traded with the natives) and baubles of minimal worth. In proportion to what they carry, as Pym's account makes clear, the crew of the *Jane Guy* expect an astronomic return on their investment.

Recording who first discovered each island and where its most convenient points of access are, Pym catalogs his observations in the manner of promotional tracts. Even when knowledge gathering is ostensibly most disinterested, as in Pym's apparently irrelevant elaborations on wildlife in the south Arctic sea, every bit of information is potentially profitable. Thus, Pym notes the flora and fauna of each island the *Jane Guy* passes and records facts essential to potential settlers, such as his observation on the largest of the Tristan d'Acunha islands: "Plenty of excellent water may here be readily procured; also cod, and other fish, may be taken with hook and line" (155). As he makes these observations, Pym occasionally slips into the second person— "Proceeding on eastwardly from this anchorage you come to Wasp Bay . . . into which you can go with four fathoms"—authorizing his American audience to identify with the explorer/colonizers (150–51). This rhetorical strategy includes the reader in the enterprise, making him a trading partner in the text, holding out to him the benefits initially recognized by the Virginia gentlemen.

Pym recounts the various voyages and claims of other explorers, noting two in particular (Jonathan Lambert and "an Englishman of the name of Glass") who seized sovereign authority over their "discoveries." He himself eagerly anticipates laying similar claims: "Of course a wide field lay before us for discovery, and it was with feelings of most intense interest that I heard Captain Guy express his resolution of pushing boldly to the southward" (162). Pym's "intense interest" (an echo of the Richmond gentlemen's "deep interest") belies the apparently objective and disinterested tone of the information recorded in his narrative, and his own earlier protestations to the contrary. It is precisely because of his "intense interest" that Pym persuades the captain of the *Jane Guy* to continue southward, despite evident danger. The decision leads to the massacre of the crew, and Pym expresses regret for the consequence of his proposal. Yet he qualifies his sorrow, explaining that "I must still be allowed to feel some degree of gratification at having been instrumental, however remotely, in opening to the eye of science one of the most intensely exciting secrets which has ever engrossed its attention" (166). As

Nancy Bentley points out, Pym here "all but confesses a causal link between the violence of [his] adventures and the project of science. . . . The tension here between the lament for bloodshed and the gratification of scientific desire is barely in check" (6).

Colonial science would hardly be "intensely excit[ed]" over areas that did not somehow stand to benefit the economy of the colony. Pym's pursuits deliver to the "eye of science" not only the news of a temperate and productive zone, but several "natural" proofs of racial hierarchy as well. Each in turn pertains directly to white economic interest. While the first discovery catalogs material and human resources ready for exploitation, the second backs a theory which would legitimize that exploitation by naturalizing "white" domination in metaphysical terms. Pratt observes that "regardless of an individual traveler's own attitudes and intentions, the Europeans in this domain of struggle [the colonial frontier] were charged with installing the edifice of domination and legitimizing its hierarchy" (127). It is not surprising, then, that racial hierarchy becomes the dominant subtext of Pym's account of the island Tsalal — an island which is particularly well-suited to the *Jane Guy*'s purposes. "Well wooded," apparently unmapped and undiscovered, the island "occasioned us great joy." Excited by the potential for profit on Tsalal, Pym has a clear interest in the "savages" he finds there.[6]

Racialist polarities structure the island of Tsalal. A Manichaean world where black and white colors dominate but do not mix, Tsalal in effect underwrites the color line of the antebellum South, and Pym's observations of the island highlight its segregated nature. Immediately he calls attention to the curious water, which was not "colourless, nor was it of any one uniform color." Pym elaborates on its striking character: "Upon collecting a basinful, and allowing it to settle thoroughly, we perceived that the whole mass of liquid was made up of a number of distinct veins, each of a distinct hue; that these veins did not commingle; and that their cohesion was perfect in regard to their own particles, and imperfect in regard to neighbouring veins" (172). Pym underscores the significance of this evidence of a natural principle of color segregation, describing it as "the first definite link in that vast chain of apparent miracles with which I was destined to be encircled" (172).

According to Pym, Tsalal replicates the natural apartheid evidenced in the water. "Indeed," he writes, "we noticed no light-colored substances of any kind upon the island" (199). He details the dark rocks and dark-skinned animals, birds, and fish. More significant, the narrative suggests that the all-black Tsalalians instinctively avoid anything white. Their surprise at sighting the crew of the *Jane Guy* signals to Pym "that they had never before seen any of the white race." Their response — they "recoil" — indicates a "natural" aversion between races, shared by black and white alike. Unlike *Hope Leslie*, *Pym* does not acknowledge the possibility that Tsalalians might regard the crew of the *Jane Guy* as "savage." Rather than exploring the reciprocity of values (isn't it interesting that the Tsalalians seem to consider white to be as evil and dangerous as we consider black?), the narrative instead employs this example to reinforce a stable, *hierarchical* opposition between white and black, equating the former with civilization, the latter with complete ignorance and savagery.

Pym's account after his escape from Tsalal continues documenting this binary opposition. As Pym, Peters, and their hostage, Nu-Nu, continue southward, the environment becomes increasingly white—"pallidly white birds" negotiate the "milky water" and sky, and "white ashy material" covers the men. Nu-Nu, physically elemental in aiding Pym and Peter's escape from the island, is semiotically elemental to the final chapter of Pym's account. The all-black Tsalalian provides both a point of contrast and a pointed message. When Pym and Peters innocently try to gain his help with a piece of white linen, Nu-Nu shudders and shrieks (202–3). Later, when the linen sail flaps in his face, Nu-Nu "became violently affected with convulsions" (204). From this point, he "obstinately lay in the bottom of the boat," refusing a "rational reply" (205). His only response, in fact, is to lift his upper lip, showing his black teeth.

These events offer a segregationalist parable: in the state of nature, black doesn't *want* to mix with white.[7] Nu-Nu provides a direct affirmation of this, convulsing and expiring in the face of an increasingly white environment. The unaccountable white monochrome of water, air, and wildlife, counterpointed by Nu-Nu's black presence and expiration, all provide Pym and his readers with a fantastic confirmation of Manifest Destiny. If the Anglo-Saxon colonist's project was to "whiten every sea," the "truth" objectively recorded by Pym revealed that the white colonist's right—physically and metaphysically— to the South Sea is already guaranteed: it *is* white.

Of Birds and Men

Tzvetan Todorov observes in a recent article that "whereas racism is a well-attested social phenomenon, 'race' itself does not exist" (171). Collette Guillaumin, in her essay "The Idea of Race and its Elevation to Autonomous, Scientific and Legal Status," clarifies this line of argument:

> The crucial fact is that the present century has seen the idea of race given legal status, alongside the older categories such as property, sex and age. The idea has emerged from the area in which it was only an *effect* of social relationships (and thus still an ideological form), and become in its turn an independent *cause*. This change has been to some extent underestimated . . . Today the question raised by the notion of race, if not of racialism, is generally thought to have been settled. The notion is supposed to correspond to self-evident physical fact; to be beyond debate, and thus something it is unnecessary or ill-bred to discuss. But the whole point is that race is not a material fact which produces social consequences. It is an idea, a mental fact, and so a social fact in itself. And if we really want to, we can find out where ideas come from. They certainly do not fall out of the sky. (41; Guillaumin's emphasis)

According to Guillaumin's analysis, we must regard "race" as a "practical relationship which has been crystallized in a pseudo-scientific form, the form of racial taxonomy and its successive historical implications" (57). Likewise, careful readers should not accept *Pym*'s fictional premise of "race" as a biological or metaphysical category.[8] In fact, the narrative itself questions and undermines this biological/metaphysical reading by revealing race as a strategic interpretive construct governed by political motives.

The *Jane Guy*'s encounter with the Tsalalians calls to mind the colonial exploitation of Native Americans. Europeans invade Tsalal and exploit the Tsalalians, bartering, as did the early North American Anglo settlers, with trinkets and beads. The scene has suggestive links as well to the colonial and antebellum South. Captain Guy, we are told, "was a gentleman of great urbanity of manner, and of considerable experience in the southern traffic" (148). The actions of the "white" crew of the *Jane Guy* on Tsalal result from the complacency of their historically proven superiority. Like their ancestors roughly two hundred years before, they take for granted their right to take fuel and refuge on Tsalal, as well as their right to forcefully exploit the apparently friendly natives.

It is significant that the pretense the crew makes at negotiating with and compensating the natives for their goods and services is a tacit admission of Anglo-European bad faith. Clearly they are not establishing mutual trust or equitable exchange, nor do they intend to do so, really. Captain Guy assures Too-wit of "his eternal friendship and good-will," at the same time knowing that the crewmen will "sacrific[e] . . . him immediately upon the first appearance of hostile design" (175). In return for a supply of food, as well as permission to establish a commercial industry on shore, the natives are presented with "blue beads, brass trinkets, nails, knives and pieces of red cloth."[9] That the exchange is merely a token mask for the real structure in play is admitted by Pym in the next sentence: "We established a regular market on shore, *just under the guns* of the schooner, where our barterings were carried on with every *appearance* of good faith" (177, my emphasis). The "appearance" is "faith"; the operative dynamic is force.

Just as power, not goodwill, is the rule of the market, so power is also the interest that rules Pym's perception of the natives. Pym assumes, for instance, that because the Tsalalians recoil from the "complexions" of the *Jane Guy*'s crew, "it was quite evident that they had never before seen any of the white race" (169). It is important for Pym to believe that the crew of the *Jane Guy* are the first white men the Tsalalians have seen in order to legitimize their claim to the island. When the Tsalalians express apparent willingness to be exploited by the white crew's proposed system of exchange, Pym unquestioningly believes what he perceives as their ignorance, "they being fully delighted in the exchange"—an exchange which the *Jane Guy* crew clearly knows is unfair (hence their pleasure in the "arrangement"), and which Pym's narrative calls attention to by detailing the precise value of the *bêche-de-mer* on the Chinese market. Pym's knowledge of Tsalalian behavior is never objective; it is always shaded by his own investment in the interpretation.

The underlying motives of Pym and the crew actually constitute a dangerous blind spot in their observations of the natives. Crew members feel assured in their assumptions about the Tsalalians' ignorance because of their confidence in their superior force (white [is might] is right). Indeed, they cling cognitively to their superiority as they cling physically to their guns. They assume that the Tsalalians "took [their guns] for idols, seeing the care we had of them, and the attention with which we watched their movements while handling them" (169). Since the crew did not demonstrate "the certain efficacy" of their weaponry to the natives, they conclude that the "savages" are unaware of their function—despite (indeed because of) the evident "awe" and fear the natives manifest in the presence of the "great guns" (181, 169). The guns, however, prove to be the *whites'* idol: despite the great faith the crew places in them, their guns are useless in the rock-slide attack. While Pym protests that the "perfidy" of the natives—their "great . . . decorum" and "extravagant demonstrations of joy"—disarm the crew, it is finally the crew's own blind sense of superiority which exposes them to ambush.

Pym cannot reconcile the Tsalalians' "deeply-laid plan" of ambush with their supposed ignorance. This event in fact negates all colonial representational certainty and undermines Pym's textual authority. Pym sidesteps the issue by shifting his cognitive framework from "ignorant" to "treacherous" to explain the event, but another level of the text suggests an alternative explanation. For instance, when Chief Too-wit witnesses the cook accidentally gashing the deck of the ship, his actions demonstrate a "sympathy" in what he apparently considered "the sufferings of the schooner, patting and smoothing the gash with his hand, and washing it from a bucket of sea-water which stood by." In the same way, the rest of the Tsalalians on board are careful to turn their spear tips up from the wood of the ship. Their actions, Pym remarks, evidenced "a degree of ignorance for which we were not prepared." Yet it was precisely *because* the colonizing crew is prepared to arrive at this conclusion that it fails to perceive the possibility of a belief system that would help it gather more precise knowledge about Tsalalian culture. That is, rather than focusing on Too-wit's extravagant ignorance, the crew might have concentrated on his obvious reverence for wooden objects. Inexplicable as that might have seemed, it might also have usefully informed the crew's subsequent actions.

Indeed, information in the narrative encourages readers to speculate on the ways in which the ship's crew violated Tsalalian cultural norms. The "great astonishment" that the natives evince when the crew members quickly clear a flat area of timber might indicate not pleasure, but displeasure—a possibility which Pym never entertains. Similarly, Pym's assumption that the Tsalalians regarded the guns as idols overlooks the suggestion that the natives knew their use, and were never fooled by the crew who everywhere proceeded "armed to the teeth" (180). This is to say that the "awe" of the Tsalalians can be read two ways: as wonder (at having never seen such a thing) or as wariness (at having seen precisely such a thing). Ironically, while the shipmen are all very poor at reading the Tsalalians' belief system, the obverse is apparently not true. The Tsalalians manage to dupe the crewmen by turning their sense of security against them. The Tsalal natives face their visitors unarmed, with a simple assertion: "there was no need of arms where all were brothers" (180). The statement is ambiguously double-barreled. At one level—the level the crew accepts—it can mean "we don't need arms because we feel like your brothers." It can also be a warning that "if we were brothers we wouldn't need arms." Furthermore, it defines their visitors as enemies—men who are "brothers" *don't* carry arms. Pym's account suggests that the Tsalalians were never duped by the crew, but rather acted on their knowledge of the use of firearms *and* the crewmen's sense of security with them in order to trick them into their deaths. Thus, these marginalized elements of *Pym* calculate the possible ramifications of the self-blinding basis of colonial "knowledge."

The Tsalalian episode highlights the expectations for dominance over the racial Other that underwrites the colonial enterprise. But another seemingly unrelated episode suggests an alternative to this exploitive social structure. Before his arrival at Tsalal, Pym pauses to describe a rookery—the curious living arrangement developed between albatross and penguins. These "colon[ies]" are described as a social system. They are carefully planned, "trace[d] out, with mathematical accuracy." Each resident must contribute to the colony's construction, which is "just sufficient size to accommodate easily all of the birds assembled, and no more—in this particular seeming determined upon preventing the access of future stragglers who have not participated in the labour of the encampment" (152). Most important, it is integrated. The penguins and albatross live cooperatively, even admitting "a variety of other oceanic birds." Pym himself signals its importance, commenting that "in short, survey it as we will, nothing can be more astonishing than the spirit of reflection evinced by these feathered beings, and nothing surely can be better calculated to elicit reflection in every well-regulated human intellect" (153).

The birds' collectivity reflects negatively on Pym's ethnocentric attitudes, which seek not cooperative integration, but exploitative segregation of humans. Pym's description of the birds also throws into relief the motives behind his delineation of human characters. He describes the royal penguin as a stately blend of grey, white, black, gold, and scarlet, whose variegation symbolizes the integration of his community. Pym also calls attention to the penguin's "striking . . . resemblance to a human figure"—so striking that it "would be apt to deceive the spectator at a casual glance or in the gloom of the evening" (151). He suggests an explicit comparison between the two groups in this passage and offers at the same time an opportunity for comparison between his reading of birds and men.

Pym's appreciation of the social mixing that he sees mapped in the rookery and symbolized in the penguin does not extend to humans. Dirk Peters is a "hybrid" of red and white, not "stately" but "half-breed," not "beautiful" but "deformed" (see 104, 55, 87). Peters' conduct, unlike that of his presumably rational white companions, "appeared to be instigated by the most arbitrary caprice alone" (100). Some *Pym* scholars have attributed the narrator's curious remark after the Tsalalian ambush that "we [Pym and Peters] were the only white men on the island" to a technical mistake by Poe.[10] It seems appropriate to suggest, however, based on his postnarrative introduction of Peters as "half-breed" that this classification is one entirely in keeping with Pym's prior cognitive strategies. As Evelyn Hinz has suggested, Pym needs an ally when faced by an island of angry "blacks," and thus his arbitrary racial delineation shifts to include Peters in the exclusive "white" club. Once back in his comfortably white-dominated world, however, Pym relegates Peters to a "half-breed" caste. Peters's changing status finely illustrates the arbitrary social basis of racial categorization.

To Be Shady/To Be White

Another level of *Pym* reveals the general failure of Pym and his colonial epistemology to represent Otherness as "radical," to inscribe a stable opposition between "black" and "white" as well as between "art" and "nature" which would support colonial knowledge. Rather, what colonial knowledge *refuses* to know becomes its structuring dynamic. The foregrounded level of meaning in *Pym* is caught in its desire to reach some sacred, final point of knowledge that would confirm the legitimacy of colonial motives. This aspect of *Pym*, then, reveals the terminal instability of colonial knowledge and identity, while it lays bare the repressive means through which colonial subjectivity and authority operate.

Barbara Johnson notes that "the transference of knowledge is no more innocent than the transference of power, for it is through the impossibility of finding a spot from which knowledge could be all-encompassing that the plays of political power proceed" (*Critical Difference*, 107). As I have suggested throughout this study, the colonial motivation to know the nature of various races of men arises from a complex symbiosis of political, economic and psychological needs. The second half of Pym's narrative in particular concerns itself with discerning essentialist racial categories but is finally unable to support them with any certainty. How racial knowledge collapses on itself in *Pym* becomes evident in a close reading of the narrative's system of binary oppositions.

Pym imposes a racial interpretation right after meeting the Tsalalians. Noting almost immediately that the "savages" who greet the *Jane Guy* are "jet black," he also notes their black accoutrement: clothing, clubs, and black stones on the bottoms of the canoes. The narrative also establishes their contrast to "the white race," semiotically linking white sails, eggs, books, and flour to the crew of the *Jane Guy* (169).[11] Seamen are not, of course, notoriously white in complexion. (It is difficult to imagine that every crewman on board the *Jane Guy* was albino.) Yet it is evidently Pym's priority to identify his group as white, in direct contrast to the "jet-black" Tsalalians.[12]

This initial identification allows Pym to develop a useful conceptual binary around which he structures his knowledge of both groups. Just as he arbitrarily represents an outward opposition, he depicts correspondingly antithetical behavior in the two groups. Thus the savages "harangue" and "jabber," while the crew communicate in "every ingenious manner we could devise" (169, 176). Pym (as well as the author of the concluding note) relies unquestioningly on these perceptual/conceptual oppositions. Closer examination, however, reveals these binaries as self-collapsing at an epistemological level — insupportable fiction, not stable opposition. As we have seen, Pym's arbitrary classification of outward appearance ignores contradictory evidence (i.e., even if we grant Pym the "blackness" of the Tsalalians, we know that "whites" are not *white*). Similarly, in order to construct a convincing essentialist argument for racialism, Pym must transform difference *within* human behavior, into difference *between* arbitrarily drawn groups of humans; he must, as Johnson puts it in *The Critical Difference*, turn ambiguity into binarity.

The conceptual strategy of binarity, as Johnson observes, "presupposes that the entities in conflict be knowable" (106). But it is precisely to combat the unknowable that Pym creates these categories. The colonial knowledge structure must codify difference in order to stabilize the identity of both the Subject/Self and the Object/Other. Pym's epistemological certainty about *both* "black" Tsalalian and "civilized" or "white" nature fails because he must know *in advance* of knowing. In other words, he must know the Tsalalians to know how the white colonizer differs, and he must know these things before he sets eyes on the Tsalalians, in order to assume the superior right of colonizer — a right assumed from the moment he began his journey. He must construct a fiction about knowing that inevitably discloses its actual failure to know.

The rigid system of color imagery in the text collapses in a similar manner. As John Carlos Rowe observes, the black/white polarizations of imagery "are only apparently oppositions" (100). Paul Rosenzweig perceptively elaborates on the significance of Pym's apparently "insignificant footnote" in the opening of the Tsalal section. In the note, Pym explains that his descriptive use of the terms "morning" and "evening" are not to be "taken in their ordinary sense." This is because the daylight is continual, it still being fall in the southern hemisphere (*Pym*, 166–67). Rosenzweig comments: "Something so basic to man's [sic] sense of reality as the cycles of day and night is here revealed as relative, a mere fiction of artistic license for much of the narrative" ("Dust," 143). Pym's complacent admission that he can neither distinguish day from night, nor dates, nor location, and his continued use of all distinctions, raise difficulties for other apparently stable oppositions. "How seriously," asks Rosenzweig, "are we to take Pym's similar light-and-dark divisions of landscapes and races? Mere figments of the mind, too?" (143).

Other aspects of the text undermine the strict black/white imagistic distinction. The final phase of the southward trip, which relies heavily on light-white/dark-black imagery, gradually erodes the strict disparity commonly acknowledged between the two. The vapor from the south is in fact repeatedly described as "gray" — a blend of white and black. Eventually the antithetical sense of the two words merges into a union. While Pym records the increasing whiteness of the environment — the "milky hue" of the water, the "fine white powder" that falls over them — he also describes the "materially increased" and "sullen darkness." Like the behavioral opposition that disintegrates under close scrutiny, the perceived opposition of black/white color imagery also dissolves in *Pym*.[13]

It would seem that any perceived opposition is inherently unstable, as Pym himself suggests earlier in the text. Reflecting on the quality of his experiences through various stages of his adventure, Pym notes that "so strictly comparative is either good or evil" that one day's suffering is another's relief (139). It is in fact Pym's nagging awareness of the unreliability of human perceptions, compensated for only by an interpretive will, that leads him late in the narrative to construct another binary, between art and nature. J. Gerald Kennedy has observed that in the "Flying Dutchman" scene, in which the mutiny survivors hope to be saved by a death ship, interpretation is revealed "as flagrant self-delusion" (*Poe*, 155). Pym and his crew members see what they want to see: a rescue ship. They persist in their interpretation, accounting for the brig's wide yawing by adding interpretive epicycles and eccentric orbits to the providential delivery they believe is coming. "She yawed so considerably," reports Pym, "that at last we could think of no other manner of accounting for it than by supposing the helmsman to be in liquor" (123). Even when irrevocably confronted with the fact that the ship will not provide a rescue, Pym and his mates do not relinquish their interpretation: "We plainly saw that not a soul lived in that fated vessel! Yet we could not help shouting to the dead for help! Yes, long and loudly did we beg" (124).

Pym arrives at a new formulation which will compensate for human short-sightedness while still confirming colonial desire for self-confirming knowledge. He comes to suspect what John Irwin calls "the larger epistemological problem . . . of whether the mind is a self-verifying apparatus." His solution is to turn to "the book of nature [as] a self-evidential text" (Irwin, 93). Pym's lingering doubts about the apparent nature of the Tsalalians, though never acted on, prove, like the Flying Dutchman, that the colonist's interpretive will must always remain suspect. In hindsight he muses:

> I believe that not one of us had at this time the slightest suspicion of the good faith of the savages. They had uniformly behaved with the greatest decorum, aiding us with alacrity in our work, offering us their commodities, frequently without price, and never, in any instance, pilfering a single article, although the high value they set upon the goods we had with us was evident by the extravagant demonstrations of joy always manifested upon our making them a present. (179–80)

Yet he had noticed earlier evidence to the contrary, with some discomfort—for instance the systematic reinforcements of Tsalalians on their first march into the village, and the contempt with which Too-wit greeted the captain's gift of blue beads, along with his obvious preference for the knife. When Pym and Peters emerge from the gorge after the avalanche, Pym reports that "luckily a half suspicion of foul play had by this time arisen in my mind, and we forbore to let the savages know of our whereabouts" (184). Although Pym tries to rationalize the deception as being the Tsalalians' fault ("we should have been the most suspicious of human beings had we entertained a single thought of perfidy on the part of people who had treated us so well," 180), it is clear that the crew's fate was the result of their own self-deception. They had, as Pym "half" suspects, seen what they wanted to see. Pym backs away from conceding that their knowledge is not absolute.

To allay his fears Pym constructs a more sophisticated binary at this point in the narrative, privileging self-evident Nature over manufactured art. In doing so he is able to displace responsibility for interpretation—the self-verifying apparatus of the mind—onto the eternally inscribed text of the world. This explains his interest in finding the hieroglyphs "altogether the work of nature," even while (and especially because) he recognizes an indenture that "might have been taken for the intentional, although rude, representation of a human figure standing erect, with out-stretched arm" (195). Pym ignores evidence of human agency—the "vast heap[s]" of "arrowhead flints" as well as the Tsalalians' demonstrated ability to effect chasms in the rock formation—to conclude on the basis of "several large flakes of marl" that the hieroglyphs must be "the work of nature" (195). He assiduously documents their scientific interest, an action which reveals the importance he attaches to their shape.

Similarly, when Peters and Pym enter a ravine, where "the surface of the ground in every other direction was strewn with huge tumuli, apparently the wreck of some gigantic structures of art," Pym concludes that "in detail, no semblance of art could be detected" (198). As with his evident fascination with the significance of the Tsalalian water, Pym looks for "natural" evidence of segregated order. To accept the hieroglyphs and surrounding ruins as the product of art—the work of man—means that they are at once suspect. The product of art *is* the product of the interpretive will, and therefore anything it "reveals" is as partial (in both senses of the word) as Pym's interpretations of the Tsalalians. If, on the other hand, the hieroglyphs can be shown as the work of nature, with the hieroglyphic figure gesturing to the white figure at the pole, then all the natural world can be seen working in concert to confirm colonial desire: the right of white. The natural domination of the "white" race of man will be guaranteed not by their own limited and suspect knowledge, but instead by the Nature of Things, irrefutable and divinely ordained.

Yet this binary proves no better at sustaining itself than the one constructed between white and black. Merely discerning between art and nature is exposed as an act of will when Pym persuades Peters on the basis of ambiguous evidence that the chasms are the work of "nature":

> I convinced him of this error, finally by directing his attention to the floor of the fissure, where, among the powder, we picked up, piece by piece, several large flakes of the marl, which had evidently been broken off by some convulsion from the surface where the indentures were found, and which had projecting points exactly fitting the indentures; thus proving them to have been the work of nature. (195)

The lacuna signaled by the semicolon marks the site of interpretive will. Pym refuses to consider the fact that the Tsalalians had demonstrated their ability to render such chasms in the wall of marl. He denies the significance of the heaps of (white) arrowheads. In this break he imposes his intention to interpret the hieroglyphs as *not* the work of man, an *interpretation* that collapses the structure of the binary as it reveals that every act of cognition is "art." "Knowledge" is inseparable from the knower's "interest." The distinction Pym wants to make between art and nature is, finally, artificial.

In *Nature*, a confident Ralph Waldo Emerson observes of "man" (presumably western, European) that "one after another his victorious thought comes up with and reduces all things, until the world becomes at last only a realized will" (20). *Pym* exposes the process by which colonial knowledge achieves this exclusive "realized will." As Emerson aptly suggests, it succeeds only by reduction: both in its willful blindness and in its attempt to repress cultural/narrative heterogeneity. The last chapters and the note emphasize how authority is established in colonial literature by limiting the structure of representation to a speaking, white Subject and a voiceless, dark Other, and by naturalizing this arbitrary division and silence.

Richard Drinnon has suggested in his impressive study *Facing West* that for Western colonial civilization, the dispossession of native peoples became a "defining and enabling experience," the means by which they "conquered an identity for themselves" (461). The death of Nu-Nu in the closing scene of Pym's narrative naturalizes the colonial structure of representation as it emblematizes colonial desire. Nu-Nu's expiration is preceded by the loss of speech in the increasingly white environment. As Pym records, "This day we questioned Nu-Nu concerning the motives of his countrymen in destroying our companions; but he appeared to be too utterly overcome by terror to afford us any rational reply" (205). The next day he remains even more passive: "he breathed, and no more" (205). Nu-Nu cannot (and must not) tell his story in the white world. His silence and death provide another proof for racialism as it confirms "white" identity.

Pym's story is authorized *by* Nu-Nu's silence as well as by that of Dirk Peters. No other versions contradict his. By a default that cannot be seen as coincidental since Pym carefully discredits any version Peters might offer in his introductory note, Pym provides the author-ized version of the journey. In a sense, then, the white identity constructed in Pym's narrative demands the silence of the Other.

The concluding note similarly assumes interpretive authority by repressing other voices. Although Pym is dead, the mysterious editor promises that Peters "may hereafter be found, and will, no doubt, afford material for a conclusion." Yet the note itself stands for this conclusion, offering a redaction that supports Pym's original colonial intents. It is striking that the interpretive strategies of the author of the note duplicate Pym's strategies even as he assumes the responsibility of pointing out Pym's oversights. Like Pym, the editor ignores the contradictory evidence contained in the narrative in order to assert that "nothing *white* was to be found at Tsalal, and nothing otherwise in the subsequent voyage to the region beyond" (208). Like Pym, he fills in gaps with certainty—literally—as he notes that while the hieroglyphic characters of the lower range "are somewhat broken and disjointed; nevertheless, it cannot be doubted that, in their perfect state, they formed the full Egyptian word . . . 'the region of the south'" (208).

The editor's interest in documenting the opposition of white and black becomes apparent in his willingness to assume that an intentional opposition is inscribed by the hieroglyphs. In fact, nothing about the hieroglyphics indicates that "to be white" obtains to the exclusion of black in "the region of the south." While the editor assumes that "to be shady" is excluded from the "region of the south" both hieroglyphically and actually, as documented in Pym's narrative, we might alternatively conclude that "to be shady" is—like the chasms that contain the hieroglyphs and the black rock they are inscribed on—all-encompassing. As we have seen, the actual region of the south documented by Pym's narrative contains both light and darkness, white and shade. Further, these terms exist in relation to each other (like bad and good); one is meaningless without comparison to the other. The conclusion suggested by the author of the note, however, that the two are mutually exclusive rather than intrinsically related, exposes the editor's own investment.

The editor has indeed an "interest" in his interpretation. "*White*" becomes the obsessive emphasis of the note, as we see in the last sentences:

Tekeli-li was the cry of the frightened natives upon discovering the carcass of the *white* animal picked up at sea. This also was the shuddering exclamation of the captive Tsalalian upon encountering the *white* materials in possession of Mr. Pym. This also was the shriek of the swift-flying, *white*, and gigantic birds which issued from the vapoury *white* curtain of the South. Nothing *white* was to be found at Tsalal, and nothing otherwise in the subsequent voyage to the region beyond. (208; "editor's" emphasis)

Here the editor focuses on white nearly to the negation of black. The structure of representation authorizes *only* whiteness, just as the interpreted hieroglyphs "point" solely toward whiteness—the final sanction of colonial domination. The text must silence and repress the Other even as it maintains the negative presence of the Other as a point of comparison ("nothing white . . . nothing otherwise"). Like the black/white binary, colonial authority is meaningless without reference to the Other.

The litany of "white" establishes the point of colonial subjectivity and authority. This subjectivity is constituted through its comparison to the Other, precisely as that Other is excluded from subjectivity. As Susanne Kappeler outlines the repressive structure of representation:

The . . . project of constituting . . . subjectivity is a serious business that has nothing to do with fictional and playful fantasy. It is the means by which the . . . subject convinces himself that he is real, his necessary production of a feeling of life. He feels the more real, the less real the Other, the less of a subject the Other, the less alive the Other. And the reality he creates for himself through his cultural self-representation is the Authorized Version of reality. (62)

Colonial subjectivity and authority, as both the ending of Pym's narrative and the appended note make clear, are premised on the presence of the Other, only under erasure: the continued death of the Other.

The (Port)Ending of *Pym*

Pym finally offers a negative social medicine, in that it subverts the basis of the model it represents without proposing an alternative. Its conclusion, however, is not solely about a "frustrating indeterminacy." The narrative emphasizes the material effects of colonial ideology while it undermines the pretensions of colonial knowledge to disinterested objectivity. Colonial knowledge, as *Pym* reveals, is nothing if not "interested" and willful. Two comments of the author of the note underscore this dynamic. First, he announces that "it would afford the writer of this appendix much pleasure if what he may here observe should have a tendency to throw credit, in any degree, upon the singular pages now published" (335). And in drawing out the confirmation of "whiteness" conveyed by Pym's narrative, the editor affirms, "Conclusions such as these open a wide field for speculation and exciting conjecture" (336). The ambiguous words "afford . . . credit" and "speculation" all highlight the pecuniary motive of colonial literature. "Interest" initiates the text, and "speculation" on whiteness provides the "conclusion"—a fiction crisscrossed by the traces of the colonial will to power through knowledge.

Despite a wide range of fairly promising reviews, Burton Pollin documents the surprising failure of *Pym* on the literary market.[14] It was perhaps the refusal of *Pym* to resolve its own issues in any specific way that frustrated contemporary readers of the work. An unsigned notice in the *New York Review* called the book "perplexing and vexatious" (Walker, 98); a London *Spectator* review complained that the book was "without any definite purpose" (Walker, 103). Sales apparently dwindled in the critical irresolution over its intentions. As one reviewer spoofed, "Arthur Pym is the American Robinson Crusoe, a man all over wonders, who sees nothing but wonders, vanquishes nothing but wonders, would, indeed, evidently, scorn to have anything to do with wonders" (Walker, 105).

However, *Pym*'s intellectual stalemate may be precisely what makes it so attractive to modern theorists of American literature. As G. R. Thompson summarizes,

> Despite the astonishing range of readings, what emerges from all the critical attention is that there is in *Pym* a coherent and symmetrical structure of events that generates a haunting ambiguity. Once regarded as an unfinished or hastily finished mistake, the arabesque romance of *Arthur Gordon Pym* exemplifies Poe's method of resonant indeterminateness and his affinities both with modernism and postmodernism. (174)

But the "affinity" that *Pym* shares with these modes of theory is not unproblematic. Nancy Hartsock has highlighted some important pitfalls in modernist and postmodernist theory in a recent article, "Rethinking Modernism: Minority vs. Majority Themes." As she summarizes, postmodernist theorists propose a "social criticism that is ad hoc, contextual, plural and limited" as a counter against "totalizing and universalistic theories such as those of the Enlightenment" ("Rethinking Modernism," 190). But, she argues, the theoretical agenda of postmodernism has more in common with "Enlightenment paradigms and values" than postmodernists would care to acknowledge. "Somehow," she observes, "it seems highly suspicious that it is at this moment in history, when so many groups are engaged in 'nationalisms' which involve redefinitions of the marginalized Others, that doubt arises in the academy about the nature of the 'subject,' about the possibilities for a general theory which can describe the world, about historical 'progress'" (197).

Pym may suggest doubt, as current poststructuralist critics claim, about the nature of the Self and its origin. But there is no doubt expressed in *Pym* about the relation of the Subject/Self and Object/Other in colonial ideology. The final pages of the narrative and the note epitomize Hartsock's model:

> The philosophical and historical creation of a devalued Other was the necessary precondition for the creation of the transcendental rational subject . . . the creation of the Other is simultaneously the creation of the transcendental and omnipotent theorizer who can persuade himself that he exists outside of time and space and power relations. (*Money*, 191, 195)

As Hartsock perceptively indicates—and *Pym* illustrates—the construction of the colonial Self is predicated upon the devaluation, the domination and the continuing destruction of the racial Other.

Overlooking *Pym*'s broadly social basis wrongly implies the unimportance of these connections between literature and material reality. Such criticism also overlooks the important challenge that it makes to any critical enterprise. Russell Reising has recently warned against theoretical tendencies to derealize literature, to denature its social basis and agenda. As he notes, "for many contemporary theorists, the question of American literature's social or historical significance is not so much engaged and transcended as it is ignored" (200). *Pym* in fact comments on the final inability of the Western colonizer to interpretively transcend the social basis of meaning. In this way *Pym* is not simply about "the duplicity of the sign" (Rowe, 107), the origin of the "writing self" in the "uncertainty between body and shadow" (Irwin, 234), or the fact that "the ultimate secret is not to be found" (Thompson, 274). Although the novel is to some degree about all those, what it also clearly emphasizes is the problematic, even violent basis of colonial knowledge (science/theory), subjectivity, and authority. It is not solely about absence of meaning, but about the impulses—social, political, economic—that undergird the construction of any system of meaning. *Pym* offers a serious examination of the questionable motives behind the interpretive will and the real, material ramifications of those interpretations. As such it should pose a difficult question to contemporary theorists about their own theorizing activities.

6

"For the Gaze of the Whites": The Crisis of the Subject in "Benito Cereno"

Involuntary Choices

Reading "race" in "Benito Cereno" has a history as fraught with contention as the debates over the meaning of "race" in the works of Edgar Allan Poe. Scholars have for decades been concerned with how "Benito Cereno" reflects on Melville's own political stance. F. O. Matthiessen, Charles Neider, Joseph Schiffman, and Sidney Kaplan have argued that the story reveals Melville's racism, however unconsciously. More recent critics—including Carolyn Karcher, Marvin Fisher, and Charles Swann—maintain that Melville's intention in "Benito Cereno" was quite the opposite.[1] They argue that in the story Melville questions and even radically subverts American racism of the antebellum period.

While the diverse conclusions of these scholars preclude any pat conclusions concerning Melville's intentions for the text, they do confirm that "Benito Cereno" has something important to say about the operations of racism. It is ultimately impossible, of course (and some would say irrelevant), to determine Melville's exact aims for "Benito Cereno," yet it does seem entirely plausible to assume, for reasons that I have detailed earlier, that his text strains in *both* directions. Again, Abdul JanMohamed's distinction between the two broad categories of colonialist literature, the "imaginary" and the "symbolic," can be helpful in tracing these countervailing tendencies in "Benito Cereno." In the narrator's portrayal of Delano's reading of events on the *San Dominick*, we see an "imaginary" text, where Delano, in JanMohamed's terms, "coalesces signifier with signified" ("Economy," 65). Delano's perception and epistemology operates through the complete efficiency of Manichaean allegory. He grants the slaves no historical causality, no human dimension other than as an essentially "genial beast," or "ruthless savage." But the *narrator's* reading of Delano's reading of "race" doubles the import of the text, much as it is formalistically doubled by the account of the Lima Court. The narrator's reading, then, operates at a different level of consciousness, and of conscious *critique* of the colonialist system that is epistemologically imposed by Delano, and reimposed by the Lima Court.[2] So the narrator's reading functions, as Jan-Mohamed would say, symbolically. It becomes "reflexive about its context, by confining itself to a rigorous examination of the 'imaginary' mechanisms of colonialist mentality" ("Economy," 66).

JanMohamed's description of these colonial texts becomes less helpful, however, in describing "Benito Cereno" in terms of the story's final import. It seems inadequate to say that "Benito Cereno," through its symbolic dimensions, manages to "free itself from the manichean allegory," as JanMohamed posits a symbolic text should do. Although I argue that Melville's narrative manages to *subvert* the Manichaean perception and epistemology of the colonial system, "free" connotes wrongly here. I would say instead that the text is *unable* to achieve a final liberation from that binary vision, even while it clearly recognizes it as a dehumanizing force.

Generally, then, "Benito Cereno" questions the dominative structure of Western conceptualization, epistemology, and representation. Through its redoubled presentation of the slave revolt on the *San Dominick*, "Benito Cereno" effectively brackets the concept of "race," disproving its ontological basis and revealing its political/social/economic genesis. Yet, even though the text incisively dismantles the colonialist construction of power through race (and gender and class) oppression, it does not go beyond its ironic critique to posit countervening antiracist possibilities for action/knowledge. On the contrary, the story is finally arrested in a consuming sense of horror that may well mitigate, or even *supersede*, the earlier questioning. In the end, "to rush from darkness to light was the involuntary choice" (292). Babo, at last, is "the black," defined, sentenced, and emblematized by "the whites."

In accounting for the arrested dynamic of the text's critique, it is helpful to look more closely at the perceptual strategies which undergird Delano's reading of events on the *San Dominick* and after.[3] We might begin by analyzing the conceptual, epistemological, and communal structures Delano employs. Then we should closely consider the evident, indeed, overwhelming relief he feels toward Don Benito when the "truth" of the matter on the *San Dominick* overcomes him. It is this "infinite pity" which he feels on behalf of his "host" that provides the clue to the fundamental structure of power in Delano's world. A careful reading of the implications following the imaginative configuration of subjectivity and power in Delano's colonial economy will help us to read the full significance of that final, horrific image of Babo's impaled head, and the complicated structure of racial representation that at once delimits "the gaze of the whites" and paralyzes "Benito Cereno."

The Grayness of Everything

In the narrator's mocking portrayal of Delano's perceptions, we can read an account of the willful nature of colonial epistemology reminiscent of that exposed in *The Narrative of Arthur Gordon Pym*. The Manichaean binarity which undergirds the colonialist conceptual structure translates to a perceptual strategy for Amasa Delano. Since Delano, differently from the narrator, is unable to question his own ideology, he too complacently trusts his own observations, not understanding them as contingent interpretation. The order of nature is, for the captain of *The Bachelor's Delight*, self-evident. Despite the narrator's observation that on the day described in the story, "everything [was] gray," Delano insists on seeing in black and white. Even when he cannot discern the nature of the curious ship he sights (it "showed no colors"), he imagines that he sees a "whitewashed monastery after a thunderstorm," inhabited by "dark moving figures . . . as of Black Friars pacing cloisters" (241). Similarly, once aboard the ship, Delano persists in forcing all evidence into his conceptual framework, despite his growing discomfort at the uneasy fit.

The conceptual binary of black and white that rules Delano's perception also organizes his interpretation of events, which in turn is governed by a body of assumptions about the essential nature of each color. Before Delano can even make out figures on the ship, his imagination is "coloring" them — transferring a dualistic scheme onto diversely colored and heretofore *unseen* humans. So when Delano boards the ship, he can take the slaves "genially," relying on his certitude that "whites" are "by nature the shrewder race" and that "blacks" are "too stupid" to worry over (279, 270). Drawing on his philanthropically benevolent "knowledge" of "blacks," then, he attributes the potentially ominous sight of the six Ashantis sharpening hatchets to "the peculiar love in negroes of uniting industry with pastime," explaining their threatening activity to himself as "unsophisticated" cymbal-crashing (243). It is impossible for Delano to entertain the notion of "black" power. It is equally impossible for him to envision a fellow "white" without it. And so he wonders at Don Benito, "this undemonstrative invalid . . . apathetic and mute," of whom "no landsman could have dreamed that in him was lodged a dictatorship beyond which, while at sea, there was no earthly appeal" (246). Delano cannot read through the will-to-power that constitutes a blind spot in colonial epistemology, and questions his own interpretations only when forced to by what he perceives as a threat to his life. But Babo clearly has done so — he counts precisely on Delano's complacent reading of "black" and "white" for the success of his plan.

Where *The Narrative of Arthur Gordon Pym* describes an attempt to naturalize racial opposition and hierarchy, in "Benito Cereno" it is a fait accompli. Like the Negro saluting the French flag in Roland Barthes's analysis of "Myth Today," Babo's evident devotion to Don Benito signals to Delano the "beauty of that relation" between black and white, "a spectacle of fidelity on the one hand and confidence on the other" (250).[4] Babo's particular history, the specific history of slaves on the *San Dominick*, and the more general history of slave oppression and Western trade are elided. Instead, just as the *Paris Match* cover coalesces the historically emptied image of the African soldier with the imperialist meaning of the French flag by means of his salute, so Babo signifies not *himself* or his own particular history but only the now-naturalized "beauty" of benevolent patriarchal relations between the euphemistically designated master ("confidence") and slave ("fidelity").

Despite the confidence of his original assessment of the situation on board the *San Dominick*, as Zagarell observes, "when Delano finally discovers the true nature of the blacks' position, he shifts effortlessly from sentimentalizing them to brutalizing them as monsters" ("Reenvisioning America," 248). Like Pym, then, Delano's recognition of the slaves "with mask torn away . . . in ferocious piratical revolt . . . like delirious black dervishes" (295) is still grounded in racist essentialism. He has learned nothing about the slaves, but has merely substituted one essentialist label for another: blacks are now not by nature innocent, but *depraved*. Thus, the conceptual strategy which structures his "revelation" *prevents* him from ever reaching a point of understanding that would comprehend the slaves' point of view. By refusing to consider a historical (local or otherwise) basis for the actions of the slaves, Delano denies the slaves Subjectivity. In doing so, he keeps them safely objectified, never having to regard them as any more than animals, either Newfoundland dogs or wolves (279, 299).

But Delano's conceptual strategies are not seamless. We see a point of instability begin to emerge in his reflections on Don Benito. As Emery observes, American cultural prejudices against the Spanish were rife throughout the periods during which "Benito Cereno" was both set and composed (61–62). Thus for Americans in both periods, "Spanish" was an unstable marker, semiotically balancing between light/fellow Westerner and dark/Other. So it is for Delano. He is eager to be welcomed by the "gentlemanly" Don Benito as an equal. But the more uneasy he becomes, the more he is drawn to reflect on Benito Cereno's "yellow hands" and "dark" complexion and moral character (243, 251, 263). We see how he is torn between considering "Spanish" as a marker of inferiority or an index of equality. Delano at one point wonders about a Spanish conspiracy, figured in terms of darkness: "Might not that same undiminished Spanish crew, alleged to have perished off to a remnant, be at that very moment lurking in the hold? On heart-broken pretense of entreating a cup of cold water, *fiends in human form* had got into lonely dwellings nor retired until a *dark* deed was done" (245, 262; my emphasis). The collapse of moral nature and physical appearance that distinguishes racist thought becomes complete when Delano laughingly muses on "the *dark* Spaniard himself, the central hobgoblin of all" (263; my emphasis). Yet earlier, at a point where he was feeling less suspicion than compassion, Delano mentally describes Don Benito as the "*pale* invalid" (258; my emphasis). The tension between his twin impulses to view Don Benito as a Spanish type ("The Spaniard") and to perceive him as equal becomes evident when he reflects that "these Spaniards are all an odd set; the very word Spaniard has a curious, conspirator, Guy-Fawkish twang to it. And yet, I dare say, Spaniards in the main are as good as folks as any in Duxbury, Massachusetts" (273–74).

The ultimate exposé on the artificiality of racist conceptualization comes from Babo. He replaces the ship's figurehead with the bleached-white bones of Don Aranda, and poses the key question, "whether, from [the] whiteness [of the bones, one] should not think it a white's" (304–5). Essentially, as Babo's gesture graphically affirms, when one gets down to the bare bones, there is *no* difference. Racial difference is, then, demonstrably superficial, its significance evidently artificial. This is a lesson that Delano simply does not comprehend and Don Benito refuses to countenance. Like every other Spanish crewman aboard the *San Dominick*, Don Cereno "covered his face" when Babo tries to make him look on Aranda's skeleton (305). As in *The Narrative of Arthur Gordon Pym*, then, the "whites" must systematically blind themselves to large portions of their experience if they are to maintain their sense of dominance.

We have seen from Delano's musings on Don Benito that "white" and "black" are perceptually interchangeable as racial markers in certain instances. We need to consider how and *why* they become interchangeable. The narrator underscores Delano's quirky deployment of white and black characterization in a passage where Delano decides to accost one of the sailors directly. Despite his earlier musings on the sailors' darkness, Delano regards them here as "whites": he proceeds onto the poop, "curiously surveying the white faces, here and there sparsely mixed in with the blacks, like stray white pawns venturously involved in the ranks of chessmen opposed" (265–66).[5] It is remarkable, given the opposition established here between the "white" sailors and the "black" slaves, that Delano proceeds to identify the first "white" sailor he observes with *darkness*. The narrator describes the sailor's contradictory appearance:

> The mean employment of the man was in contrast with something superior in his figure. His hand, black with continually thrusting it into the tar-pot held for him by a negro, seemed not naturally allied to his face, a face which would have been a very fine one but for its haggardness. Whether this haggardness had aught to do with criminality, could not be determined; since, as intense heat and cold, though unlike, produce like sensations, so innocence and guilt, when, through casual association with mental pain, stamping any visible impress, use one seal—a hacked one. (266)

Appearance, the *narrator* underscores, is equivocal, and as such it is insufficient evidence for evaluation. Delano's "reading" of the sailor is more complacent: Delano decides the sailor's moral character to be as black as the pitch his hand is in. Whether he looks "black," or not, Delano's perceptions of his actions and motivations are determined by that classification.

We begin to see from these examples the influence of *class* in Delano's judgment and how "race" functions as a (doubled) metaphor of inferiority. While Delano's reflections on Benito waffle, his favorable characterizations are associated predominantly with the "nobility" or aristocracy. Delano muses, for instance, on "the pale history of the voyage, and [Benito's] own pale face," which calls to Delano's mind an "image of an invalid courtier" (251). When most suspicious of Benito, Delano wonders if he is "some low-born adventurer . . . an imposter" (258). Shortly he resumes his more positive assessment of the Spanish captain as he becomes convinced of the authenticity of Don Benito's "ennobled" and aristocratic profile.

But the goodwill that Delano extends to the Spanish Don Benito does not encompass his Spanish crewmen, whom Delano much more consistently associates with darkness, and therefore vice, thievery, and subterfuge, as the narrator highlights:

> Because observing so singular a haggardness combined with a dark eye, averted as in trouble and shame, and then again recalling Don Benito's confessed ill opinion of his crew, insensibly he was operated upon by certain general notions which, while disconnecting pain and abashment from virtue, invariably link them with vice.
>
> If, indeed, there be any wickedness on board this ship, thought Captain Delano, be sure that man there has fouled his hand in it, even as he now fouls it in the pitch. (266)

Delano's suspicions of Don Benito lead him to reexamine his prejudices against Spaniards. The same is not true for the crewmen, and in fact, their Spanishness seems to have very little to do with Delano's negative assessment of them. Rather, Delano's characterization of the crew serves to naturalize another system of domination in a way that precludes questioning it. Inferiors on the socioeconomic scale deserve their status because of their self-evidently debased (dark) nature. For Delano to believe that his own status, his "progress as king-at-arms" (265) is merited, he must perceive those whom he dominates as deserving of their less fortunate position. Accordingly, by describing (and perceiving) the sailors as "dark," Delano uses a metaphor of "race" to naturalize an exclusive socioeconomic hierarchy.[6]

It is telling that Delano describes the white sailors as "pawns" — social inferiors and, as such, objects for his purposes. This characterization confirms my point: even while "race" can operate as a governing metaphor, Delano's position of dominance and authority is *not* constructed on solely racial terms. Earlier, when Delano is musing on Don Benito's indifferent reception of Delano's aid, he notes that "even the formal reports . . . made to him by some petty underling, either a white, mulatto or black, [Don Benito] hardly had patience enough to listen to" (247). The category "petty underling" conflates racial categories, and, significantly, "white" is an interchangeable term within the overall group. This is to say that Delano's epistemological structure does not simply oppose white to black, but rather opposes a certain group of "whites" to a much larger group composed of whites, mulattoes, and blacks.

A Privileged Spot

As Sandra Zagarell notes, of all Delano's worries while on board the *San Dominick*, "uppermost . . . is a strong-minded devotion to preserving a highly vertical institutional organization" ("Reenvisioning America," 249). The exercise of authority is elemental to the maintenance of hierarchy, and Delano is troubled, in part, by what he perceives as a lack of proper authority on the

San Dominick: "What the *San Dominick* wanted was, what the emigrant ship has, stern superior officers. But on these decks not so much as a fourth-mate was to be seen" (247). The captain of *The Bachelor's Delight* expects a reflection of "good order" in "armies, navies, cities or families, in nature herself" and his mental appeals to providence and a higher order mark his faith in the natural sanction of such hierarchy (244; see also 272, 293). Delano is especially disturbed by Don Benito's apparent reluctance to assume a rigorous command. "I know no sadder sight," Delano muses, "than a commander who has little command but the name" (253). He is reassured by some tokens of his counterpart's dominance. Atufal's padlocked figure provides a recurring comfort to Delano, along with other "signs" of order: "Atufal's presence, singularly attesting docility even in sullenness, was contrasted with that of the hatchet-polishers, who in patience evinced their industry; while both spectacles showed, that lax as Don Benito's general authority might be, still, whenever he chose to exert it, no man so savage or colossal but must, more or less, bow" (288). These markers of Don Benito's authority remain nonetheless "equivocal," and Delano alternately attributes his doubts to Don Benito's "icy though conscientious policy" of command (246) or his ill health.

Delano's continuing unease with Don Benito is compounded by Benito's apparent refusal to grant some sort of reciprocal recognition of Delano's authority. Assuming from the first that his "host" will appreciate "a brother captain to counsel and befriend," Delano is "not a little concerned at what he could not help taking for the time to be Don Benito's unfriendly indifference toward himself" (245). He is comforted somewhat by noting that the "pervading reserve" of Benito's manner extends to all on board and is not manifested exclusively toward himself (247). We might note that Delano cares little about how others on the ship receive him. The only opinion he cares for is Benito Cereno's, as we see when Delano muses just before leaving the ship that "after good actions one's conscience is never ungrateful, however much so the benefited party may be" (293). The majority of those on board have *clearly* exhibited their appreciation of the relief provided by Delano. But he is concerned only with the withheld recognition of Don Benito.

One way social hierarchy is maintained is through the visible alliance of superiors. Delano encourages every sign of intimacy between himself and Cereno. He seeks constantly that "privileged spot" where two captains can converse on equal footing, such as the "sociable plan" Babo proposes for the two captains to continue in conversation while Don Benito is shaved (248, 277). Delano is anxious to establish a *reciprocal* relationship of obligation and camaraderie, as when he invites Don Benito to board his ship: "Come, all day you have been my host; would you have hospitality all on one side?" (290). And when Don Benito at last displays a willingness to bid a courteous farewell to Delano, that captain registers a "pleased surprise," and "reciprocally advanced . . . with *instinctive* good feeling" (293; my emphasis). The tension between Delano's need to recognize Don Benito's authority and his need to have Don Benito recognize his lends a crucial insight to the dynamics of the power at stake in Delano's world.

The "fraternity" that Delano seeks is not simply a display for inferiors, but an ongoing confirmation of the superior status and control of the captains. Eric Sundquist has suggested that the most compelling aspect of "Benito Cereno" is that "authority . . . is caught in point of crisis and held in precarious suspension" ("Suspense," 87). As Sundquist explains, Delano as guest must defer to the locally superior authority of his host, Benito Cereno. Don Benito's exercise of power, however, is enigmatic, and therefore problematic for Delano, whose position on the ship is suspended then between guest and victim. Increasingly worried that rather than recognizing his guest's authority Don Benito seeks to usurp it, Delano begins planning to assert his own authority. He decides to withdraw the command from Benito Cereno, who "evidently, for the present . . . was not fit to be intrusted(sic) with the ship." Relieved of his duties, Delano reasons, Don Benito will "be in some measure restored to health, and with that he should also be restored to authority" (264). This line of thought allows Delano to assume that Don Benito's curious actions stem from a temporarily displaced authority, not a malign use of it. Once he has rested, all will be aright with Don Benito, and the proper relation between the two captains will be restored.

These thoughts, as the narrator frames them, are "tranquilizing." Echoing Delano's penchant for black and white, the narrator observes with a certain irony that "there was a difference between the idea of Don Benito's *darkly* pre-ordaining Captain Delano's fate, and Captain Delano's *lightly* arranging Don Benito's" (264; my emphasis). The difference is, of course, that he suspects Cereno of malign motives, while Delano only seeks to restore "good order." But does he? The narrator subtly makes it clear that Delano has "no small interest" invested in his transactions—social and business—on the *San Dominick* (239). He is looking for compensation at least for his generosity, as he politely intimates after his meal with Don Benito. Finally, his pursuit of the renegade ship belies his "interest." Despite Don Benito's warnings, Delano appoints his chief mate, suggestively described as a "privateer's man," to head up the capture. To encourage the sailors he explains that the ship's captain "considered his ship good as lost; that she and her cargo, including some gold and silver, were worth more than a thousand doubloons" (297). His assumption that Cereno has surrendered responsibility for the ship is apparently based on Cereno's warnings against pursuit; at any rate, his hasty conclusion here underscores his primary motive—money—and his willingness—even eagerness—to participate in a system that exploits human life for profit by capturing the escaping slaves.

Earlier Delano avers that he "cannot call" Babo a slave; rather he terms him "friend"—a term which, interestingly enough, he also applies to Don Benito (250, 290). He pleads on behalf of the enchained Atufal and observes, with pity for Babo's cut cheek, "this slavery breeds ugly passions in man!" (256, 283). Yet despite his protestations of cross-racial sympathy and friendship, it is unthinkable to Delano that a "white" could be "so far a renegade as to apostatize from his very species, almost, by leaguing in against it with negroes" (270). Delano also offers to buy Babo, a curious gesture for a man who cannot call Babo "slave"—apparently not, at least, until he owns him (265). Further, when Delano realizes what is *really* taking place on the slave ship, he turns with immediate violence against Babo. This moment is critical: Delano realizes that Babo is not trying to kill him but Don Benito, and he is *angrier* because of that realization. How can Babo be more dangerous to Delano as Don Benito's assailant?

The answer to this lies in how Delano formulates his sense of self and relation to others, which is, as this discussion has suggested, based on a hierarchical model of domination. Questions of power, as Nancy Hartsock has observed, are intrinsic to questions of community, and at the same time to questions of epistemology. Hartsock explains:

> Theories of power are implicitly theories of community. To examine . . . theories of power is to involve oneself in the questions of how communities have been constructed, how they have been legitimized . . . perhaps more important, efforts to explain how power operates inevitably involve larger questions as well, and different theories of power rest on differing assumptions about both the context of existence and the ways we come to know it. (*Money*, 3)

As Hartsock delineates, if we understand Delano's conception of power, we can understand his model for interpersonal relations, how he constructs a sense of Self in relation to community. This in turn should lead us to an *epistemological* understanding of just what is at stake for Delano on the *San Dominick*.

As we have seen, Delano is certain about his own power and where to expect to find it reciprocated even before he boards the *San Dominick*. Delano exercises his expectations as he overlooks in a "first comprehensive glance . . . those ten figures, with scores less conspicuous," seeking impatiently "whomsoever it might be that commanded the ship" (243). Delano credits only Don Benito's rendition of the events leading to the disrepair evident on his ship: "the best account would, doubtless, be given by the captain" (247). And we have seen that for Delano, issues of power are tied intrinsically with issues of ownership, as when he asks of Don Benito, "You are part owner of the ship and cargo I presume" (254). The construction of community among ship captains is based ultimately on economic issues. Delano boards the ship to offer assistance. Once he does so he prolongs his visit in order to discuss remunerative arrangements. And he is frankly surprised that Don Benito "appeared to submit to hearing the details more out of common propriety, than from any impression that weighty benefit to himself and his voyage was involved" (286). Benefit and profit are apparently the bottom of the matter for Delano. Hospitality is but a prelude to business, the real reason for interrelating in Delano's world. This would explain why Delano is so concerned that Babo be excluded from discussions of "pecuniary business," as well as why he is particularly puzzled at Cereno's reluctance to comply. Community is constructed by and through economic relations, constituted by selected and isolated individuals seeking profit. Interrelation occurs through "a brief association on the basis of [a] momentary conjuncture of interest": Delano has what Don Benito needs (Hartsock, *Money*, 44).

But community formed on the basis of capital or market exchange can be only, in Hartsock's words, "instrumental and arbitrary" (44). Delano's model is what Hartsock would term a "fragile community." Its fragility is compounded not only by its instrumental temporality, but by its exclusivity. In Delano's model for community, the slaves are part of the cargo, not part of any potential community. Nor are the sailors accorded equal status as members of Delano's community, as we see when he begins wondering "how come sailors with jewels?—or with silk-trimmed undershirts either?" Ownership is connected intrinsically with the power of command; sailors are not in command. Therefore they must have stolen the valuables: "Has he been robbing the trunks of dead cabin-passengers?" (261). The sailors are closer in status to the captain than to the slaves—Delano does consider consulting various sailors when Don Benito is not forthcoming. Yet they are just as easily overlooked. Most people on the ship are, in short, "pawns"—objects used by the captain of a ship for profit and gain. Delano assumes an asymmetrical Subject/Object structure where, in Kappeler's words, "the role of subject means power, action, freedom, the role of object powerlessness, domination, oppression." Clearly, as Kappeler observes, "the two roles are not equally desirable" (52).

A Bachelor's Delight

Within Delano's epistemology, then, the status of Subject is derived from supremacy, not intersubjectivity. As we have seen, community is constituted along at least two axes of domination: race and class. At this point it is important to consider a third: gender. While scholars have long focused on race and class, few have commented on the aspect of gender in the construction of power in this story. Observing that commentators have traditionally referred to the "homoerotic coloring" that Delano attributes to the relationship of Cereno and Babo, Sandra Zagarell argues instead that "grounded as it is in a reversal of power, the relationship actually reveals the literal instability of gender." Melville makes this point to prove that not only are race and gender cultural constructs, but "all meaning in his readers' world derives from convention" ("Reenvisioning America," 251).

It may be true that the point is the instability of meaning, but it is important to see that a *very stable* set of expectations is associated with the concept of gender in "Benito Cereno." While women are hardly present in the action of the story, they are *imaginatively* present in nearly every instance of domination, and their metaphoric significance cannot be overestimated. The Subject-position is equated with male status, the Object with female. We see this imaginative system at many points in "Benito Cereno." Most often noted, of course, is the scene where Babo has just appeared, bleeding from a cut he says was inflicted by Don Benito. Delano ruminates on the ugliness of slavery, but when the master and slave reappear, "as if nothing had happened," Delano thinks, "but a sort of love-quarrel, after all" (283). As Zagarell points out,

Babo's behavior toward Don Benito blends "feminization with domestication" ("Reenvisioning America," 251), behavior which Delano finds reassuring.

Delano also derives a great deal of satisfaction from viewing a negro woman and her infant. The sight not only provokes a philosophical reflection on "naked nature" and the reproductive traits of "uncivilized women," but it "insensibly deepened his confidence and ease" (268). It is possible at this point to suggest that the sight deepens Delano's confidence and ease—both shaken by his doubts about his position on the *San Dominick*—because they reconfirm his status as Subject. The "slumbering negress" is doubly objectified in Delano's epistemology: both woman and African, she is two times a servant.

Delano is similarly "charmed" by the sight of the chained Atufal (292). Although Atufal himself is an undoubtedly masculine figure, "like one of those sculptured porters of black marble guarding the porches of Egyptian tombs," his role is feminized by the symbolic value of his chains and his subservience to Don Benito (287). Babo elucidates for Delano: "the slave there carries the padlock, but master here carries the key" (256). Delano absorbs the significance of the key "suspended by a slender silken cord from Don Benito's neck," and with a smile observes "So, Don Benito—padlock and key—significant symbols, truly." Delano is offended this time at Don Benito's reaction. Don Benito, it seems, either didn't get, or did not appreciate the joke, Delano's "playful allusion to the Spaniard's singularly evident lordship over the black" (257).

Symbolic relations of gender domination are also present in Delano's musings on the mulatto servants. In a patriarchal, capitalist system, miscegenation had only one permissible (i.e., legal) equation: white (Subject) owner-male plus black (Object) slave-female. In this context, Delano's interest in seeing improvement in the offspring of this interaction is ironically revealing: "For it were strange, indeed, and not very creditable to us white-skins, if a little of our blood mixed with the African's, should . . . have the sad effect of pouring vitriolic acid into black broth" (284). Even the imagistic metaphor he chooses is suggestively gendered.

Woman as a gender category is most clearly objectified in metaphors for the ships in "Benito Cereno." The use of gendered pronouns, an "accepted" practice among seamen, coupled with dominative verbs reinforces patriarchal cultural praxis. The name of Delano's ship underscores this principle: *The Bachelor's Delight*. Delano's interpretation of other ships' movements are based on gendered conjecture. He surveys the stranger ship in the opening passages of the story with uncertainty: "she" is indecisive, and "it seemed hard to decide whether she meant to come in or no—what she wanted or what she was about." Delano at last comes to a decision. "Surmising . . . that it might be a ship in distress, Captain Delano . . . prepared to board her, and at the least, pilot her in" (240). We see the archetypally indecisive woman "mastered" by this captain. Elsewhere, Delano compares his boat to a "New-foundland dog," a comparison he has earlier made to blacks, completing the association between women, slaves and service-objects (271).

These aspects of gender metaphors and domination combine in "Benito

Cereno" to confirm what Hartsock explains as the "symptomatic . . . cultural confusion of sexuality, violence and domination" (*Money*, 165). More specifically, she explains sexuality as a "gendered power relation" (164). The association of power and maleness with Subject-status in "Benito Cereno" thus become most clear in the court deposition when it focuses on the role of the "negresses" in the revolt. These women, who unlike their male countrymen remain unnamed, declare their Subjectivity in the revolt through their assertion of power and even violence. Their actions are apparently so far in excess of their gender that they are restrained by the (presumably male) "negroes" (310), as the deposition records. Perhaps worse than their physical actions, the African women use the power of their voice willfully to inflame the violence. These women who vocalize and act with violence are arguably the largest threat to the system ascribed to by Delano and Don Cereno, for they most radically call into question the racist, classist, and sexist underpinnings of the legal and social system that has enslaved them.

As Zagarell notes, there are only two positions in Delano's ideological system: victor or victim. All relations are based on dominative and *gendered* power relations, but the only exercisers of power are those accorded status as Subject—that is, as male, non-African owners of capital. That Delano expects power plays between Subjects becomes evident in his persistent suspicions of Don Benito. But the largest threat to his epistemological system is precisely the one that is unthinkable for him: the challenge issued by Objects in the system, black "cargo." *This* provides the answer to the question posed earlier, of why Delano becomes angrier when he realizes that Babo is trying to kill not Delano, but Don Cereno. If Babo is defending Don Benito by trying to kill Delano, his actions provide direct confirmation of Benito's subjectivity, thereby upholding Delano's epistemological system. On the other hand, Babo is trying to kill his "master," he is directly challenging the system that affords him only Object status; that is, he is acting to seize his own Subjectivity. As such, his actions are profoundly threatening to Delano as well as to Benito Cereno. Delano's reaction—both the physical and the mental blow to Babo along with the "infinite pity" he feels toward Don Benito—simultaneously confirms his Subject-status and his place in the Subject community with Don Benito (and by extension, all other "white" male owners of capital).

The problem for Don Benito is somewhat larger and more destructive. He has been forced to exchange places with Babo: Babo is in actuality the thinking/acting Subject and Cereno is the Object of the ex-slave's manipulations. Further, Babo makes a travesty of Don Benito's former Subject-status by *forcing* him to assume the role he once *commanded*. While Delano perceives Don Benito's "lordship" over Atufal and Babo, the worst indignity he apparently suffers, as many commentators have observed, is being emasculated via his secret status as Object, signified by the "artificially stiffened" scabbard that he sports, not a real sword at all. Rather it is Babo who carries the "alert . . . dagger" (306), which he shows Don Benito to command his submission. While Delano recognizes only momentarily a real threat to his status as Subject, and is able quickly to repress the danger, Cereno is for a time fully robbed of his, a horror which, from his subsequent actions, is clearly unbearable. For this reason, Don Benito cannot afterward stand to face Babo, living evidence of the arbitrariness, the temporality of the racist ideology he shares with Delano and the court of Lima. He cannot "identify" Babo in court, since that power—the power of naming, of authorship—is the power of the Subject. All he has left, as Carolyn Karcher incisively notes, is blame for the inadequacy of the Subject community upon which both he and Delano have relied. "You were with me all day," he accuses Delano,

> stood with me, sat with me, talked with me, looked at me, ate with me, drank with me; and yet, your last act was to clutch for a monster, not only an innocent man, but the most pitiable of all men. To such degree may malign machinations and deceptions impose. So far may even the best man err, in judging the conduct of one with the recesses of whose condition he is not acquainted. But you were forced to it; and you were in time undeceived. Would that, in both respects, it was so ever, and with all men. (*Shadow*, 314)

Cereno still clutches at racist essentialism, at the Subject community. Denying the historical dimension of the situation, and, ergo, his particular responsibility for it, he whines of abstract "malign machinations." Just as Delano expected interrelation between Subject-captains, so did Don Benito rely on Delano's understanding. Don Benito can cover his face from the bleached bones of Don Aranda, but ultimately he cannot avoid acknowledging the frailty of his power, his Subjectivity, his community, his epistemology, testified to by the subjunctive in his last sentence, "*would that . . . it was so ever, and with all men.*"

More and more Don Benito retreats into silence, silence being in "Benito Cereno" the marker of Object-status. Delano, upon first boarding the ship, notes the "noisy indocility" of the slaves: whenever the Object speaks without the command of the Subject, she/he speaks out of turn (245). Even Babo's "conversational familiarities," ostensibly in service of Don Benito, begin to annoy Delano (256). Conversely, though Atufal's muteness is sign of his resistance (he will not beg pardon), it is also a sign for Delano, combined as it is with his complete obedience, respect and general docility, of "royal spirit." In short, though he will not ask forgiveness, his silence marks him as a good slave. Because Delano cannot comprehend the reversal of roles on the *San Dominick*, he does not understand that silence can be subversion as well as submission.

Likewise, he does not comprehend the reversed dynamics of communication between sailors and slaves—for instance, the "old Barcelona tar" whom he decides to consult for information. The sailor at first attempts to escape attention, then reluctantly confirms Delano's queries. The narrator notes that "the negroes about the windlass joined in with the old sailor; but as they became talkative, he by degrees became mute, and at length quite glum, seemed morosely unwilling to answer more questions, and yet, all the while, this ursine air was somehow mixed with his sheepish one" (267). Robbed of his Subject-status by the reversal of power in the revolt, the sailor gradually loses his voice, his position an unfamiliar combination of dominant bear and powerless sheep. Much in the same manner and unable to recover from his trauma,[7] Don Benito progressively sinks into silence. The communication systems utilized by the patriarchal and colonialist epistemology which dominates Don Benito's world are inadequate to communicate his experience of Objectification. Yet this epistemology is upheld and reconfirmed by the legal and aesthetic discourse in "Benito Cereno." Indeed, these two systems of communication actively sustain and propagate the epistemology according to which Delano operates, reproducing the power of the white male Subject.

The Beauty of That Relationship

Arguing that Western representation is a sexist and racist system of communication, Susanne Kappeler observes that within the traditionally conceived Western representational system, there "is the structure of production and consumption represented by two white men." She elaborates: "There is collusion between the two white men of the picture. They look at each other. One is the host, the other his guest. There exists a structure of identification and solidarity, a common purpose, a shared understanding, a communicated pleasure between them. What is more, there are further white men: in the courts" (15). While the interrelation or mutual confirmation of power and Subject-status that should have happened on the *San Dominick* between Delano and Don Benito fails initially, this failure is recoupled by the Lima Court. As Kermit Vanderbilt has observed, the Lima Court "succeeds Delano's crew as the narrowly vindictive . . . instrument of white oppression" (318). The court documents duplicate and magnify the impersonal, ahistorical and essentialist tendencies of Delano's epistemology. "Race," in the court deposition, is an appendage, a marker of less-than-Subject (or human) status. "The negro Babo" rings repeatedly through the text, "negro" brought to fore as the court in effect renames the slave, his "legal identity" confirmed by the "testimony of the sailors" (315). Conversely Don Aranda and Don Benito are identified racially only in the context of Babo's quoted remarks; otherwise they are named simply Don Aranda and Don Benito. The linguistic structure of naming in the court document becomes reminiscent of a common feature of language: man/(wo)man, where the prefix marks essential Otherness, and Object-status. Thus, in every instance identified as "the negro Babo," the slave is denied Subjectivity and historicity, and is thereby essentialized.

It is also striking, as Vanderbilt points out, that the court views the blacks but not the whites as "defendants in a 'criminal cause'" (318).[8] As Object-Others in a white, male legal system, the slaves are silenced; nowhere is their testimony solicited, except through the medium of white male hearsay. It is significant, then, when a peculiar phrase appears near the end of the extract from the deposition: "that all this is believed, because the negroes have said it" (310). Confirming as it does the acquiescence and willful participation of all the slaves both male and female in the revolt, this "testimony" is strategic.

The voice of the defendants is (indirectly) invoked only in terms of self-indictment.[9] The passive construction of the sentence is no accident, conveying a universal and objective judgment on behalf of a very limited, very interested group.

The power of legal discourse is recognized by the slaves as well. Halfway through their revolt, they seek to draw up a "paper," a legal contract between the slaves and Don Benito and his crew, promising not to kill any more in exchange for a safe voyage to Senegal and the ship and its material cargo. Legal language, then, is one of the many patriarchal/capitalist apparatuses that the slaves seek to subvert and manipulate to their purposes, having recognized its efficacy in the "master's" system. Charles Swann discusses Melville's fascination with the active power of legal discourse. "Here is a language," Swann notes, that unlike the powerlessness of novelistic discourse "does, frighteningly, have effect, that can speak—and enact—'capital sentences'" ("'Benito Cereno,'" 10).

The court of Lima both figuratively and literally enacts a sentence on Babo, which confirms the purpose of the trial. We should note, however, that the purpose of the trial was not to find the slaves guilty—that is a given. Rather, the sentence is enacted to prove that the "whites" on the ship were in every way responsible to the community of fellow white male Subjects, as the deposition at one point observes: "these statements are made to show the court that from the beginning to the end of the revolt, it was impossible for the deponent and his men to act otherwise than they did" (311). Babo's punishment becomes the emblem of "white" guiltlessness.

In ordering Babo's head to be affixed to a pole for the "gaze of the whites," the legal discourse of the Lima Court merges with another kind of discourse prominent in "Benito Cereno"—that of the aesthetic. The two types of discourse exist in a symbiotic relation; legal discourse sanctions power for an elect group, while aesthetic discourse defines pleasure. Babo's head as a legally produced artistic object both symbolizes this power and provides its viewers a pleasurable sensation of power. To understand how this is so, we must first turn to Delano's seemingly benign reflections on "beauty" in "Benito Cereno."

As the court's language employs a mask of disinterested universality, so do Delano's aesthetic observations convey a passive reception of beauty that emanates spontaneously from the object. Beauty, that is, is an object-function; it does not originate in the viewer-Subject, but is simply recognized by him. Delano's attention "had been drawn to a slumbering Negress." He is (passively) led to notice her, to recognize her as an object of beauty: "Ha, there now's a pleasant sort of sunny sight." As Delano watches her, she "started up, at a distance facing Captain Delano." "Not at all concerned at the attitude in which she had been caught," she proceeds to ignore Delano and kiss her child (267). The language in this passage is important, suggesting as it does a certain artistic setting. "Facing" the viewer or artist, the object of interest, the "mother," is "sight[ed]" and "caught." This scenario establishes the artistic vantage point: apparently unconscious of Delano's gaze, the mother continues in "maternal transports." He sees her, she remains oblivious to him; he has "caught" her unaware, much as an artist recognizes and captures his artistic object.

The scene continues:

> There's naked nature, now; pure tenderness and love, thought Captain Delano, well pleased.
>
> This incident prompted him to remark the other negresses more particularly than before. He was gratified with their manners: like most uncivilized women, they seemed at once tender of heart and tough of constitution; equally ready to die for their infants or fight for them. Unsophisticated as leopardesses, loving as doves. Ah! thought Captain Delano, these, perhaps, are some of the very women whom Ledyard saw in Africa and gave such a noble account of.
>
> These natural sights somehow insensibly deepened his confidence and ease. (268)

Delano recognizes the other women as objects of admiration and beauty *just as* Ledyard did before him. Like the sight of the original "slumbering negress," these other "noble women" commonly (if speculatively) viewed by both men afford pleasure "insensibly."

Jan Mukarovsky has outlined the social function and construction of aesthetic norm and value. He argues that there is a "relation between social organization and the development of the aesthetic norm" (49). This is to say that "aesthetic value is not inherent in an object: in order for the objective pre-conditions to be effective, something in the arrangement of the subject of aesthetic pleasure must correspond to them" (28). The subject—artist/viewer—must be either individually or socially motivated to "discover" beauty in any object. For this reason, then, although any particular aesthetic norm "strives to attain universal validity, it can never achieve the force of natural law" (26), simply because it is a social and therefore a dynamic construct.

Mukarovsky comments also on the *pleasure* associated with the aesthetic: "Another important feature of the aesthetic function is the pleasure which it evokes. Hence its ability to facilitate acts to which it belongs as a secondary function, as well as the ability to intensify the pleasure connected with them; cp. the use of the aesthetic function in child-rearing, dining, housing, etc." (22). Using Mukarovsky's comments as a guideline for our analysis of Delano's reflections on the "slumbering negress," we can now begin more clearly to understand the social dynamic of the aesthetic function for Delano in "Benito Cereno."

As Delano revealingly notes, the "sight" is "sunny . . . [and] quite sociable, too" (267). While the language of the passage, in its passive construction, pretends to a universal and disinterested recognition of beauty in the women, it also contains evidence of its political and social agenda. I have suggested that part of the appeal of this sight for Delano rests in its confirmation of his superior racial, gender, and class position. Another reason for its appeal is the *community* it constructs between Delano and another man, Ledyard, in their common (disinterested and therefore objective) recognition of beauty. As Mukarovsky delineates, another aspect of the aesthetic value of the scene

Delano views lies in its imperative to certain types of action, its naturalization of certain kinds of social relationships. Thus Delano aesthetically idealizes the woman ("naked nature") as "uncivilized" in her position as social inferior, "negress" in her role as slave, and "mother" in her reproductive (and therefore profitable) capacity.

Clearly the focus is less on the O/object than on the advantageous social arrangements and sensations that result from viewing her for the artist/viewer/Subject. Kappeler suggests that this is because the picture or artistic Object is always "the true icon of its author" (52). She illustrates her argument by using language as a metaphor: "As a speaker, I am always present as the subject of my speech: I may represent myself by means of the pronoun 'I' within my utterance, or I may never say 'I' or 'me' at all, and yet I am implicitly present, the author of my speech, the speech the token of my presence" (52). Likewise, the artist is the "speaking I" of the representation, communicating to "another subject—the spectator or reader," his "guest." Artistic representation, like language, is a communicative structure that creates and confirms community between the artist and viewer, speaker and listener, between two Subjects. Through aesthetic recognition, then, the viewer identifies himself with and confirms his place in the Subject community.

We can see the structure of this community if we analyze another of Delano's reflections on beauty. Shortly after Delano boards the *San Dominick*, he prods an explanation of the ship's plight from Don Benito. As Don Benito attempts to recount the exemplary behavior of the slaves on board, he falters repeatedly, apparently weak. He finishes by commending Babo above all the slaves, whereupon Babo humbly protests that "Babo is nothing; what Babo has done was but duty." Here Delano congratulates Don Benito on such a "faithful fellow" and pauses to reflect: "As master and man stood before him, the black upholding the white, Captain Delano could not but bethink him of the beauty of that relationship which could present such a spectacle of fidelity on one hand and confidence on the other. The scene was heightened by the contrast in dress, denoting their relative positions" (250). Once again we have an artistic "scene," an objective and passive recognition of "beauty." This time the important difference is the physical presence of a white in the "scene." We should observe, however, the position of Don Benito. He may be physically supported by Babo, but to Delano this is further proof of Don Benito's Subject-position relative to Babo's placement as Object. If we reexamine the verbal transaction just before this "snapshot," this dynamic will become clear. Don Benito has just testified to Babo's efficacy in subduing the other slaves. This is to say that at a point of incipient rebellion among the Objects on the ship, Babo alone remained submissive to his Object status, acting on behalf of his "master" in maintaining the Subject-status of Cereno. In the face of this compliment, Babo does not assume authority; rather he is explicitly self-effacing, confirming his passiveness, accepting his powerlessness. Delano responds to this *by congratulating Don Benito*, cementing the Subject-community by acknowledging Cereno's dominance and ownership of Babo. Thus, in the scene that Delano admires, Don Benito is the artist; *he* has created the "beauty of that relationship." Delano joins with Cereno in admiring the Object that he has created, the happily dominated slave Babo.

Kappeler comments incisively on the relation between representation and reality, fact and fiction. Rather than being disjoined and mutually exclusive, Kappeler argues that they exist in symbiotic relation, one feeding the other. Representation *is* acting in the world: the "subjectivity of viewing goes over seamlessly into agency in the world" (58). Critics have made much of Delano's "repudiation" of slavery (when he reflects on Babo's cut cheek) and the subsequent irony of his offer to buy Babo. As I hope this analysis would indicate, there is *no* irony in his offer to buy Babo. He very clearly identifies himself with Cereno, imaginatively occupying the same Subject space as privileged, dominant, owner–master. It is not contradictory, then, for him to offer to buy the slave from Don Benito. Rather, it is only the seamless extension of his appreciation of "the beauty of that relationship," the validation of his Subjectivity.

We are now in a position to return to a consideration of that final image of the impaled head of Babo as a *reprisal* of the scene just analyzed. As I have argued, Babo's head is placed on the pole by the Lima Court as an *artifact*, a *re*-presentation of his sentence, as an(other) emblem of "white" guiltlessness. His punishment, then, is marked by a structure of representation strikingly similar to that suggested above, and to another which Kappeler presents as part of her framing argument in *The Pornography of Representation*. In a section entitled "Fact and Fiction," Kappeler analyzes the photographic evidence of the torture and death of black South African Thomas Kasire. Kasire, who had been recently employed on the farm of the "white" van Rooyen, was accused by him of being a supporter of the South Western People's Organization. As Kappeler summarizes, van Rooyen one weekend invited his drinking pals to the farm, took Kasire hostage, and for two days, they systematically tortured and eventually killed Thomas Kasire. Kappeler argues that the photographs, which were used as evidence in van Rooyen's trial, were an intrinsic part of the torture:

> The coincidence of this kind of violence and its representation is no accident. It is no curiosity in the domain of representation. The pictures are not documentary evidence, snapped by a journalist or observer by chance in the right place at the right time. The pictures are compositions, deliberate representations, conforming to a genre. The victim is forced to 'pose'; the perpetrator of the torture positions himself in the other picture with reference to the camera. Another white man is behind the camera, framing the picture. (6)

Like the photographs of Thomas Kasire, the impaled head of Babo is also part of a "genre," a recognizable structure of representation which carried a certain host of associations, and a certain positioning of participants. Babo's torture and death, like that of Kasire's, plays out a sophisticated structure of representation: through that re-presentation, the "whites" reaffirm their dominance, enact the structure of representation in their viewing, and carry it seamlessly into their realities. Just as Delano recognized the "beauty" of the master/slave relation and offered to buy Babo, the "white" audience of Babo's torture and execution identifies with the scenario constructed by the court of Lima. They enact its sentence physically, as they participate in Babo's torture, and metaphorically, as they "gaze" on his head, the "gaze" constituting their Subject-community. Thus the "final tragedy" of "Benito Cereno" is not, as Eric Sundquist would have it, that Delano cannot identify with Cereno ("Suspense," 100). Just the opposite: neither Delano nor Benito Cereno can identify with the humanity of Babo. Both men—Delano only momentarily, Cereno much more fully—experience the dehumanization of being subversively rendered Object/Other under Babo's authority. But neither the Spanish nor the American captain is able to identify with the horror of dehumanization when it is reimposed on Babo through the legal authority of the Lima Court. To the contrary both men resume their place as Subjects and participate in asserting the universality of (white male) Subjectivity. The Africans' actions graphically reveal, through its reversal, the violent basis of Western domination. But their subversion of that power structure is rendered, through Western legal discourse, an *aberration*; the power structure itself remains intact and unquestioned. Slavery and racism, as Western institutions, are *not* the horror of the story for Delano and Cereno. Rather, it is the specter of the possible assault on their status as Subjects presented by one anomalous African. As such, Babo's severed head embodies this horror for them while it reifies white male Subjectivity and its essentializing structure of representation.

His Voiceless End

The final tragedy for the narrator seems different. His might be described as an overwhelming sense of entrapment in the ruthless will to power of the racist system which reproduces its dominance by beheading Babo. Of all the texts considered in this study, "Benito Cereno" is the most incisive in its recognition of the conceptual, epistemological, and representational structures that support the racist economy. As diverse commentators have noted, however, in "Benito Cereno" the text of the narrator reaches a point of paralysis, where "past, present and future seemed one."[10] "Black" and "white" may be artificial and even dangerous conceptual constructs, but grey is not a positive alternative in this text. It functions only as a state of irresolution, of uncertainty, an antecedent to the necessity of black and white interpretation. In the "voiceless end" of Babo, "Benito Cereno" acknowledges the inadequacy of the racist, patriarchal, and capitalist structure of communication in representing the experience of the Object of that system. But the narrator is not able to voice an alternative to the essentialist dilemma, and we are left with the silence of Babo. The final vision of the text is that of a despairing (even sinister) collapse of history into timeless, repeated and unavoidable oppression.

I have suggested frequently in this study that if we see conflict in a "resisting" text, it may be an index of the repressed politics of the writer, who is consistently accorded the privileges of a colonizer by the very system she or he is critiquing. "Benito Cereno," more than any other text in this study, brings this dynamic to the fore. In the final section of his story, the narrator allows Delano to describe his own "providential" blindness, ironically highlighting his willful refusal to confront his own role in a vicious system of domination. Yet the final paragraphs of the narrative display the narrator's own inability to free himself from the imaginative economy that he satirizes through Delano.

Through the narrator's direct mention in the closing paragraphs of the story, we see how Babo's "plot" has, in effect, been the narrator's plot. Babo is deprived of both his literal body (it is "burned to ashes") and his figurative plot (in that he cannot or will not speak his story), and the narrator's textual embodiment of each draws attention to how both body and text become vehicles of resistance to an oppressive system. We see Babo scheme to physically fight his enslavement, until he no longer can, when unable to "do deeds [he] will not speak words." The narrator takes up for him, though, making both Babo and his "plot" *textual* figures of defiance.

At the same time, the narrative highlights how both body and text can be sites of domination. Babo's body, formerly enslaved, is severed from his head on orders from the Lima Court. The narrator's text thus finally and paradoxically embodies Babo's sentence: his literal deprivation of body. But the text does more than that. It *reproduces* the terms of the sentence, and it *represents* its product—Babo's severed head, on a pike, unabashedly fronting "the gaze of the whites" (315). Thus, it can also be said that the narrator *participates* in the sentence and the gaze of the Lima Court at the same time he makes it possible for his readers to do the same. The narrator's final sentences host the enactment of Babo's sentence. The narrative restages the scene of domination.

Here question of the narrator's perspective becomes problematic. Lacking any explicit qualification, the closure of the narrative could seem tacitly to endorse the verdict of the Lima Court. Yet this would be inconsistent with the critique of the dominative epistemology that the narrator has steadily developed. The question might rightly become whether the narrator recognizes the contradictions of his position: Voicing neither explicit criticism nor alternative action, does the narrative provide by *default* an endorsement of Babo's sentence? We might approach this question by examining the narrator's deployment of the final line of the text: "Benito Cereno, bourne on the bier, did, indeed, follow his leader" (315).

The line alluded to, "follow your leader," has been radically dialogized by the very different contexts in which it has earlier been uttered. Readers of the narrator's text first see the line dramatically revealed as the slaves on the *San Dominick* make a dash for open sea. The covered figurehead, which Delano has assumed to be under repair, is accidentally revealed and we see a human skeleton, under which the portentous words are chalked. We learn from Don Benito's agonized wail that the bones are those of Don Aranda and therefore, we can assume, a product of the slaves' revolt. Shortly thereafter we hear Delano's mate reinterpret the slaves' phrase of resistance: the "skeleton . . . seemed beckoning the whites to avenge it. 'Follow your leader!' cried the mate" (298). Belatedly, in the court documents, we learn the context of the slaves' intentions for the phrase. According to the testimony of Don Benito, Babo's message to the crew was pointed: "Keep faith with the blacks from here to Senegal, or you shall in spirit, as now in body, follow your leader" (305).

It is striking that the deployment of the phrase is wholly different when uttered by Babo or the first mate. Babo's gesture, meant to intimidate the Spanish crew into submission, at the same time subverts the idea of essential "racial" difference, as I have discussed earlier (essence, then, is *sameness*). On the other hand, the exhortation of the first mate to his "white" crewmen, to "follow your leader" puts back into force the very notion of racial difference that Babo's utterance has called into question (essence is *difference*). Thus, while a superficial reading of the final line of the narrative would seem to indicate simply that Don Benito had "followed his leader"—Don Aranda—"in spirit" by dying, a more careful reading must take into account the conflicting intentions of the line's earlier usages. If we also recall that *Babo* has served, for a time, as Don Benito's leader—precisely the experience that enervates and finally finishes Cereno—then the possible resonances of those final words become even more discordant.

In this closing line the narrator encapsulates the ironies of his reading of Babo's "plot." Babo himself can only resist the violence of his enslavement by utilizing violence, subversively threatening, but precisely threatening, the Spanish crew members with the bleached bones of a "fellow" crewman. The "whites" categorically refuse to confront the underlying epistemological challenge of Babo's actions, and the first mate spontaneously colonizes the slaves' radical intentions for the phrase to his own rapacious and correspondingly violent ones. Both levels of experience—his enslavement, and his subsequently restored dominance—become unlivable for Don Benito. Neither level of experience phases Delano. At last meaning seems mastered by brute force. The Lima Court orders Babo's head, that "hive of subtlety," severed from the body that succumbed immediately to Delano's superior brawn. Even legally, then, might makes right. The narrative suggests this fact particularly through its references to the replaced figurehead, into which we can appropriately read two levels of meaning: the carved figure on the bow of the ship *and* a person placed in a key position whose authority is hollow or undeserved. The latter also calls forth the image of Don Benito's "artificially stiffened" scabbard, suggesting the way in which he served as a figurehead—perhaps before the rebellion as well as during Delano's stay on the ship. But conjoined as this image of the scabbard is in the last paragraphs with the depiction of Delano quickly mastering Babo, a more pointed reading of the "artificially stiffened" figurehead becomes possible: Might is *not* "right"—the figurehead/leader exercises an always arbitrary authority.

Finally, though, the narrator offers no alternative to the conflicts embedded in the parting line. The imperative—follow your leader—is ineluctable. Echoing the command for his own closure, the narrator ironically reveals his entrapment in the imaginative economy of white male subjectivity. His perspective for the narrative—telling it largely through Delano's eyes—has allowed him to comment on Delano's ethical stance and has enabled him to analyze the exclusive structure of Subject-community in Delano's world. (As the narrator observes, after the trial the "fraternal unreserve" of the "two captains" is fully restored.) Moreover, the narrator's strategy allows him to underscore how the structure of Delano's world precludes Babo himself from ever representing his "plot."

But there is one certain limit in the narrator's perspective: Babo's story, told through Delano's eyes and through Don Benito's deposition, objectifies Babo as fully as the sentence of the Lima Court. The narrative perpetuates the same *structural* exclusivity of white male subjectivity in its own necessarily limited portrayal of Babo's motives and goals, and ultimate humanity. This perspective can present Babo only as a type—it can offer the reader no insight into the scope of Babo's humanity. In the end, the narrator provides no alternative to "follow[ing] his leader," which the *narrator* has done in following, with however much irony, the accounts of Delano, Cereno, and the Lima Court. The narrator's horror thus seems to be at his own imaginative dead end. He can expose Delano's fraudulent philanthropy but is stuck in the cul-de-sac of those very terms. As Eric Cheyfitz has recently observed, "One cannot articulate a critique of one's own place unless one can also stand in a radically different place" (xiv).[11] The irresolution of "everything . . . gray" signals the narrator's inability to think outside of the epistemological prison-house of black and white, just as Babo's silence resonates with his failure to imagine an intercultural dialogue. Relying on the structures of knowledge generated by the community that privileges him to speak, and speaking within that community, the narrator cannot avoid sentencing Babo as Other any more than he can see a way out of the dilemma of reading "race" in black and white.

7

"Read the Characters, Question the Motives": Harriet Jacobs's *Incidents in the Life of a Slave Girl*

The Meaning of "Race"

"The meaning of race," as David Brion Davis observes in a recent review essay, "remains curiously elusive." He asks "to what extent is race an ideological construction?" ("Ends of Slavery," 34). The aim of this study has not been to answer Davis's question definitively, but to suggest the texture of the Anglo-American literary dialogue which concerned itself with the exploration of "race." It has not been my goal to reduce these texts to their least common denominator; rather, I have been concerned with exploring the variances between these texts, to investigate the literary uses of "race" as—to use Raymond Williams's words—an "active history, made up of the realities of formation and struggle" (210). As I have argued, literature plays a formative role in shaping material and social reality, in conceiving of and suggesting strategies for dealing with the problems of "race."

It seems difficult (and even unfair) to generalize about a group of texts as different in strategy and historical positioning as those represented here—texts chosen precisely for their diversity. One feature that must be considered, however, is their common appeal to what each text variously constructs as a "white" audience. *Newes from America* enthusiastically extols the opening of new land to its British audience; "Benito Cereno" incisively castigates the dominative social structure of its Anglo-American audience. Each text considered here, no matter what its social or political ends, establishes a structural bridge between a "white" author and a "white" readership.

Kenneth Burke argues that the function of "rhetoric" is "to confront the implications of division" between people (*Rhetoric*, 22). While the subject matter of each text *ostensibly* addresses the divisions among racial groups in America, each text *rhetorically* addresses divisions among "*white*" readers over the issue of race—between colonizers over Christianizing Indians or slaves, between citizens in the city and on the frontier, between postwar

Americans who fueled racial prejudice and those who fought it (and even within the *individual*, as we have seen in "Benito Cereno," between colonizing and resisting Self). Clearly there was never a consensus on "race" among Anglo-Americans; each text proposed a kind of model, a perspective on "race" for its conflicted readership.

But finally, this rhetorical positioning, "white" author to "white" reader, seems to lead to an ineluctable cultural conservatism—or even protectionism. No matter how progressive the impulse of the text—in discussions of "racial" intermarriage from Byrd's *Histories* to Child's *A Romance of the Republic* for example—or how suggestively the text deconstructs its own racist privilege— as we have seen in *Nick of the Woods* or *The Narrative of Arthur Gordon Pym*—the final perspective always maintains at least some last vestige of "white" privilege. This fact is most concretely figured in the exclusive communicative structure between author and readership. Like the oppressively constructed community that is modeled and critiqued in "Benito Cereno," this reading community constitutes Subjectivity between author and reader over and against an objectified Other. As a result, texts like "The Negro Christianized" nonetheless affirm the superior right of white accumulation; likewise, *A Romance of the Republic* unquestioningly endorses "white"-bourgeois class structure and culture. What we see here confirms the inevitable conservatism of what Todorov has called the "third-person" variety of representation: the racial Other, not a Subject by merit of participation, but only ever the subject for discussion in these texts, remains trapped, forever an Object. The communicative/ideological structure remains Self-reflecting—whether uncritically— as I argued in my readings of Underhill, Jefferson, and Mather—or critically— as I have indicated in my analysis of "Benito Cereno." The lesson might be, then, that in order for there to be a truly constructive confrontation of the issue of "race," there must be a direct dialogue with the heretofore objectified Other—a move which immediately collapses his/her status as Other. As Sedgwick insisted in *Hope Leslie*, "whites" must learn to occupy a more humble position, and seek out the voices and experiences of the victim/object of American racial history and representation. Perhaps Anglo-America's failure to do so—both in literature and social practice—has been the problem from the very start.

Slavery, Sympathy, and Social Change

In his recent discussion of "the political responsibility of the critic," Jim Merod argues that "texts are records not only of verbal or conceptual possibilities, but no less of communal and interpersonal possibilities" (100). The texts considered in this study construct a vision of community in different ways, some including and others excluding the racial Other discussed. Yet in every vision of community, segregated or integrated, an exclusive "white" communicative structure remains entrenched. I have suggested that this rhetorical design (in both senses of the word—as artistic pattern and secret scheme) underwrites a cultural conservatism in a way that subtly but inevitably reinforces the hegemonic interests of the dominant Anglo class. Although it would take a different book to explore this possibility fully, it seems appropriate to consider briefly another text, this one addressed by its "black" author to a "white" audience: Harriet Ann Jacobs's *Incidents in the Life of a Slave Girl*.

Evidencing, in Abdul JanMohamed's words, a "sustained negation of the attempted hegemonic/ideological formation" ("Negating," 246), *Incidents* effectively undercuts racialist epistemology of the pre–Civil War era. In so doing, it presents an incisive reading of the distribution of power and Subjectivity in the slaveholding society, as well as a highly nuanced analysis of the potential power and actual limitations of an abolitionist, interracial sisterhood. Jacobs's text reveals how *both* of these models for community perpetuate race and gender oppression by constituting identity through ideas of essence, whether of master/servant or of woman/mother. Jacobs's narrative refutes the first model and reformulates the second by insisting on the social, political, and economic axes along which power is distributed and identities are constructed. In its analysis of women's community, *Incidents* critiques and redefines the "sympathetic" framework for understanding that featured prominently in both domestic and abolitionist texts of the period. The text reformulates sympathy so that it can recognize common bonds of humanity while acknowledging and respecting differences among people, and offers this model as a more viable means for real social change.

My Master Had Power and Law; I Had a Determined Will

Abdul JanMohamed has outlined in a recent article how the dominant culture attempts to school members of subordinate cultures to accept their own less-than-human status—in fact, to acquiesce to their own negation as social subjects. He observes that "the most crucial aspect of resisting hegemony consists in struggling against its attempt to form one's subjectivity, for it is through the construction of the minority subject that the dominant culture can elicit the individual's own help in his/her oppression" ("Negating," 247). For slavery to function as an efficient social system, the slaves must to some extent agree with their degraded status. Orlando Patterson has shown how a slave's sense of dishonor has always been a crucial aspect of any slave system: the slave is required simultaneously to accept the standards of the oppressor's value system, and the responsibility for his or her exclusion thereof.[1] As Patterson is the first to point out, while slaves are forced to at least superficially acquiesce to their "dishonor," they covertly maintain a fierce sense of honor. But where the white master's honor is a given, the slave's honor is hard bought. An important aspect of Linda's story, then, is detailing how she creates a sense of honor as she rejects her social negation. Her struggle provides the basis for a strong critique of the Subject-space she has been denied within the social system of the Old South. As she stakes out a clear position of Subjectivity for herself, she carefully reconstitutes it in a way that highlights its diverging epistemological space, and *value*.

That positioning has not only to do with Linda's "racial" status. Slavery in the United States existed in a complementary relationship to patriarchy: the smooth functioning of the system depended also on gender subordination. One of the mainstays of the Southern social system was its rigid *ideal* of "True Womanhood." Recent scholarship has highlighted how this social model could provide a definite basis for women's power in a patriarchal society. But it is also true that to a certain extent, this behavioral code served to objectify all women, "white" and "black."[2] The slave woman was inevitably most fully affected by the negative aspects of the construct.

For the Anglo "lady," True Womanhood functioned as a positive objectification—a stereotype that, hypothetically at least, she could achieve and profit from.[3] The cult of True Womanhood may have extracted a heavy psychological toll on the Southern "lady," encouraging her to repress her sexuality, yet it compensated her in ways that "allowed the white mistress to live her contradictory position" (Carby, *Reconstructing Womanhood*, 31). As Elizabeth Fox-Genovese points out, this objectified gender role "merged seamlessly" with the "social roles and sense of identity" of the Anglo woman (192). She could at least experience True Womanhood as protection, and could at best partake of the material benefits of the status she reflected for her husband. If her chastity was ultimately a commodity, the product of her sexuality served the positive good of the society that simultaneously objectified and exalted her. Her reproductive role was "glorified," and her children, as Hazel Carby notes, "were heirs to the economic, social, and political interests in the maintenance of the slave system" (31).

For the slave woman, however, True Womanhood operated as a *negative* objectification—a model that was unattainable and offered her neither protection nor benefit. This cultural ideal for the "black" woman served as a double negation, branding her with dishonor. First, as for the "white" woman, the imaginative ideal of True Womanhood required an ostensible denial of her full sexuality. But, second, because of the rape and enforced cohabitation institutionalized under slavery, True Womanhood functioned as a negation of the slave woman's ability to live up to that ideal of absent sexuality. So her *enforced* sexuality defined her failed status as "woman." The stereotypes attached to "black" women either cast them as breeder (Mammy), or presented them as wantonly promiscuous (Sapphire). Either stereotype, as Carby points out, served to obfuscate the operative dynamic by displacing responsibility for slave women's sexuality from the party whom it benefited to the victim. Thus, "the white slave master was not regarded as being responsible for his actions toward his black female slaves" (Carby, *Reconstructing Womanhood*, 27). The system worked to ensure for the slave master that, as Jacobs puts it, "licentiousness shall not interfere with avarice" (76). For the slave woman, it served to negate her entitlement to her own "womanhood" as that concept was culturally constructed.

Incidents focuses insistently on the victimization of women, and most particularly on the victimization of slave women. If patriarchal slavery is fueled by the oppression of blacks and women, then the profoundest victim, as *Incidents* repeatedly underscores, is the slave woman. Linda's narrative and commentary highlight this "double jeopardy" of sexism and racism as it portrays her owner's attempts to "master" her.[4] Flint harasses Linda with sexual innuendoes and (presumably) pornographic letters. Because of the vigilant jealousy of his wife, he is prevented from acting out his obsession for Linda. Consequently, he devises plans to build a house for Linda several miles away, where she will live in exchange for light labor (see 53, 83). His "promise" to "make a lady" of her by keeping her as a private prostitute exposes the social construction of "lady" and how its fluctuating definition worked to serve white male interest: "white ladies" are valued (by "white" men) for their sexual chastity; "black ladies" are valued (by "white" men) for their sexual permissiveness. Linda responds by taking the "white" Mr. Sands as lover and father to her two children. Her observation that "it seemed less degrading to give one's self, then to submit to compulsion" ironically underscores the fact that her action only redistributes her bondage; she is in fact exploited by *both* men.

The mixture of "race" that Linda's union with Sands highlights—the "tangled skein" of slave genealogy (78)—provides a point of resistance to racial definition. *Incidents* repeatedly documents that the perceptual opposition of black and white is unreliable and ultimately invalid. Linda drives this point home when she relates how her uncle Ben is able to escape from slavery: "For once his white face did him a kindly service. They had no suspicion that it belonged to a slave; otherwise, the law would have been followed out to the letter, and the *thing* rendered back to slavery" (24). But even though slaves like Ben might be able to use their fair complexion as a ticket to freedom, within the South's epistemological system a "white" complexion was also the slave's badge of dishonor, a dishonor which paradoxically refigured his or her social negation. It was a marker of the slave mother's sexual "transgression," taken as evidence of her lustful and consenting "nature" and justification of her continued debasement. The force of this white social standard could serve to draw the slaves themselves into negative self-judgment, encouraged thereby to acquiesce to their supposedly uncontrolled sexuality as well as to their stereotyped "desire" to *be* "white."[5]

Linda chronicles how she for a time accepted slaveholding society's logic in "A Perilous Passage." In this chapter Linda details the emotional crisis and course of action that Flint's sexual overtures force her to. She insists that "I wanted to keep myself pure; and under the most adverse circumstances, I tried hard to preserve my self-respect" (54). Linda repeatedly apologizes to her Northern audience for her lapse in moral character, for her loss of womanly virtue in accepting Sands as lover and father to her children. While these apologies may be read as strategic to her larger purposes, it does seem that Linda for a time accepts the Anglo reading of "womanly virtue." When she reveals the fact of her pregnancy to Flint, Linda recalls that she "felt wretched . . . my self-respect was gone! I had resolved to be virtuous though I was a slave. I had said, 'Let the storm beat! I will brave it till I die!' And now, how humiliated I felt!" (56). She is at this point compliant with the slave system's attempt to negate her selfhood, accepting patriarchy's version of her corrupted virtue and debased self-respect—her failure as a True Woman.

Yet alongside the apologies, she details how the conventional morality of True Womanhood fails the slave woman. In fact, this passage subtly provides an alternative reading which suggests that Linda has maintained her virtue *precisely* through her liaison with Sands.[6] Linda had hinted earlier in her narrative a reading that resisted the one imposed on her by white patriarchy when she observed that "it is deemed a crime in [the slave girl] to wish to be virtuous" (31). "A Perilous Passage" offers a confession of "failure" that is countered by the success of her resistance of Flint (and slaveholding patriarchy more generally), through an act of self-assertion. "I knew what I did, and I did it with deliberate calculation" (54). Although she wavers during the actual event (rather than the "triumph" over Flint that she expected, she feels shame), the mature Linda who narrates *Incidents* is able to counter the negation of her Subjecthood under the Southern social system by negating the basis on which it was formed. "The condition of a slave," she insists in retrospect, "confuses all principles of morality, and, in fact, renders the practice of them impossible" (55). As Barbara Johnson observes, while "identities are lost through acts of negation, they are also acquired thereby" (*World of Difference*, 4). If the constituent elements of slave society are "the slave's 'social death,' his [*sic*] utter powerlessness and his overwhelming sense of dishonor," Linda's "Passage" powerfully marks her revision of self and claims her honor, counter to the self-negating imperatives of white social hegemony (see JanMohamed, "Negating," 248).[7]

In narrating how she reconstitutes her Subjectivity, Linda levels a critique against the epistemological structure of the system which denies her. Her narrative delineates the construction of white male subject status in the slaveholding community differently from the narrator in Melville's "Benito Cereno." That narrator spoke from the vantage of fellow Subject, while Linda speaks from the position of victim. Thus it is from the margin (rather than the center) that Linda learns to understand as well as actually to manipulate the dominative structure of identity required by the slaveholder to confirm his Subject status. As Linda recounts Flint's seduction/harassment, we see the extent to which his mastery of her depends on *her*. Repeatedly he asks her to recognize his dominance: "he told me I was his property; that I must be subject to his will in all things" (27). In a key scene of confrontation in the narrative, where Linda confronts Flint to ask for permission to marry, Flint asks Linda: "Do you know that I have a right to do as I like with you—that I can kill you, if I please?" Linda responds: "You have no right to do as you like with me" (39). Her answer infuriates Flint, who commands "Silence!" and proceeds to compare his own behavior as master to those of others who might "have killed [Linda] on the spot." In this response, he asserts the prerogative of the Subject over the Object—to silence, to kill. But Flint *could not* kill Linda before she has confirmed his mastery of her (her symbolic death). His own identity depends on her recognition of it. He apparently cannot feel his mastery until she reflects it to him.[8]

Flint's attempt to dominate Linda revolves around making her an object for his sole pleasure. He repeatedly tries to isolate Linda from the scrutiny of the community, and from access—visual or otherwise—to other men. He bars Linda from her free black lover, commenting, "I'll soon convince you whether I am your master, or the nigger fellow you honor so highly" (39). After he learns of the first pregnancy, he attempts to threaten Linda into ending her relations with Sands: "You must henceforth have no communication of any kind with the father of your child. You must not ask anything from him, or receive any thing from him. I will take care of you and your child. You had better promise this at once" (59). When he learns of Linda's second pregnancy, his reaction is to shear off her hair, a gesture that obverts his attempts to veil her from the public eye by removing her from the community, but replicates exactly those intentions by controlling how she will appear. In his final attempt to win Linda's submission, Flint assures her that she will gain freedom: "and you can obtain it only through me" (83). All of Linda's actions, however, challenge Flint's designs. She clearly maneuvers for some kind of freedom from Flint through her liaison with Sands, and at the same time rejects any recognition of Flint's ultimate mastery over her.

In his first offer to build a small house outside of town, Flint promises Linda both to give her a home and to make her a lady. Her return strategy, to take a white slaveholder as a lover, illustrates her penetrating insight into the structure of the slaveholder's Subject community. Linda explains her choice to her reader: "It seems less degrading to give one's self, than to submit to compulsion. There is something akin to freedom in having a lover who has no control over you, except that which he gains by kindness and attachment" (55). But her calculations extend beyond that. She might have become pregnant by a fellow slave, or by a free "black" man. Her choice—a "white" man of obvious status in the community (Sands goes on to win a spot in Congress)—has clear strategic value in her "competition in cunning" against Flint. Flint's first question after the birth of Linda's child is indicative: "I command you . . . to tell me whether the father of your child is white or black" (59). A fellow white—a fellow white *slaveholding* male—is the one category of humanity whom Flint cannot hope to command to submission in this social system. Sands—the anonymous white lover—checks Flint's domination of Linda. Linda herself has maneuvered the pieces into position, playing master against master, king against king.[9]

Sisterhood and Sympathy

Linda successfully exposes and rejects the identification with mastery required of her by Flint. In her protracted escape from slavery, she analyzes and qualifies another kind of identification: that which occurs through sympathy. Many have commented on how *Incidents* draws its structure from popular sympathetic or domestic fiction, producing an appeal to Northern women to identify with and act on behalf of their enslaved "sisters." But while it enlists the productive energy of that genre, it carefully interrogates the power structure implicit in popular configurations of sympathy.

Perhaps the most vivid contemporary example of the narrative deployment of identification through sympathy comes from Harriet Beecher Stowe's *Uncle Tom's Cabin*. Stowe's narrative asserts a primary locus of identification: the actual and/or imaginative experience of motherhood. In one key scene she models how sympathy can cross racial boundaries and can become a stimulus to both cross-cultural understanding and effective social resistance. Mrs. Bird is arguing the contradictions of the fugitive slave law with Christian principle when the fugitive slave Eliza Harrison appears on the Bird's doorstep. The situation is loaded: after Mr. Bird's assertions about his duty in upholding the law, we do not know how he will react to Eliza's attempt to escape. He quizzes her, learning that she had a kind master and mistress, and finally asks, "what could induce you to leave a good home then, and go through such dangers?" (149). Eliza responds by looking to Mrs. Bird for aid, appealing to their shared experience of motherhood:

> The woman looked up at Mrs. Bird, with a keen, scrutinizing glance, and it did not escape her that she was dressed in deep mourning.
> "Ma'am," she said, suddenly, "have you ever lost a child?"
> The question was unexpected, and it was thrust on a new wound; for it was only a month since a darling child of the family had been laid in the grave.
> Mr. Bird turned around and walked to the window, and Mrs. Bird burst into tears; but, recovering her voice, she said,
> "Why do you ask that? I have lost a little one."
> "Then you will feel for me." (149)

The experience of motherhood cements their sympathetic identity bilaterally. Eliza sympathizes with Mrs. Bird's lost children, understanding Mrs. Bird's bereavement without being told, and concomitantly Mrs. Bird sympathizes with Eliza's potential loss of her child. It is through the operations of sympathy that Mrs. Bird most particularly recognizes Eliza's humanity, that moment marked by an eruption of tears. The sympathetic framework is then extended to reader-mothers, as the narrator appeals: "And oh! mother that reads this, has there never been in your house a drawer, or a closet, the opening of which has been to you like the opening again of a little grave?" (153–54). The model can work as well on nonmothers: Mr. Bird, too, through his love for his wife, is able to identify and sympathize with Eliza to the point that he acts against his avowed political principles in helping her to escape. And he cries too, with his back turned.

Incidents valorizes this same model as being *potentially*, but not axiomatically, liberational. Through repeated restagings of sympathetic exchanges, *Incidents* reads the real practice of sympathy more critically, questioning its actual efficacy, and suggesting that it too can be subtly (and not so subtly) coopted by social models of domination. In fact, the text's first sympathetic scene underscores its basic unreliability. Linda's mother, as she recounts, is the foster sister to her mistress, and Linda's subsequent owner. We learn that the mother's sister/mistress makes a promise to Linda's mother on her deathbed, that her children "should never suffer for anything." The mistress does in fact shelter Linda and her brother, so well that Linda describes her as "almost like a mother to me." But despite their common experiences of womanhood and motherhood, the mistress does not fulfill the spirit of her deathbed commitment to Linda's mother. Linda's comments show how the mistress's understanding is compromised by the dominative system of slavery that she profits from: "My mistress had taught me the precepts of God's Word: 'Thou shalt love thy neighbor as thyself.' 'Whatsoever ye would that men should do unto you, do you even so unto them.' But I was her slave, and I suppose she did not recognize me as her neighbor" (7–8). The imperatives of Christianity as well as sympathy call for an egalitarian structure of human relations, but the social system of slavery *blinds* those who benefit from its power, so that the mistress is unable, in fact, to *see* Linda outside of the context of domination. The seduction of power precludes a sympathetic recognition.

In another important scene we see again how a hierarchical distribution of power can corrupt the sympathetic relationship. Mrs. Flint asks for an account of her husband's behavior from the young Linda. Hoping, through such an exchange, to establish a common bond with Mrs. Flint, and thereby to gain some protection from her master, Linda tells her story. Mrs. Flint, listening, "wept and sometimes groaned," which inspires tears of sympathy in *Linda*, who avers, "I was touched by her grief." She is shortly disappointed to discover Mrs. Flint's sympathy narcissistically directed back toward herself, the power relation not subverted but maintained. While Mrs. Flint remains seemingly untouched by Linda's suffering, Linda herself does not reject the *potential* for sympathetic identification, and she closes the scene by noting that "I could not blame her. Slaveholders' wives feel as other women would under similar circumstances" (34).

While Linda gains a certain measure of moral superiority here, she does not gain the physical protection that she needs. The point is clear: Mrs. Flint is unable to identify sympathetically with other women because that would entail surrendering *her* identification with Mr. Flint. Karen Sanchez-Eppler's analysis of Mrs. Flint indicates how fully Flint had accomplished his mastery of his wife. Subsequently forcing Linda to sleep in her room at night, Mrs. Flint whispers "as though it were her husband who was speaking" (34), trying to catch Linda in an admission of guilt. Sanchez-Eppler observes that through this we see how, for Mrs. Flint, "the discourse of female sexuality or female power finds itself hopelessly mired in the master's words" (25). Her full identification with her husband's mastery bars her from confronting him with his seduction of Linda. Because she is so completely invested in her hierarchical relation with her husband, she cannot comprehend an alternative to domination. Rather than leaguing *with* Linda to achieve both their purposes, she lords *over* Linda in a way that leaves them both isolated in the face of Flint's power.

While Linda does not surrender hope in the power of sympathy, she does become highly suspicious of it. In depicting Linda's relationships with the two Mrs. Bruces, Jacobs offers a redemptive vision of sympathy while extending her careful critique. On her arrival in the North, Linda confesses that "I longed for someone to confide in; but I had been so deceived by white people, that I had lost all confidence in them. If they spoke kind words to me, I thought it was for some selfish purpose." Linda cannot bring herself immediately to trust the first Mrs. Bruce, as Eliza had Mrs. Bird. But gradually she found that "the gentle deportment of Mrs. Bruce and the smiles of her lovely babe were thawing my heart" (169). Still, it is some time later, and only in the face of imminent danger, before Linda finds the courage to risk revealing her history to Mrs. Bruce. Valuing Mrs. Bruce's "good opinion," Linda hesitates to lose it. But Mrs. Bruce discerns Linda's distress, and encourages her to share her trouble to which she listens "with true womanly sympathy" (180). She confirms the fullness of her sympathy in her parting gesture before Linda flees town to escape once again. Observing that Linda had taken off her own flannel skirt to make a coat for her poorly clad daughter, Mrs. Bruce's eyes fill with tears. She departs, returning shortly with a coat and shawl for Ellen. Replicating Mrs. Bird's gesture of supplying clothes for Eliza's Harry, Mrs. Bruce confirms the bond of sympathy through motherhood.

Linda's positive experiences with the first Mrs. Bruce lead her to more easily trust the second. This woman, too, proves a "true and sympathizing friend" (190), and when Linda again finds herself in danger of being captured, Mrs. Bruce sends off her own daughter with Linda, epitomizing in this gesture motherly sympathy as active resistance. She explains to Linda, "if they get on your track, they will be obliged to bring the child to me; and then, if there is the possibility of saving you, you shall be saved" (194). Her act of sympathetic identification evokes emotion in Linda even as she recounts it: "The noble heart! The brave heart! The tears are in my eyes while I write of her" (194).

Yet the reciprocal identification of sympathy, the ostensible equality that it promises to establish between Subjects, is subtly qualified by the terms Linda chooses in describing the events that close her narrative. Having politely and carefully rejected Mrs. Bruce's offer to buy off her pursuers, Linda cautions that "such a great obligation could not easily be cancelled" (199). Linda realizes, as Patterson puts it, that "relationships are structured and defined by the relative power of the interacting persons" (1). She sees how this gesture would assert Mrs. Bruce's relative social and economic power over Linda in a way that would ineluctably define their relationship. But Mrs. Bruce proceeds to buy Linda without her knowledge or consent, which she announces to Linda when it (or she) is a done deed. Their reunion follows the sympathetic model: "When I reached home, the arms of my benefactress were thrown round me, and our tears mingled." Crying and embracing, Mrs. Bruce insists that Linda has misinterpreted her motives: "You wrote me as if you thought you were going to be transferred from one owner to another. But I did not buy you for your services" (200). Nonetheless Mrs. Bruce is here designated "benefactress," rather than "friend." Although Mrs. Bruce acts sympathetically in purchasing Linda's freedom, her action prohibits Linda from achieving the *quality* of freedom that she wants most. Mrs. Bruce sympathizes, but she does not *understand*, and as Andrews points out, her action removes Linda from "one marginal status, that of the unfree freedom of the fugitive slave, to another kind of marginality, the obligated freedom of a charitably purchased slave" (261). Linda's closing sentences echo this irony: "It is a privilege to serve her who pities my oppressed people, and who has bestowed the inestimable boon of freedom on me and my children" (201). Serving, whether under compulsion or privilege, remains servitude; the structure of this sympathetic identification is one of hierarchy, not equality.

Lives Receive Their Hue from Circumstance

It is from the point of view of the victim that *Incidents* constructs a critique of two models of identification, dominative (master/slave; male/female) and sympathetic (woman/woman; mother/mother), underscoring how the equality of the latter can subtly slip into the hierarchy of the former. Moreover, the text reveals how *both* models depend on ideas of "essence." The "patriarchal institution" hinges on essential distinctions between races and gender, just as the popularly constructed sympathetic community of women assumes a womanly and/or motherly essence that elides *any* difference. Linda's narrative undercuts notions of essence at every level. Her observation, that "lives . . . receive their hue from circumstance" is strikingly double-valenced. It deconstructs the essence of color—a perceptually invalid but epistemologically enforced distinction between "white" and "black" people—by asserting the *historical* basis ("circumstance") of what is perceived as *essence* ("hue"). It hereby challenges essence of identities ("lives") constructed and assumed based on this model of color. Similarly, the narrative challenges essential constructions of womanhood.

For instance, while Linda hides in the house of the white slaveholder's wife, Flint puts her children in jail to draw her out of hiding. Betty, the wife's cook, would visit the children and report back to Linda, who repeatedly cried over them. Betty, sympathizing with Linda's desire to escape, responds, "Lors child! what's you crying 'bout? Dem young uns vill kill you dead. Don't be so chick'n hearted! if you does, you vil nebber git thro' dis world" (101). Linda underscores the limitations of Betty's sympathy, observing:

> good old soul! She had gone through the world childless. She had never had little ones to clasp their arms round her neck; she had never seen their soft eyes looking into hers; no sweet little voices had called her mother; she had never pressed her own infants to her heart, with the feeling that even in fetters there was something to live for. How could she realize my feelings? (101–2)

Womanhood does not automatically situate common understanding, a fact which Linda understands and excuses. In a later scene we see the balance reversed. As Linda finally makes her escape to Philadelphia, she discovers a friend on board the boat. She and Fanny embrace in astonishment, bursting into tears. Fanny relates to Linda her story of escape, and the painful separation from all her children who had been auctioned away from her. Linda tells Fanny her own story, concluding, "we have the same sorrows." Fanny's response is pointed: "No . . . you are going to see your children soon, and there is no hope that I shall ever even hear from mine" (157). These moments assert the important differences in women's experiences that should not be overlooked in the moment of sympathy. Similarly, though the ship's captain makes clear his sympathy to the two escaping women, he is offended that Linda refuses to fully trust him. His sympathy, Linda notes, is not equivalent to understanding: "if he had ever been a slave he would have known how difficult it was to trust a white man" (158). *Incidents* refigures the sympathetic model in a way that shows how *contextual* identities are. These series of examples emphasize the message circumspectly conveyed in the final chapter: sympathy assumes *sameness* in a way that can prevent an understanding of the very real, material *differences* that structure human experience in a society based upon unequal distribution of power.

Reader, If You Have Never Been a Slave, You Cannot Imagine

Incidents is, finally, remarkable for the way in which it extends this challenge to its readers. The text repeatedly appeals to the sympathy of its readers, but at the same time it warns them to be careful about the motives and critical of the results of that sympathetic identification. Beginning in the preface, the narrative begins its double enterprise:

> I have not written my experience in order to attract attention to myself. . . . Neither do I care to excite sympathy for my own sufferings. But I do earnestly desire to arouse the women of the North to a realizing sense of the condition of two millions of women at the South, still in bondage, suffering what I suffered, and most of them far worse. . . . Only by experience can any one realize how deep, and dark, and foul is that pit of abominations. (1–2)

Linda is willing to use her story to create a locus for the sympathetic identification between (white) women of the North and enslaved women of the South. While encouraging that contact, Linda also implies that a Northern woman who responds imaginatively to the text does so from a different context entirely, and cannot assume that she *understands* the perspective of her slave sister: "only by experience" would this be possible. Repeatedly she asks her reader to realize the inadequacy of her experience to understand the perspective of the slave: "What would *you* be, if you had been born and brought up a slave, with generations of slaves for ancestors?" (44).

Seldom does Linda invite the reader to sympathy without such careful qualifications. For instance, in a passage developed around obvious sentimental conventions, Linda makes an appeal: "Reader, it is not to awaken sympathy for myself that I am telling you truthfully what I suffered in slavery. I do it to kindle a flame of compassion in your hearts for my sisters who are still in bondage, suffering as I once suffered" (29). Sisterhood becomes the valence for sympathetic identity. While Linda situates her white Northern readers as part of that sisterhood, she also encourages them, through a subtle narrative strategy, to confront their own possible complicity with the patriarchal social system.[10] Linda proceeds to tell a fable of two sisters, "one . . . a fair white child; the other . . . her slave." She briefly chronicles their lives:

> The fair child grew up to be a still fairer woman. From childhood to womanhood her pathway was blooming with flowers, and overarched by a sunny sky. Scarcely one day of her life had been clouded when the sun rose on her happy bridal morning.
>
> How had those years dealt with her slave sister, the playmate of her childhood? She, also, was very beautiful; but the flowers and sunshine of love were not for her. She drank the cup of sin, and shame, and misery, whereof her persecuted race are made to drink. (29)

Linda here forces in her reader a recognition of a preexisting, corrupt "sisterhood" between women of both "races," not "white" and "black," but master and slave. This strategy allows her both to evoke moral indignation in her readers while reminding them the differences between them and slave women are sheerly social, not racial. Notably the slave sister, in contrast to her "fair" owner, is nowhere identified by her skin color, but only in terms of her social status. More important, the narrative is able to suggest that the injustice suffered by the slave woman is at least partially the fault of her free sister, who fails to live up to the responsibilities of sisterhood.

The passage, with its direct appeal to its readers, is strategically juxtaposed to the chapter entitled "The Jealous Mistress." Its opening lines carefully hark back to the previous passage, asserting that Mrs. Flint "had no sympathy" for her slaves. She did, however, have "the key to her husband's character" (31). While she might have used that knowledge to shield her slave sisters, she fails to offer them the protection her status could afford. Here Linda makes explicit what she left implicit in the previous passage: women who have more power in the system have a moral obligation to protect their "sisters" — women who are even more victimized. And having begun by evoking a sisterly bond between her readers and slave women, Linda's parable about sisters manages obliquely to suggest that free women must understand how their sympathetic response to the slave sister of the story can be compromised by their own relationship with the existing social system.[11] Like the "fair sister," they too may be enjoying a life "overarched by a sunny sky," *reading* with sympathy, but failing by omission of *action* to render the protection to slave sisters.

In what is perhaps her riskiest appeal for sympathy, Linda again insists on her point. In the chapter where she chronicles how she resisted Flint's machinations, Linda must reveal her failure to live up to the codes of True Womanhood. Potentially this failure could disqualify her from the sympathy of her free sisters. Linda acknowledges this, but here calls upon her reader to use sympathy *unconventionally*, to try to understand the very different way a slave woman experiences the world. She prefaces her "confession" by exhorting her reader: "O, ye happy women, whose purity has been sheltered from childhood, who have been free to choose the objects of your affection, whose homes are protected by law, do not judge the poor desolate slave girl too severely" (54). She calls on her reader to suspend her understanding of True Womanhood, to see it as culture-bound. Linda concludes her confession even more strongly: "Pity me and pardon me, o virtuous reader! You never knew what it is to be a slave; to be entirely unprotected by law or custom; to have the laws reduce you to the condition of chattel, entirely subject to the will of another" (55). This structure epitomizes the way in which *Incidents* projects its sympathetic model—by asking the reader to become aware of her *own* social position and biases before she feels qualified to try to understand the very different difficulties of another.

The book's model for sympathy does not stop here. Linda frames her entire confession with comments that suggest an alternative reading of this episode in her life, different than the one afforded by standards of True Womanhood. "The influences of slavery had had the same effect on me that they had on other young girls; they had made me prematurely knowing, concerning the evil ways of the world. I knew what I did, and I did it with deliberate calcula-tion" (54). Linda's assertion is strikingly ambiguous. Young slave girls can be "prematurely knowing" in terms of their own sexuality, which by the social standards of True Womanhood would implicate them in "the evil ways of the world." *Or*, we might read this as a comment on how slave girls are victimized in a way most other girls are not by "the evil ways of the world." The latter reading seems finally most consistent with Linda's critique, particularly as she concludes her confession by asserting, "still, in looking back, calmly, on the events of my life, I feel that the slave woman ought not to be judged by the same standard as others" (56).

In this way *Incidents* begins to structure an alternate vantage of understand-ing, an alternative epistemology, that mirrors Linda's reconstituted Subjectiv-ity. Linda makes clear that she has a different way of knowing the world, a difference which is structured by her experiences. She repeatedly insists that her perspective is important to any understanding of the slave experience and any formulation for social change. Linda therefore presents a different sympathetic model. Sympathy ideally should *bridge* the gap of difference be-tween sisters. Yet it neither can nor should *collapse* the differences that it bridges. We see this reading of sympathy epitomized in one particularly strik-ing address to the reader late in the narrative. Linda has finally been united with her son, Benjamin. "O reader, can you imagine my joy?" she queries in what initially seems simply a rhetorical question at a climactic moment in the text. Of course the reader can identify with being separated from a loved one. Of course the reader shares her joy. But the next line tersely asserts, "no, you cannot, unless you have been a slave mother." Here the reader is called on almost simultaneously to experience the full collapse of sympathy *and* to re-member the crucial differences that comprise the way women experience the world.

This moment is, we might say, a condensed lesson in *Incidents'* reformula-tion of the convention. Sympathy should contribute to an active strategy of social reform, but it cannot accomplish its goal of community based on equal-ity until it is able to *acknowledge* and *value* the different perspective of the slave "sister"—her different experiences in, and hence different knowledge of, the world. In fact, as the text suggests at several points, it may be the knowledge of the slave woman that *most* effectively critiques the structure of domination under slavery, is best able to point up how the good intentions of free women are unconsciously compromised by their investment in the oppressive system they ostensibly fight.

Linda's narrative carefully suggests that her marginal perspective is *central* to the goals of the sympathetic community of women. But just as Linda's desire for freedom is sympathetically misappropriated by Mrs. Bruce, the text predicts its own misappropriation by the reader.[12] Mrs. Bruce's actions give her a clear sense of philanthropy. And while they *are* helpful for Linda, as she acknowledges, they also limit the sense of autonomy she worked so hard to preserve while in reach of Flint. Mrs. Bruce's well-intended actions here call to mind Child's scheme for American postwar regeneration, whereby "whites" would lift up ex-slaves into middle-class society through a system of patronage. This, put in the most ungenerous terms, soothed the consciences of Anglo-Americans, allowing them to recoup their sense of guilt over their complicity with the slave system. And, as I have pointed out, it preserved a class structure which ensured the continued cultural (and economic) domination of the Anglo-American majority. But perhaps its most serious ramification was the way in which it assumed *Sameness* between Anglo and African Americans. This assumption constitutes precisely the difficulty that *Incidents* so effectively warns against: as long as the dominant class cannot acknowledge and accept difference on a horizontal scale, it will be perpetuated and even enforced on a vertical one.

As a corrective, *Incidents* reformulates sympathy as a communicative bridge that could effectively equalize the distribution of power, the deployment of knowledge and the structure of community. Its radical vision, however, depended on the willingness of its audience to listen and to accept the challenge of self-critique; it seems that its message might be just as relevant today.

Notes

Preface

1. See, for instance, Michael Omi and Howard Winant, *Racial Formation in the United States* . . . , who argue that sociologists "should treat race in the United States as a fundamental *organizing principle* of social relationships" (66; authors' emphasis). Ringer and Lawless propose that racism has undergirded the nation's politics in a similar manner: "The Founding Fathers sanctified two political models," a "colonial" model that upheld liberty for the Anglo-American population, and a "colonialist" model that sanctioned the oppression of "others." They conclude that "America's historic treatment of its racial minorities has been both an expression and a product of the dialectical tension between these two models" (xiv).

2. In *The Mismeasure of Man* Stephen Jay Gould observes that "biologists have recently affirmed—as long suspected—that the overall genetic differences among human races are astonishingly small. Although frequencies for different states of a gene differ among races, we have found no 'race genes'—that is, states fixed in certain races and absent from all others" (323). Winthrop Jordan, who, in his 1968 landmark study discusses "the concept of race" in terms of science, observes that "recent advances in the study of race have done little to settle certain important questions concerning racial differences in physiology and anatomy—let alone the slippery problem of mental abilities. . . . It is ironic that a scientific problem which has been acknowledged for several millenniums still remains unsolved, and, further, that scientists have not yet been able to fit one of the most socially explosive facts of human biology securely into the framework which now supports the study of human races" (585). For other informative sources, see: Collette Guillaumin, "The Idea of Race and Its Elevation to Autonomous, Scientific and Legal Status"; Michael Banton and Jonathan Harwood, *The Race Concept*; Nancy Stepan, *The Idea of Race in Science*; and Anthony Appiah, "The Uncompleted Argument: Du Bois and the Illusion of Race." It is important to note the work of Martin Barker ("Biology and New Racism") and Lucius Outlaw ("Toward a Critical Theory of Race") who remind us, in Outlaw's words, that despite its scientific discreditation, "'race' continues to function as a critical yardstick for the rank-ordering of racial groups both 'scientifically' and sociopolitically, the latter with support from the former" (67).

3. This is only a partial rendering of Foucault's discussion here of the concept "apparatus" (*dispositif*). For a fuller discussion, see pp. 194–97; for an illustrative elaboration, see his *History of Sexuality*. My adoption of Foucault's "apparatus" as a critical tool has much in common, I think, with David Theo Goldberg's recent proposal that we study race as a "field of discourse." See his essay "The Social Formation of Racist Discourse" in *Anatomy of Racism*, esp. p. 296.

4. The suggestion that race is a "fiction" has triggered a huge debate. Although its scientific basis has been painstakingly discredited, some literary and cultural critics have become alarmed over the implications of discrediting the political and concrete experience of race. This aspect of the controversy has been outlined in the debate between Joyce Joyce, Henry Louis Gates, Jr., and Houston Baker in *New Literary History*, and in a separate article by Houston Baker in *Critical Inquiry*. The surge of interest in ethnicity, spearheaded by Werner Sollors, has sparked a parallel debate about whether "race" should be subsumed or subordinated to ethnicity. For an insightful and helpful reading of both these debates, see Diana Fuss's chapter on "Poststructuralist Afro-American Literary Theory," in her *Essentially Speaking*.

5. Henry Louis Gates, Jr., in a well-known essay has argued that "race has become a trope of ultimate, irreducible difference between cultures, linguistic groups, or adherents of specific belief systems which, more often than not, also have fundamentally opposed economic interests. Race is the ultimate trope of difference because it is so very arbitrary in its application" ("Writing 'Race,'" 5). Eric Cheyfitz also argues in favor of viewing "race" as a literary construct: "Just as existence is a product of language, race, a political effect of existence, must also be a matter of language. To become white, that is to become a real human being, is not a physical problem, it is a political problem" (125).

6. "Sociological criticism" is posited by Kenneth Burke as a criticism of literature which would "seek to codify the various strategies which artists have developed with relation to the naming of situations" (*Philosophy*, 301).

7. See, for example, the interview "Truth and Power" in *Power/Knowledge*.

8. As Paschal Bruchner puts it in his provocative book, *Tears of the White Man*, we should be able "to love ourselves without being conceited" (151).

Chapter 1

1. In the title to this chapter, "uncommon need" alludes to Winthrop Jordan's remarks on Thomas Jefferson's public stand on African inferiority. Jordan argues that "it is clear that only one man in the South felt compelled to take [an essentialist] position publicly. Jefferson alone spoke forth, and this fact in itself suggests, at very least, strong feeling on his part, an uncommon need to discourse upon the subject" (457). This observation seems widely applicable to the need of the Anglo-colonialist to discourse upon the subject of "race."

For a fascinating discussion of the developing genre of European travel literature, which provides the backdrop to Columbus's "discovery" mission, see Mary Campbell's important study *The Witness and the Other World*. In chapter 2, "'Wonder Books' and Grotesque Facts," she discusses the influence of fictional accounts on actual explorers.

2. Here Cotton justifies the profit mission of colonialism. Curiously his example, taken from Matt. 13:44–46, reverses the direction of Christ's parable, which compares the wise who recognize true value and sell all their material belongings to aspire to be good Christians. Cotton uses this example for an opposite lesson, comparing good

Christians to those who are "wise . . . and . . . sudden" enough to seize material gain in the New World.

3. I use the gendered pronoun advisedly. Interest in female natives was always only secondary, as we see, for example, in the pronouncement of Comte de Buffon on the "American savages": "They lack ardour for their females" (qtd. by Thomas Jefferson in *Notes*, 58–59).

4. See Nash, *Red, White, and Black*, 27–39. Nash suggests that Spanish accounts of native genocide may have "suggested that when Europeans met 'primitive peoples,' slaughter was inevitable." As Benjamin Ringer notes, however, while they may have unconsciously molded their *fears* around Spanish representations of the natives, the British colonists did not model their colonial *system* on that of the Spanish (36). The term "positional superiority" is Edward Said's. He describes it as a strategy which "puts the Westerner in a whole series of possible relationships with the Orient without ever losing him the relative upper hand" (7).

5. As Winthrop Jordan points out in *White Over Black: American Attitudes Toward the Negro, 1550–1812*, there seems to be a "fog of inconsistency and vagueness enveloping the terms *servant* and *slave* as they were used in England and seventeenth-century America" (52–53), and that the evidence surrounding the usage of those first Africans in Virginia is sketchy at best. However, the wording of legal documents and evidence of freed Africans indicate an evolving trend from treating Africans as servants to their very definite status as lifelong slaves by 1659 (see Ringer, 65).

6. In fact, many colonial artist/engravers ignored conceptual evidence of physiognomic difference, portraying Africans and Native Americans with facial features and bodily structure identical to Anglo-Europeans. Kupperman provides detailed analysis of early colonial representations and writings on this subject in *Settling with the Indians*. See "Indian Appearance," 33–44. She notes particularly that for the early colonial ethnographers, "color itself was a manipulable attribute. Writers mostly referred to the tan color of the Indians as the "Sun's livery. . . . However the color was produced [i.e., by sun or walnut stain], the important fact was that Indians were naturally white. . . . Their darker color was part of a deliberately produced identity which the Indians chose for themselves, because they considered it beautiful or to protect themselves from the elements" (37).

7. See Alden Vaughan, "From White Man to Redskin," 920; Winthrop Jordan, 9–11. Nancy Stepan marks an important historical shift in the emphasis on and uses of blackness in her 1982 study entitled *The Idea of Race in Science*. She argues that the absence of a racial system of slavery among the Greeks and Romans was probably owing to "the absence of any obvious colour or racial prejudice," and further notes that as Europe became invested in a racial system of slavery, "slowly blackness itself, which in the ancient world had often been associated with positive qualities such as physical or moral beauty, came to be associated negatively with the degraded condition of slavery" (xi–xii).

8. Goldberg's work supports my analysis. He notes that while "the concept of race crept into European languages in the fifteenth century, and its scientific and popular usage peaked in the eighteenth and nineteenth centuries . . . the ethnocentrisms of socioepistemic conjunctures prior to the seventeenth century, although forerunners of racism, were not themselves forms of racist expression" (295, 298).

9. See Vaughan, "White Man." Similarly, Richard Drinnon, in *Facing West*, documents a lexical shift in the adjectival use of "brutish" to describe Native Americans, to the nominative "brute" during this period (50).

10. V. Y. Mudimbe also locates an epistemological/representational shift in the

seventeenth century that simultaneously collapses difference by establishing a "white" norm, and articulates distinctions from that norm by "an accumulation of accidental difference, namely nakedness, blackness, curly hair, bracelets, and strings of pearls." The cumulative effect of this is to remove from perception "physical and cultural variations, while maintaining and positing surface differences as meaningful of human complexity" (9).

11. Winthrop Jordan's comments are representative: "The concept of Negro slavery there was neither borrowed from foreigners, nor extracted from books, nor invented out of whole cloth, nor extrapolated from servitude, nor generated by English reaction to Negroes as such, nor necessitated by the exigencies of the New World. Not any one of these made the Negro a slave, but all" (72).

12. See also Thomas S. Kuhn's *Structure of Scientific Revolution*, which presents an account of the fundamental conservatism at the heart of any scientific "revolution."

13. In fact, as Butterfield further notes, Copernicus was perhaps driven as much by his personal desire to usurp Ptolemy as by objective disputes based on observation. Says Butterfield: "It would appear that Copernicus found a still stronger stimulus to his great work in the fact that he had an obsession and was ridden by a grievance. He was dissatisfied with the Ptolemaic system for a reason which we must regard as a remarkably conservative one—he held that in a curious way it caused offence by what one can almost call species of cheating" (37).

14. John Milton, *Paradise Lost*, VIII: 65–172. As Merritt Y. Hughs notes in his detailed introduction to Milton's work, debate has long raged over whether Milton threw his support to the geocentric camp, or, for the sake of convenience and convention, depicted a geocentric universe while theoretically acknowledging the implications of heliocentricity (see esp. 186–88). Despite the imaginative difficulty of surrendering the idea that Man was at the physical center of the universe, Karl Guthke argues that by far the more threatening implication of Copernican thought was the implication that there might be a plurality of worlds which would work to undermine theological and epistemological anthropocentrism. See his chapter entitled "The Renaissance," esp. pp. 43–66.

15. David Theo Goldberg notes that "classification is established as a fundament of scientific methodology only as a function of the '*esprites simplistes*' of the seventeenth century and the Enlightenment" (301). See Nancy Stepan, *Idea of Race*, 1–19, for a historicized reading of the ideological permutations of the Great Chain as a racist scientific model.

16. Thomas Gossett observes that "just as astronomers before Galileo had assumed that angels governed the movements of the planets, so scientific thought in the seventeenth and eighteenth centuries usually assumed that the Creator must personally have attended to the fabrication of every animal and plant on earth" (33–34).

17. Stephen Jay Gould argues that this "propensity for ordering complex variation as a gradual ascending scale" is one of the most pervasive fallacies of Western scientific history—a fallacy which he titles "the mismeasure of man" (24–25, 31). Christian Delacampagne forwards an argument that is in impulse similar to mine, that racism "progressed hand in hand with the very foundations of Western rationalism" (83). See also Peter Fitzpatrick, who likewise proposes that "racism was, in short, basic to the creation of liberalism and the identity of the European" (249).

18. Similarly, Robert Berkhofer, Jr., suggests that "exploration and expansion overseas resulted from and reinforced nationalism at the same time that it promoted an overall collective vision of a Europe in contradistinction to the rest of the world" (23).

19. There is some disagreement over the actual proportion of "gentlemen" to artisans and laborers, ranging from 3 : 1, to 1 : 3. See Ringer (40) for a discussion.

20. Morgan identifies this contradiction in policy as "the American Paradox."

21. In an alternative analysis of the "paradox," Benjamin Ringer and Elinor Lawless do not try to resolve the inconsistencies, but rather propose that the political system of the United States did in fact develop around two standards, a "colonist" system, which applied to the self-governance of the yeoman/farmer; and the "colonialist" system, which applied to the enforced governance of African slaves (see 106). Paul Hoch, in his important and little-known 1979 study entitled *White Hero, Black Beast*, argues somewhat differently that racism begins "as an assertion of masculinity—the claim that the superior warrior manhood of the conquerors justifies their economic exploitation of the conquered" (115), adding that the development of racial hierarchies "eventually crystallized class structures *within* societies that led to the state" (114). His argument is suggestive; it is certainly possible to see how the legal entrenchment of racial slavery served as some kind of placebo to the lower (and still disenfranchised) Anglo classes.

22. This coincidence of massacre and benign mission later becomes a leitmotif in U.S. literature, as Philip Fisher trenchantly argues in his analysis of Cooper's fiction:

> In Cooper's plot we could say that on the way to the marriage of Chingachgook and Hist there was, incidentally, a massacre. At a saturated moment of history every intention—such as the intention to take a journey or to marry or to farm a piece of land—will again and again register the same individual secondary outcome: and on the way to Oregon, and on the way to marriage, and on the way to farming 240 acres in Kansas, there was a massacre, there was a massacre, there was a massacre. (73)

23. For a very different reading of the Pequot War, see Alden T. Vaughan's *New England Frontier: Puritans and Indians, 1625–1675*, 134–38.

24. As Alden T. Vaughan points out, Captain John Stone, notorious among colonists for his hijacking/pirating adventures, had been banished by the Plymouth Colony (*Frontier*, 124).

25. Philip Fisher observes that "the provisions of subcategories for one side and their collapse for the other is one of the most far-reaching political acts of narrative since it controls the issue of collective responsibility or innocence and legitimizes violence on an indiscriminate basis. It is in fact the inner mechanism by which 'justice' and the punishment of individual offenders spreads out, under a collapse of differences, into extermination" (34).

26. Michael Paul Rogin provides an extended psychoanalysis of this general Anglo cultural trend to represent Native American warfare as childish. See "Liberal Society and the Indian Question," 144–47.

27. It is worth noting that Underhill, like Winthrop in his *Arbella* sermon, turns specifically to Old Testament precedent, which authorizes a vengeance denied by the focus of the New Testament on mercy.

28. See Drinnon, *Facing West*, 55. John Mason records in his account of the Pequot War that afterward, when the number of the surviving Pequots was reduced to somewhere between 180 and 200, the Pequot sachems petitioned the Puritans for mercy in return for their submission. Mason records that "the Pequots were then bound by Covenant, That none should inhabit their native Country, nor should any of them be called Pequots any more" (40).

29. See Ann Kibbey's brilliantly insightful reading of the map itself.

30. All references to Query XVIII are drawn from Jefferson, 162–63. Of this particular quote, Winthrop Jordan notes that "the depth of [Jefferson's] feeling was apparent

for he rarely resorted to exclamation marks and still less often to miracles without skepticism." Jordan's extensive reading of Jefferson's pronouncements on African Americans in *White Over Black* remains one of the finest and most nuanced. Even though the conclusions of my analysis and Jordan's have much in common, our analyses of the relative interpretive value of the two slave passages differ substantially.

31. Winthrop explains this incongruity by arguing that Jefferson made a distinction between soul/morality and intellect. The former was common to all humans, but the latter individuated groups of humans. This reading does apparently reconcile Jefferson's seemingly contradictory statements on African-Americans in *Notes*; however, it does not explain why Jefferson felt compelled to argue for such a split, consistently ignoring (as Winthrop himself observes) contradictory evidence.

32. Similarly, as Mitchell Robert Breitwieser observes, Monticello was built out of the labor of a slave economy but was structured architecturally to efface evidence of slave labor. This would explain "the hidden stairways; the slave passages to the kitchen; laundry and stables hidden . . . beneath terraces; the dumbwaiters, invisible within the fireplace, that obviate the need to have wine carried into the room; the ladder that folds so that it does not look like a ladder; and the seeming door that revolves to reveal shelves of hot food, but conceals the servers" (317).

33. See Diggins for a fuller discussion, 224–28. Nancy Stepan notes this strategy — of displacing onto Nature what was in fact a moral issue — as a more general Western formation in her excellent *Idea of Race* (see xiii). I should also note, as others have more extensively discussed, that Jefferson applies precisely the opposite argument to Native Americans in *Notes*, that their supposed cultural inferiority was not evidence of an inferior nature, but of lack of nurture. See Winthrop, Drinnon, and Breitwieser for fuller discussion and debate.

34. Jordan argues convincingly for the specifically gendered aspect of Jefferson's position, arguing for a direct link between the Virginian Statesman's attitudes toward hierarchy, sex, and race: "Jefferson laid uncommonly great stress on the physical distinction between Negroes and whites. This emphasis derived partly from his emotional responses to women but also from a pervasive temperamental characteristic, a habit of mind not unconnected with his views of the opposite sex" (475; see also 461–69).

35. It is interesting that the similarity (and differences) between Jefferson's comments here, and those made by Benjamin Franklin some forty years earlier in *Observations Concerning the Increase of Mankind*: "And while we are, as I may call it, scouring our planet, by clearing the American woods, and so making this side of our globe reflect a brighter light to the eyes of inhabitants in Mars or Venus, why should we . . . darken our people? Why increase the Sons of Africa, by planting them in America, where we have so fair an opportunity, by excluding all blacks and tawneys, of increasing the lovely white and red?" (234).

36. Kenneth Burke argues that 'beauty' must be conceived as the site of a struggle, between a "situation and a strategy for confronting or encompassing that situation." Thus, as Lentricchia concludes, "beauty cannot be conceived monistically, but only dialectically as always an act in the world, always involved in the administration of political medicine" (see Lentricchia, *Social Change*, 156).

Chapter 2

1. As various scholars have noted, it is not until Anglo-Europeans were firmly committed to economic and geographic expansion overseas that they become interested in developing theories of "race." Both Jordan and Gossett comment extensively on the

development of Anglo racism toward Africans. Alden T. Vaughan discusses how the growing emphasis on Native American racial difference paved way for more aggressive Anglo-American territorial policies in "From White Man to Redskin: Changing Anglo-American Perceptions of the American Indians." Dorothy Hammond and Alta Jablow note a similar dynamic toward Africans in their study of British colonialism.

2. Currently Abdul JanMohamed and Homi Bhabha are debating the status of "ambivalence." See Homi K. Bhabha, "The Other Question — The Stereotype and Colonial Discourse" (18–36), and JanMohamed's "The Economy of Manichean Allegory" (esp. 59–61) for a sample of this debate.

3. For an excellent survey of early theories of the color of Africans, see Jordan's *White Over Black* (esp. "The Bodies of Men," 216–65).

4. This phrase has a history which further complicates Mather's use as a less-than-naive contradiction of his earlier argument. It alludes specifically to Jeremiah 13: 23 ("Can the Ethiop change his skin / or the leopard his spots? / No more can you do good / you who are schooled in evil"), a passage which suggestively links skin color to moral condition. Furthermore, according to Winthrop Jordan, "Elizabethan dramatists used the stock expression 'to wash an Ethiop white' as indicating sheer impossibility" (15). Yet it is also important to note, as Forrest G. Wood points out, that in its original context, this comment did *not* designate Ethiopians as being unworthy of redemption. Rather, during biblical times, the Ethiopian's dark skin functioned as a metaphor, but did not reflect on the state of his or her soul. This is an attitude, Wood further notes, that changed for the worse over the next ten centuries as both Christians and Muslims increasingly viewed dark skin as evidence of moral inferiority (see 50).

5. Abdul JanMohamed notes:

> [T]he dominant model of power- and interest-relations in all colonial societies is the manichean opposition between the putative superiority of the European and the supposed inferiority of the native. This axis in turn provides the central feature of the colonialist cognitive framework and colonialist literary representation: the manichean allegory — a field of diverse yet interchangeable positions between white and black, good and evil, superiority and inferiority. ("Economy," 63)

6. In the closing essay of *Mythologies*, Roland Barthes schematizes the semiological system of mythology through his explication of a cover on a copy of *The Paris Match*:

> On the cover, a young Negro in a French uniform is saluting, with his eyes uplifted, probably fixed on a fold of the tricolor. All this is the *meaning* of the picture. But, whether naively or not, I see very well what it signifies to me: that France is a great Empire, that all her sons, without any color discrimination, faithfully serve under her flag, and that there is no better answer to the detractors of an alleged colonialism than the zeal shown by this Negro in serving his so-called oppressors. (116)

In order for the final stage — "the presence of the signified through the signifier" that is myth — to occur successfully, the signifier must undergo a process of dehistoricizing and depoliticizing. It must become a form, argues Barthes, where "meaning leaves its contingency behind; it empties itself, it becomes impoverished, history evaporates, only the letter remains" (117). The negro soldier thus loses his individuality and his cultural identity. He becomes generic and exchangeable, an (almost) empty signifier in a system of communication, ready to be imbued with colonial meaning. Because of its prior emptying, the signifier becomes transparent to the signified; the saluting Negro *stands for* French imperialism.

7. We might also question the striking superficiality of Mather's plan. In a culture where religious profession was considered a deeply *intellectual* matter, and where

children were catechized only as a preamble to more extensive study in their adulthood, Mather's method—outlined at the end of the tract—is clearly either assuming that negroes can't learn much after all, or is lacking in real commitment to the enterprise.

8. Mather apparently names his slave after the Onesimus of Paul's Epistle to Philemon, wherein Paul converts the slave, and sends him back to his master. As Forrest G. Wood notes in his massive study of the racist structure of Christianity in America, the example of Onesimus is a perfect one for the "Bible-quoting slaveholder" (70).

9. See *Invasion of America*, where Francis Jennings argues that the so-called Indian Menace was, in fact, "a boomerang effect of the European Menace to the Indians" (37).

10. Gary Nash points out that the early eighteenth century saw an increase generally of colonial literature about Native Americans that was "linked by the basic assumption that the Indians' culture was worth examining on its own terms," this owing largely to the subsiding threat from Native Americans as their numbers decreased drastically from wars and disease.

11. For those natives who remain, the public *History* outlines an interesting course of action: subjugate them through trade—particularly of firearms. Thomas Morton may have been persecuted by the Puritans for selling rifles to the Indians, but Byrd insists that providing firearms is a *good* idea "because it makes them depend entirely on the English, not only for their Trade, but even for their subsistence" (116). Practically speaking, arrows are silent, and therefore more dangerous—unlike the noisy rifle shot, which alerts the unsuspecting colonist immediately.

12. Parrington discusses the social leveling associated with the lubberland in frontier literature in *Main Currents in American Thought: The Colonial Mind*, i:139–42. Richard Slotkin, in his study *Regeneration Through Violence*, provides a reading of Byrd's account of lubberland that, while similar in focus, diverges somewhat from my own (see 218–20).

Chapter 3

1. William Ellis argues that herein Cooper "instances what would be, in the nineteenth century, a central problem for the American novel . . . the unstable mixture of realism and uncritical, because abstract, 'romance'" (149).

2. Jane Tompkins's work on Cooper represents an important break from earlier critics who focus on the archetypal or psychological experience of the individual on the frontier. She argues in her essay "No Apologies for the Iroquois" that Cooper is a "profound thinker, one who was obsessively preoccupied not with the subtle workings of individual consciousness, but with the way the social world is organized," and also with exploring the dangers of sameness and difference within a given social order (99, 118). Tompkins urges us to see *The Last of the Mohicans* and similar works as "agents of social formation" (119).

Richard Slotkin's second major work, *The Fatal Environment*, is also an important contribution to sociopolitical studies of frontier novels and has provided an important springboard for my discussion in this chapter.

3. Ellis makes a comment in reference to Cooper's depictions of Anglos of differing classes that is similarly suggestive. Asserting that Cooper's most "despised characters are often his vivid ones," Ellis goes on to argue that what he is aiming for is

to identify a weakness in Cooper's work that has sometimes been taken as a virtue because it is "romance"—when I think it really is an unwillingness or inability to put certain ideals at risk by embodying them in credible characters who might invite an ambivalent response. That is why I have called the symbolic embodiments of these ideals [i.e., the protectors of "civilization"] ideological, or symbols of emotional safety. (149)

4. Homi Bhabha provides a helpful discussion of the flattening effect of colonial depictions of the Other, and its production of "a regime of truth, that is structurally similar to Realism," in "The Other Question . . . The Stereotype and Colonial Discourse" (23).

5. As Slotkin explains, "the Myth of the Frontier is the American version of the larger myth–ideological system generated by the social conflicts that attended the 'modernization' of the Western nations, the emergence of capitalist economies and nation states." The Metropolis—"the center of national life and activity"—was extended by each new Frontier, which "made possible a progressive improvement: an increase in wealth, and occasion for technological invention, a new source of productive resources, a new outlet for the production of the Metropolis itself" (see *Fatal Environment*, 33–36).

6. R. W. B. Lewis has said that Cooper's contribution to American literature was to bring the hero to life by taking him out of society ("the cities and cellars") and "putting him where he belonged—in space" (98). This comment may apply more accurately to a large portion of Cooper *criticism* (and frontier romance criticism in general) in this century. Beginning with D. H. Lawrence, who, utilizing a psychoanalytic approach, discussed the "dream world" and "wish fulfillment" dynamic of Cooper and his novels, criticism has tended to focus on the abstract, or interior psychological values of frontier romance that transcend immediate social concerns. Most often the action of the novel is considered a dramatic tableaux against which the individual plays out eternal conflicts and discovers absolute moral qualities. Lewis, for instance, discusses Cooper:

> The drama Cooper constructed for [his] actors on the spatial scene resulted from his trick of poising that scene upon the very brink of time. In the characteristic adventure of a Cooper novel . . . the personality of the Adamic hero is made to impinge upon the products of time: the villages lying a little inland . . . social institutions with their precedents and established practices; relationships inherited through the years. (99)

Society, however, is just what the heroic individual avoids, according to Lewis: "These are things the hero has to cope with in the course of his dramatic life, but which he must eventually stay clear of, if he is to remain faithful to the spatial vision" (100). In the "space" of the frontier, the Adamic hero must play out mythic conflicts, for instance, in *Nick*, where the Adamic, "innocent man of love" meets, and is transformed by a "collision with evil," becoming "the outraged Adam" (107–9).

All three novels fall under the rubric of Richard Chase's definitions of "romance," either the historical romance which follows the lead of the British Scott, or the darker, psychological strain of the genre which produced such an influence on Melville and Hawthorne (20). For Chase romance as a genre under either definition is ultimately anticultural. Instead it defers to larger truths: "the very abstractness and profundity of romance allow it to formulate moral truths of universal validity" (xi). Further, its characters "will not be complexly related to each other or to society or to the past. Human beings will on the whole be shown in ideal relation—that is, they will share emotions only after these have become abstract or symbolic" (13).

Leslie Fiedler rejects Chase's arguments in *Love and Death in the American Novel*. "To speak of a counter-tradition to the novel, of the tradition of 'the romance' as a force in our literature, is merely to repeat the rationalizations of our writers themselves; it is certainly to fail to be specific enough for real understanding" (29). Fiedler's view is more monolithic, but if his arguments differ from Chase's, the implications are much the same. American literature does not have counter strains, but is itself counter to the American social reality:

> Our fiction is not merely a flight from the physical data of the actual world, in search of a (sexless and dim) Ideal; from Charles Brockden Brown to William Faulkner or Eudora Welty . . . it is, bewilderingly and embarrassingly, a gothic fiction, nonrealistic and negative, sadist and melodramatic—a literature of darkness and grotesque in a land of light and affirmation. (29)

Fiedler, in his analysis of the bourgeois genre of the novel, discovers a "turning . . . from mythology to psychology, from a body of communal story to the mind of the individual" (40).

Fiedler acknowledges a concrete social reference for Chingachgook, as the embodiment of communal (white) guilt for the violence against Indians. The task of the Leatherstocking Tales, he argues, is precisely to exorcise that guilt (195). The contemporary value of the process is abstracted into the mythic: "The primitive, good or evil, Cooper never lets us forget is past history and a present dream" (199). In the end, and despite a nodding acknowledgement to the notion that Cooper might somehow have addressed a social conflict between two cultures, Fiedler discusses Cooper's Indians as symbolic interactants of a white psyche.

Influential critics like Lawrence, Lewis, Chase, and Fiedler have established what A. N. Nikolyukin calls a "subjective–idealistic conception of literary development— Freudian, mythic, existential, and so forth" (575), which persistently deflects attention from literature's social/material inception. Even when a critic begins with some attempt to foreground real social concerns, the pressure to abstract the discussion seems irresistible. Joel Porte, who pinpoints Cooper's racial consciousness as centrally "American," notes that "Cooper commenced his writing career at a point when the notion of race began to have special interest for an American writer" (8) during the Jacksonian era that saw Indian resettlement become national policy (and pastime). Yet Porte quickly sidesteps the issue of social reference by arguing that "the notion of race ultimately became for Cooper . . . a way of meditating on good and evil" (9). Thus Cooper does not mediate an actual social reality, but provides the artist with a means to contemplate the (universalized) Nature of Experience: "The American hero is simply facing his own duplex nature—the light and darkness within himself—and the duplex nature of experience generally" (10).

7. Philip Fisher notes that Cooper's *Deerslayer* (1840) appeared in a decade which "mark[ed] out the . . . plateau from which the structure of the American past [concerning Native Americans] was suddenly unmistakable." The same is obviously not as true of *The Last of the Mohicans*, appearing as it did before the great decade of Indian Removal.

8. Jane Tompkins observes that "the two key events in understanding American attitudes toward race relations during this period are the founding of the American Colonization Society in 1816 and Monroe's policy of Indian removal formulated in 1824" (110).

9. For example, there is Duncan Heyward in *The Last of the Mohicans,* and Mr. Matthews in *The Yemassee*, who, though currently living in the country, is clearly inexperienced and ignorant of its dangers, particularly the "habits" of its native inhabitants. Interestingly, the motif of the ignorant city dweller in frontier literature, especially in *The Last of the Mohicans* and *Nick of the Woods*, reverses the "country bumpkin" theme, producing a type of "city witling."

10. Bird ambiguously claims to recollect an actual story that corresponds to Na-

than's: "The author remembers, in the published journal of an old traveller—an Englishman, and, as he thinks, a Friend; but he cannot be certain of this fact, the name having escaped him and the loose memorandum he made at the time having been mislaid—who visited the region of the upper Ohio towards the close of the last century, an observation on this subject, which made too deep an impression easily to be forgotten" (34). Whether or not Bird fictionalized the event, his placement of the Slaughter family in the northern region of the Susquehanna Valley during this period is historically appropriate.

11. This exchange provides a fictional example of the Western scientific attitude V. Y. Mudimbe has described in his recent book as "epistemological ethnocentrism." In a fascinating analysis of Carl Sagan's commentary on Dogon astronomical knowledge, Mudimbe details the persistent qualities of the belief that "scientifically there is nothing to be learned from 'them' unless it is already 'ours' or comes from 'us'" (see 13–15).

12. What Pratt calls the "timeless present" is similar in concept to what Berkhofer calls the "ethnographic present" (see 29).

13. It is interesting that *The Yemassee*, with its attention to a hierarchy of attractiveness between and among the races, anticipates the racist phrenological and physiognomical scientific theories which were developed more fully later in the century, while *Nick of the Woods*, by associating Indians with children, prefigures late nineteenth-century recapitulationist theories of race (and gender) difference. For a discussion of these theories, see Gould, chapters 3 ("Measuring Heads") and 4 ("Measuring Bodies"), esp. 113–22.

14. Simms makes a similar comment, with a double emphasis (see 63, 244).

15. This strategy is mirrored in the title of Cooper's last Leatherstocking tale, *The Deerslayer*, where, as Fisher notes, "Cooper's title swerves away from direct announcement of its central matter" (35).

16. William Ellis has recently criticized Cooper on a slightly different basis. More than just ignoring the implications of Natty's social position, Cooper cannot see the "struggle of the gentry and its opponents in complex social, historical, and moral terms." His reliance on "romance" as a strategy becomes an evasive ideological devise for Cooper: "he came to see [the struggle] only in the simplistic terms of the romance, as Chase described them—an opposition of Manichean dichotomies and categorical alternatives" (147).

17. As Michael P. Rogin observes, "not the Indians alive, then, but their destruction, symbolized the American experience. The conquest of the Indian made the country uniquely American" ("Liberal Society," 137–38).

18. David Simpson argues that this ambivalence extends generally to all of Cooper's novels, which "speak for a consciousness divided by precisely the tension that informed so much of the theory and experience of the Jacksonian period, that between innocence and expansion" (154).

Chapter 4

1. In a careful analysis of one of Child's short stories, "Slavery's Pleasant Homes," Karcher documents the radical yet careful craft of Child ("Rape, Murder and Revenge"). In "Censorship American Style: The Case of Lydia Maria Child," Karcher examines the opposition Child met with from booksellers and publishers, and argues that while rejections of Child's manuscripts were often couched in terms of "public taste" and "demand," the motives for the dismissals were probably quite different. In a careful analysis of sales figures and correspondence, Karcher argues that, in fact,

Child's more radical work was fairly popular with the reading public, who frequently bought out what they could get—when they could get it. Rather, it was the *booksellers* who refused to promote the abolitionist works. The public, Karcher suggests, may have been "more receptive to radical views than the publishing industry" ("Censorship," 287). Looking closely at this phenomenon, Karcher documents the financial links between the publishers and booksellers and between Southern interests and pro-Southern interests in the North. She suggests that the publishers' concerns were more for "alienating powerful patrons rather than masses of readers, North or South" ("Censorship," 296). This pressure drove Child, who relied professionally and financially on her writing, to modify her work to meet the covert censorship of American presses.

2. To wit, a three-day national conference on "Race, Gender and Sentimentality" was held at Cornell University in 1990.

3. Similarly, Freibert and White conclude that frontier novels by women as well as by their male colleagues, "served as a form of expiation" (104).

4. Ann Douglass (Wood), in her 1971 article "The 'Scribbling Women' and Why They Wrote" apparently takes Sedgwick's disclaimers at face value, asserting that "in fact cooking was the only accomplishment of which [Sedgwick] admitted to being vain." But as Kelley's sensitive reading in *Private Woman, Public Stage* suggests, Sedgwick's relationship to her work was much more serious than she was comfortable admitting publicly—a fact that probably amplified her discontent as a female author in a male-dominated establishment. Kelley traces Sedgwick's anxiety throughout the testing period of each new book, and it becomes clear that Sedgwick took her writing and her reputation as author very seriously, despite her nonchalant assurances to family and friends (see esp. 199–206).

5. Qtd. in Walsh, 67. See also Kelley, *Private Woman*, 290.

6. As Sandra Zagarell notes, *Hope Leslie* "characterizes . . . the solidification of the Massachusetts Bay Colony, as being grounded in a legalistic patriarchy in which domestic and external policy—masculine dominance in the home, the obliteration of the Indians—are two sides of the same coin." Sedgwick thus demonstrates, as Zagarell incisively puts it, "that gynophobia gives way to genocide" ("Expanding America," 233, 237).

7. As Mary Kelley's notations to the Rutgers edition of *Hope Leslie* attest, Sedgwick read widely in preparation for her fictionalization of colonial New England, drawing apparently on diverse sources.

8. We should also note, as Zagarell has pointed out, that Sedgwick takes a sly dig at Cooper in naming Faith's Pequot husband: "Sedgwick knew from the Puritan histories she read, Uncas was *not* 'the last of the Mohicans,' and one of his sons was named Oneco" ("Expanding America," 239).

9. The political dimensions of Hope Leslie's behavior in this respect have often been overlooked, or sentimentalized by the novel's critics. Michael Davitt Bell's analysis of *Hope Leslie* characterizes the novel's heroine as thoroughly "conventional," used by Sedgwick in a "conventional" way to personify her "view of the essential movement of American history." Gossett and Bardes counter astutely that Bell's formulation is limited in that it fails to "consider what it means to embody the spirit of American history in a woman who breaks laws" (29, n.29). They argue that Hope Leslie's illegal actions speak powerfully to the fact that "a woman may be driven by her sense of political powerlessness to undertake civil disobedience" (21).

10. As Mary Kelley notes, the epigraph is taken from John Robinson, quoted in William Bradford's *History of Plymouth Plantation* ("Introduction," 41, 357).

11. Shirley Samuels, private correspondence to the author, September 12, 1989.

12. As Christopher Castiglia observes, "Sedgwick extends the subversion of male myth/history" by showing the two to be "indistinguishable" (12).

13. It might be plausible to argue that Sedgwick is proposing simply to reverse the historical record, to replace one voice with another, rather than to create a dialogue. I would point out, however, that the quoted sentence is attributed to Everell, who's been "touched" by Magawisca and whose position is obviously partial at this point. Rather, I think Sedgwick's larger point is that *any* version is an interested version; thus the inherent necessity of constructing history out of a dialogue.

14. In a carefully argued analysis of "Sentimental Liberalism and the Problem of Race in *Huckleberry Finn*," Gregg Camfield traces "how sentimentalists wished to define . . . that slippery term 'realism.'" What that meant for philosophers of sentiment like Thomas Hume and Adam Smith was, argues Camfield, a kind of "psychological mimesis," which could be "no more than felt through the power of sympathetic imagination, a human power superior to logos." Camfield's ultimate point—that the sentimentalists were subscribers to a type of realism, but one defined much differently from our contemporary understanding of it—supports the metahistorical suggestions made by Sedgwick's narrator in this section: the emotionally authentic perspective of the victim of persecution provides the truer, more sympathetically realistic history.

15. See Todorov, section 3, "Love" (*Conquest*, 127–67). Deborah Root analyzes incisively the imperialist implications of Todorov's own argument in her article "The Imperial Signifier: Todorov and the Conquest of Mexico." Root argues that "Todorov would maintain the Aztec radical 'Otherness' to serve a pedagogy cleansed of imperialism," which, rather than *neutralizing* difference, depoliticizes it. As a result, Todorov becomes uncritical of his own reductive generalizations and the ways in which his own analysis reduplicates and perpetuates colonialist discourse, particularly in its desire to master and silence the racial Other: "Despite Todorov's claim to have engaged in a dialogue with the Other (and to have expressed a neutral acceptance of difference and a recognition of equality), in *The Conquest of America*, the voice of the Other is evoked only to be, again, silenced" (197, 219). In this way it would seem that Todorov's own analysis of the "prejudice of equality" might be suggestive in terms of his own work.

Todorov obliquely defends his stance in "'Race,' Writing and Culture." Here he clarifies his position that "whereas racism is a well-attested phenomenon, 'race' itself does not exist." His focus is rather the attribution of *cultural* differences to "race" and the difficulties of assessing the importance and import of cultural difference:

> Racialism has affinities both with relativism and with universalism. . . . The excessive universalism takes the form of refusing cultural differences in the name of the unicity of the human species and the diversity of individuals. We are so busy battling stereotypes . . . that we end up refusing these Others any specificity at all. . . . The restricted universality of the past should be opened up as much as possible, until it is able to account for both the diversity of cultures and the differences which exist within one and the same culture. (*Conquest*, 174–75)

Collette Guillaumin finds such a stance, however generously intended, problematic. She argues that an "anti-racist" position, which uses as its "central argument culture and the right to cultural identity, is not so far removed from what it counterposes. This position, she argues, still means "postulating some being specific to human groups, and it is of minor importance whether that being is to be encouraged or saved: the fact remains that groups are being regarded in light of essences and not relationships" (63–64). Hazel Carby would agree: "Culture is the terrain of struggle *between* groups . . . there is no whole, authentic, autonomous black culture which lies outside of these relations of cultural power and domination ("The Canon," 43).

16. Of course we must also note that her most heroic action serves to save her

beloved for Hope Leslie. Furthermore, while her "symbolic act of liberation," as Castiglia observes, "is brutally ritualized here by the literal loss of the site of control"—her arm—Hope Leslie's parallel action of sucking the venom from Craddock's snakebite is powerfully liberatory *without* physical penalty (11–12).

17. As Castiglia observes, the entire thrust of the novel establishes Hope herself as an alternative to this paradigm: "Sedgwick creates a heroine who can dwell in the wilderness without becoming a 'rugged' (i.e., racist, misogynistic, antisocial) individualist, but can also enjoy the best of nineteenth-century domesticity without becoming, in Barbara Welter's words, a 'hostage in the house'" (5).

18. *Vacuum domicilium*, a justificatory principle for British dominion, argued that the colonialists had a right to any lands left agriculturally undeveloped by the Native Americans. For a characteristic discussion, see John Winthrop's "Reasons to Be Considered for Justifying the Undertakers of the Intended Plantation in New England . . . ," (420–25).

19. The narrative shortly after notes the "little garden patches" of "the savages," in which were planted "beans, pumpkins and squashes; the seeds of the vegetables, according to an Indian tradition, (in which we may perceive the usual admixture of fable and truth,) having been sent to them, in the bill of a bird, from the south-west, by the Great Spirit" (86). Here again we see the careful maintenance of what Edward Said has termed "positional superiority"—through which the Anglo-American can contradict herself without surrendering the position of authority.

20. I am of course referring to Annette Kolodny's important work, *The Land Before Her*, in which Kolodny explores the less aggressive and heretofore ignored visions of frontier women, who projected garden, rather than rape and conquest metaphors onto the American wilderness. In her preface Kolodny observes that "I have long ceased to lament the absence of adventurous conquest in women's fantasies before 1860 and have come now to regret men's incapacity to fantasize tending the garden" (xiii).

21. As Carolyn Karcher notes, Child's argument against all kinds of racial discrimination, including antimiscegenation laws, was a bold move for a woman in the nineteenth century and signaled her continuing commitment to "avant-garde ideas about race and gender" ("Rape, Murder and Revenge," 324).

22. *Romance* is in fact so little noted that it is frequently overlooked altogether. Neither the *Cambridge Handbook of American Literature* (1986) nor *The Columbia Literary History of the United States* (1988) acknowledges the novel in its summary of Child's work. Nina Baym, who was responsible for the section in the *Columbia History* on nineteenth-century women writers, seems entirely unaware of the book's existence. She neglects to mention it in her study of *Woman's Fiction*, and in her *Columbia History* essay "The Rise of the Woman Author" states that after *Hobomok*, Child "wrote only two more novels," *The Rebels* (1825) and *Philothea* (1836, 294). Nor does Patricia G. Holland, in her essay on "Lydia Maria Child as a Professional Author," find the book worth any extended mention. Aside from an important new essay by Karcher (1989), there is very little critical comment on the work. Alexander Cowie mentions it in his *Rise of the American Novel*, arguing that the book "should logically have been her best fiction" but that, suffering in "the hampering grip of propaganda" the novelist could not "emancipate her fictional characters from ideological bondage" (182). In a somewhat more extended analysis, William S. Osgood arrives at similar conclusion. He professes to be surprised "that a woman of Mrs. Child's intellect did not adapt her 'novel-making' to current literary tastes" (145). Arguing that "the material for a realistic story was present in Child's novel," Osgood complains that Child "chose to

package it with sentiment and suspense . . . [and] preferred to embellish real life, thereby magnifying the story out of proportion" (145). The reviewers, as Osgood notes in conclusion, ignored the work, and rightly so as Child neglected her opportunity, as he asserts, to "comment frankly on the world around her," and fails therefore to 'discharge the universal debt . . . [of] making useful books'" (158). Notably, both scholars criticize Child for *not* pandering to the public taste, the reverse of the charge leveled against sentimental or domestic writers of the preceding decades.

23. It is likely, as Karcher points out, that many of the innovations in *A Romance* from Child's earlier works come as a result of her attention to African American writers like Jacobs, and William Wells Brown. See Karcher, "Romance," 84–88.

24. As I completed the original draft of this chapter, Karcher's excellent article on *Romance* appeared in *Slavery and the Literary Imagination* (1989). In it Karcher focuses on Child's use of miscegenation in the novel, and the visions and limitations of its critique of racial prejudice. Having been so influenced by her earlier work on Child, as well as on Melville and issues of race, I was not surprised to discover that while our approaches to the novel differ significantly, many of our conclusions about its strengths and limitations are the same.

25. Laws in Louisiana, as in most slave states, proscribed the legality of any marriages entered into between slaves and Anglo-Americans.

26. Karcher notes how Child turns away from the more visionary possibility of an egalitarian marriage hinted at between King and Rosa, instead allowing King to dominate their marriage as well as the second half of the novel's plot. That being so, there is yet a glimmer of a conscious critique of King. Certain suggestive comments might be construed as an indictment of King, along with the other male characters (Bright perhaps excepted), in the dominative structure of patriarchy that seems even less likely to be defeated than racial prejudice. King's connotative connection to Royal is suggested in the way each describes his awakening love for Eulalia and Rosa, both first being attracted through "fascination of the senses" and only later noting the "true womanhood" embodied in the object of their affection (see 19 and 170). King, it should also be noted, after "gazing" approvingly on Rosa's "peculiar" complexion (9), abandons any romantic dreams of her immediately after reflecting on the prejudiced attitude of his "good mother." Blaming his own reluctance on his mother, King will later in the novel, after learning of Fitzgerald's clandestine purchase of the two girls, reflect despairingly, "[O], what would he not have given for such an opportunity as Fitzgerald had!" (169). When he finally does marry Rosa, he indicates his willingness to respect her own designs for her life. But after a lapse of years, when the two reappear, King dominates the relationship as unambiguously as did Fitzgerald. Child's failure to portray an alternative to a paternalistic marriage—consciously or unconsciously—certainly signals the resilience of patriarchy and a gloomy assessment for women in the postbellum United States.

27. Notably, in locating this scene's sentimentality in Blumenthal, *A Romance* makes it very clear that sentiment is not the sole province of women.

28. This point becomes even clearer when, later in the novel, we learn that Bruteman deliberately destroys Tulee's legally obtained "free papers" in order to sell her for a profit.

29. For a full range of examples extracted from pamphlets and newspapers of unfortunate "white" slaves, see Child's 1860 tract.

30. But, as Karcher astutely notes, while the slave spiritual sung in the final tableaux documents growing white middle-class interest in African American oral culture, the fact that Child "chose to have the slaves sing not a song of their own composing

but the pale imitation a white poet had produced of one, testifies starkly to the stranglehold that the genteel canons of white middle-class culture continued to exert on her imagination" (*Romance*, 99).

31. See note 22 in this chapter.

Chapter 5

1. Paul Rosenzweig notes that "most seem unable to resist the lure of ascribing an illuminating meaning to both the figure and ending" ("Dust," 137). Conclusions vary on the meaning of Pym, and any summary would be lengthy, so a quick categorization must suffice here. By far the most thoughtful and extended analysis of *Pym* is John Irwin's nearly two-hundred-page treatment in *American Hieroglyphics*. Here he considers Pym as a metaphysical exploration of the relation of being, knowledge, and death. For analyses of *Pym* as death wish, see William Peden; as hoax: David Ketterer ("Singular *Narrative*"; *Rationale*), Richard Kopley, J. V. Ridgely; as bildungsroman/mythic journey: Leonard W. Engel, Roger Forclaz, Richard Levine, Kathleen Sands, John Stroupe, Grace Farrell Lee; as metaphor of artistic process: Daniel Wells; as metaphysical negation: Paul Rosenzweig ("Search"), Joel Porte; as metaphysical affirmation: Curtis Fukuchi; as metacommentary on origin of reading/writing: Jean Ricardou, J. Gerald Kennedy (*Poe*), Dennis Pahl, Michael J. S. Williams; as social satire: Evelyn J. Hinz, Hinz and Teunissen, J. Gerald Kennedy ("Preface as Key"); as social commentary: Harry Levine, Sydney J. Kaplan ("*Pym*"), Edwin Fussell, Eric Mottram; as psychoanalytic treatment: Marie Buonaparte, Leslie Fiedler; as epistemological search for knowledge: Paul John Eakin, John Carlos Rowe, Joan Dayan, A. Robert Lee; as epistemological negation of knowledge: Paul Rosenzweig ("Dust"). For a more thorough consideration of trends in criticism on Poe, see Douglas Robinson's useful article.

2. Many thanks to Professor Bernard Rosenthal for extensive personal correspondence outlining the history of the controversy since the publication of his essay in 1974.

3. As JanMohamed explains, "The 'imaginary' is a preverbal order, essentially visual, that precedes the 'symbolic,' or verbal, order" ("Economy," 86, n.15).

4. I should note here that my focus on science differs significantly from Limon, who is less concerned with the social context of the science and Poe's attention to it than with Poe's career-long relationship to philosophies of science, and his attempt to position himself as writer within an increasingly professionalized scientific discourse.

5. It is important to note that the year of *Pym*'s publication coincides with the beginning of the U.S. Exploring Expedition (1838–42). Led by Charles Wilkes, the project would survey and chart hundreds of Pacific Islands, the Oregon territory, and the coast of Antarctica. As the recent Smithsonian exhibit booklet points out, the expedition "helped to establish the natural sciences as professions in America." (Many thanks to Nancy Bentley for sending this information to me.)

6. Pym's account here bears striking similarities to the narrative strategy that Mary Campbell uncovers in Columbus's *Letter to Sanchez*. Tracing the tradition of romance that undergirds Columbus's perceptions and his narrative of what he sees, Campbell notes that Columbus "praises [the natives'] virtue and generosity and innocence with the hand that writes romance, and with the other includes them in the *Letter*'s closing list of the islands' commodities, between wood and rhubarb" (184–86).

7. Sydney Kaplan, for one, is convinced that *Pym* is a record of Poe's intention to defend slavery:

In the decade of the founding of Garrison's *Liberator*, of Nat Turner's conspiracy, of the formation of the American Anti-Slavery Society, of Theodore Weld's *The Bible Against Slavery*, he felt called upon to say a more basic piece—to show that slavemasters "violated no law divine or human" to defend the pigmentocracy in his own way. . . . It was the "will of God" that Poe tried to present in his allegory of black and white at the end of *Pym*. ("*Pym*," 163)

8. Many readers have uncritically made this mistake. The comments of John Stroupe indicate the general trend of such analyses: "Pym does not die, and it is not necessary that he die to escape the savages of Tsalal, who are black (i.e., evil). . . . Thus, if the Tsalalians do not only appear evil, but are evil, then, by contrast, the white figure who destroys the savage is a representative of good—an affirmation. Perhaps Poe is suggesting that Pym comes to an affirmation of life through the confronting of evil . . . " (320). Similarly, Fukuchi observes that the "Tsalalians exemplify greed and primitive ignorance [and] are condemned to live in darkness" (155), while Richard Levine comments that "Tsalal is the island of blackness, the sphere of total depravity. The island is strange and the natives exist on an animal level . . . depraved individuals whose very teeth are black" (31). By the same standard, critics like Joseph Moldenhauer characterize Dirk Peters as "an important embodiment of the perverse, dramatizing the imp in all its ambiguity" (269).

9. Christopher Miller's analysis of a French explorational story, "Brief history of the navigations of M. Jehan Prunaut of Rouen to the land of said blacks and the colloquy of their language," is strikingly relevant to this section of Pym's narrative. Says Miller: "The text is a mercantilist dream, with blackness, nudity, fear and difference in general offset by the presence of 'precious commodities' and the formation of an alliance *by the desire of the natives*" (50–51; Miller's emphasis).

10. Burton Pollin, in his impressive annotation of *Pym*, suggests that "perhaps Poe had vaguely intended to revise in earlier portions Peters' Indian ancestry and neglected to do so" (355, n.21, 7B). He elaborates in his introduction that "the instinctive workmanship of Poe . . . prevented him from constructing an entirely artless book" but that "without question, in style *Pym* is Poe's least careful, least polished work (14, 12).

11. It is important to observe, as J. Gerald Kennedy points out, that Pym himself does not make this connection explicitly in his narrative. Like the crew's oversight of the tribal respect for wood and trees, Pym's mistake, notes Kennedy, "in classifying the objects [e.g., sails, egg, open book] as 'harmless' rather than white has far-reaching consequences" (*Poe*, 168).

12. Sydney Kaplan's introduction to *Pym* provides an informative discussion of John Cleve Symmes's theory of a habitable space inside the earth and a psuedonymously authored novel, *Symzonia*, which detailed a perfect and perfectly white race of people who inhabited the South Pole. Both were probably important influences for *Pym*. See 150–52.

13. Christopher Miller carefully traces this general confusion and collapse in Western racial discourse. As he notes, "the history of Africanist writing is the history of the collapsing-together of black and white—of their inability to remain as meaningful opposites—and the frustration of meanings attached to them" (30). Calling to mind the "resolution" of Pym's narrative, Miller further observes that the semiotic meeting point of "black" and "white" is in the "void," where they also in fact, reverse: "if white is an empty fullness (fully luminous but *void*), then black is a full emptiness (*total* absence). Both are *blank*, absent, the null set of color" (31).

14. See Pollin, "Poe's *Narrative*," "Three Notices," and particularly "Pym's *Narrative*," in which Pollin queries, "Considering the total two dozen American reviews by

now found and recorded, the question again arises: Why did Harper and Brothers have to acknowledge that their sales of so promising a book by so 'accomplished' writer were so low?" (10).

Chapter 6

1. Matthiessen pays only brief notice to "Benito Cereno." Although he regards it highly ("one of the most sensitively poised pieces of writing [Melville] had ever done" [373]), he faults Melville for a certain naiveté in his "theatrically" drawn slaves: "Although the Negroes were savagely vindictive and drove a terror of blackness into Cereno's heart, the fact remains that they were slaves and that evil had thus originally been done to them. Melville's failure to reckon with this fact within the limits of his narrative makes its tragedy" (508). Seven years after Matthiessen's comments, Charles Neider argued that in altering Delano's actual account of the mutiny, "Melville glosses over extenuating circumstances in his effort to blacken the blacks and whiten the whites, to create poetic images of pure evil and pure virtue" (10).

In 1962 Sidney Kaplan was to formulate this position most explicitly in response to the question he posed for himself: "What did Melville mean?" ("Benito Cereno," 16). For Kaplan, "Benito Cereno" represents a regression from Melville's earlier, more liberal and humane stance on racial issues. "The reverse symbolism of *Moby Dick*, it must be concluded, is simply not present in 'Benito Cereno.' . . . [L]ooked at objectively, the tale seems a plummet-like drop from the unconditionally democratic peaks of *White Jacket* and *Moby Dick*" (23). For a time Kaplan's arguments seemed powerful enough to persuade Joseph Schiffman, who had earlier argued for "Benito Cereno" as a condemnation of slavery (1950). In his 1962 introduction to "Benito Cereno" in *Three Shorter Novels of Herman Melville*, Schiffman equivocates on his earlier stand, concluding that "in highlighting the savagery of the rebellion, Melville sullied his tale with racism—an element which detracts from the stature of 'Benito Cereno'" (235).

In her exhaustive study of Melville's attitudes toward race and slavery, Carolyn Karcher argues that "Benito Cereno" is foremost "an exploration of the white racist mind and how it reacts in face of a slave insurrection" (*Shadow*, 128). She takes up Joseph Schiffman's suggestion in 1950 that "'Benito Cereno' as a story flows from two sources: first from Don Alexandro's mistaken belief that his slaves were tractable, and, second, from Delano's inability to perceive that a slave rebellion was occurring under his very eyes. . . . In depicting the short-sightedness of those who thought slavery was acceptable to other people, Melville was condemning slavery" (321). Karcher, discovering a deep ambivalence in Melville, carefully qualifies her own conclusions: "While disputing the claim of some critics, that Melville champions the cause of slave revolt in 'Benito Cereno,' one can nevertheless exonerate him from the charges of racism that others have leveled at him for having exhibited slave revolt in such an appalling light" (143). Scholars since have generally accepted and followed Karcher's careful historical and contextual analysis. Charles Swann's recent work ("Whodunnit?", "'Benito Cereno'") tackles the issue again, qualifying the findings of both Kaplan and Karcher. He finds that Melville "deconstructs" his racist readers, "unmasks by unbalancing the ideology" of racism ("'Benito Cereno,'" 10). "The more the Southern reader accepts Melville's picture of the blacks—that the smiles of servitude may be masks and that one cannot tell the difference—the more unstable his world picture becomes and the more destabilizing Melville's seeming assent to the dark part of that divided world picture" (12). While "Benito Cereno" is not a radical gesture, Swann concludes, it is a "nudge in the right direction." Two books provide a representative sample of this debate through 1964: *Melville's "Benito Cereno,"* John P. Runden, ed. (1965); and *A "Benito Cereno" Handbook*, Seymour L. Gross, ed. (1965).

2. For a very different reading of epistemology in "Benito Cereno," see Nancy Roundy.

3. Marvin Fisher has called "Benito Cereno" a "remarkable study of the problems of perception" ("'Benito Cereno,'" 31). Recent scholars have attempted to understand the basis for Delano's obviously limited perceptions. Thomas Zlatic describes a naive if obtuse Delano, who "is faithful and has confidence in an optimistic and rational view of an orderly and beneficent universe," whose consequent "faith makes him incredulous of anything which does not conform to that view" (335). For Zlatic, then, Delano "is not mercenary nor ruthless, but he nonetheless exploits the docility of the blacks, not so much for monetary gain but for corroboration of his moral and metaphysical outlook" (339). Emery sees Delano's perceptual strategies somewhat differently as the embodiment of "the interventionism of mid-century Americans," describing him as "jaunt[y]" and "bold" and motivated finally by "a simple desire for financial gain" (53–54). Sandra Zagarell expands Emery's reading of Delano in her analysis of Delano's ahistorical and apolitical ideology. "Elaborating a complex ideology, [the story] also dramatizes the epistemological fancy footwork Delano must perform in order *not* to understand what is amiss on the San Dominick" ("Reenvisioning America," 246). In rewriting Delano's *Narrative*, Zagarell argues, Melville "reverses the real Delano's portrait of himself as a moral innocent, recasting him as a minor originator of the self-celebrating hypocrisy that allowed Americans to think themselves historically unique" (247).

4. See note 6 in chapter 2.

5. Ironically, Delano relies on a conceptual strategy that opposes white to black in a power play without considering the logical extension of his metaphor, that the black side too must have a king contesting for dominance.

6. We might note at this point how the narrator's description of Delano's equitable distribution of water on the *San Dominick* ("he complied, with republican impartiality as to this republican element, which always seeks one level, serving the oldest white no better than the youngest black") is qualified, not only by Delano's reserving more water for Don Benito ("whose condition, if not rank, demanded an extra allowance"), but by his reserving the best of the food, not just for Don Benito, but for "the whites" more generally (see 275).

7. His situation is much like that of a rape victim, as Sandra Zagarell astutely observes ("Reenvisioning America," 251).

8. While Vanderbilt offers an interesting argument, I must state that I have profound reservations about his conclusion, that the point of the story is the "merging intimacy and identity" between oppressor and oppressed (316), that through their actions on the *San Dominick*, the slaves implicate themselves in the same structure of domination and oppression as that which they seek to overthrow. Superficially this conclusion seems sound, but to find slaves therefore complicit in their slavery (or the slavery of history, see 319) is a process of rationalization much like that seen in the court documents of "Benito Cereno," where the voice of the blacks is credited only where it indicts them. It seems much more to the point to historicize the motives for action on either side; where the whites in the story act clearly for economic gain, the blacks strike from a very different motive: they desperately want their freedom.

9. We might also speculate that in this usage, as just previously, "negroes" is intended to refer only to the male members of that group, in contrast to "negresses,"

thereby allowing the male slaves to confirm their subjectivity over the females (who are thereby doubly silenced) by voicing their condemnation.

10. Commentators have long marked Melville's "realistic" approach, which refuses simple resolution (see, for instance, Miller and Phillips in Gross). More recently critics have studied Melville's text less for its stylistic than for its epistemological implications. Edgar Dryden observes that "if the theme of 'Benito Cereno' is in part the fictitiousness of social, political, and religious forms, its method is a demonstration of the illusory nature of the architectonic fiction. As the limited point of view in the first part of the story reveals, the intricacies of human life can never be revealed by the carefully rounded and self-contained fiction . . . the subversive nature of truth forces all meaningful fictions to end in 'disappointing sequels'" (208–9). Both Zagarell and Emery elaborate on Melville's historic vision, which was "less pleasantly 'progressive,' more grimly repetitious" (Emery, 67). Vanderbilt concurs that in the end, the vision of "Benito Cereno" does not transcend to an alternative strategy, but "coils endlessly" on "inquisitorial" violence and oppression (322). David Leverenz concurs: "The really disorienting malice of the story exposes the drive for dominance in all human relations, and the presumption of dominance in narration itself" (95). Karcher's observation that Melville was "as tragically paralyzed as most of his contemporaries in the face of the nation's most pressing moral and political dilemma" (*Shadow*, 143) certainly applies to the narrator of "Benito Cereno."

11. My arguments about the narrator's dilemma coincide with those that Cheyfitz makes about the paralysis that dominates U.S. political and cultural attitudes today:

> Those of us who live within the privilege of Western patriarchy live in an increasingly narrow psychic and social space. For we cannot afford to enter most of the social spaces of the world; they have become dangerous to us, filled with the violence of the people we oppress, our own violence in alien forms we refuse to recognize. And we can afford less and less to think of these social spaces, to imagine the languages of their protest, for such imagining would keep us in continual conflict, in continual contradiction within ourselves, where we are increasingly locked away in comfort. Terrorizing the world with our wealth and power, we live in a world of terror, afraid to venture out, afraid to think openly. Difference and dialogue are impossible here. We talk to ourselves about ourselves, believing in a grand hallucination that we are talking with others. (xiv)

Chapter 7

1. As Patterson explains, "[T]he counterpart of the master's sense of honor is the slave's experience of its loss. The so-called servile personality is merely the outward expression of this loss of honor" (11–12). In this formulation we must also understand, as Patterson continues, that "there is absolutely no evidence from the long and dismal annals of slavery to suggest that any group of slaves ever internalized the conception of degradation held by their masters. To be dishonored—and to sense, however acutely, such dishonor—is not to lose the quintessential human urge to participate, and to want a place" (97).

2. Katharine Fishburn observes that "a woman who is a 'lady' is no longer an individual human being; she is an idea . . . [and] like the lady, the sexual black woman was a myth, an object" (10). As she points out, either way women's identities were conflated with their biology: "whereas the [white] lady was deprived of her sexuality, the black woman was identified with hers" (11).

3. I mean this term "positive objectification" only as a conceptual handle. Of course *no* objectification is good, but it is important to be able to differentiate here in order to understand what was at stake for different groups of women.

4. The term is used by Gloria Wade-Gayles. As she elaborates:

Unlike other groups in white America, black women are twice burdened. Because they are *black*, they are denied the pedestals and petticoated privileges a racist and sexist society assumes to be appropriate "gifts" for women. Because they are *women*, they are denied the power and influence men enjoy as the "natural" (or God-decreed) heads of families and leaders of nations. Black women are thus confined to both the narrow space of race and the dark enclosure of sex. This "double jeopardy" has created a complex, painful, and dehumanizing reality in which they have struggled for both freedom and selfhood. (4)

5. Conversely, as scholars like Karcher have observed, the "white" face of slave women was employed in abolitionist fiction as a marker of their increased worthiness to be treated with the privileges of True Womanhood.

6. Yellin notes here that "Jacobs's narrator does not characterize herself conventionally as a passive female victim, but asserts that—even when young and a slave—she was an effective moral agent" ("Introduction," *Incidents*, xxx). And as Carby observes, "*Incidents* entered the field of women's literature and history transforming and transcending the central paradigm of death versus virtue. The consequences of the loss of innocence, Linda Brent's (and Jacobs's) children, rather than being presented as the fruits of her shame, were her links to life and the motivating force of an additional determination to be free" (*Reconstructing Womanhood*, 59).

7. See also Valerie Smith's discussion of Jacobs's narrative in *Self-Discovery and Authority in Afro-American Narrative*. Smith observes that despite the limitations imposed by Jacobs's use of the sentimental novel and her address of a white audience, "yet she seized authority over her literary restraints in much the same way that she seized power in her life" (28).

8. This need of the slave master to see his mastery recognized by the slave may provide a point of resistance against slavery, but it does not, as Hegel implies, create what Patterson terms an "existential impasse" for the master. The master's Subjectivity was most fully confirmed, as Patterson notes and my previous chapter carefully delineates, by other masters. But the psychology of "mastery" is certainly both frail and complex, and the dynamic between Linda and Flint, as Jacobs depicts it here, is one that certainly existed and is worth examining for its implications (see Patterson, 99).

9. We must note that her triumph here is by no means total. Later in the narrative, when Sands buys Willie and Ellen, promising to free them, his actions bespeak a different purpose, and Linda laments: "So, then, after all I had endured for their sakes, my poor children were between two fires; between my old master and their new master! And I was powerless" (138).

10. The role of this interracial "sisterhood," both in a general historical sense, and as suggested in this particular text, is a hotly debated issue among scholars of women's history and literature. Gloria Wade-Gayles sees a "problematic assumption" in a recent "tendency to see black and white women as 'sisters' in oppression." She elaborates on this general issue:

The difficulties here are obvious. White women have participated actively, and without coercion, in the oppression of black men and women. They have been "ladies" who lived in leisure because black women have been "mammies." They have been protected and pampered, while black women have been dehumanized, brutalized and devalued as blacks and as females. . . . White women were victims of the peculiar institution of slavery, but they were beneficiaries as well, and it is as beneficiaries that black women see them. (9)

Many recent *Incidents* scholars have argued that Linda's perspective is coincident with Wade-Gayles' conclusion: as a black woman, Linda (and Jacobs) does not see (and perhaps does not hope for) a "sisterhood" between the white and black women in the novel. For example, Minrose Gwinn argues that *Incidents* is a "vehicle of rage directed toward her former mistress," in which "Jacobs flogs her powerless former mistress over and over throughout her narrative" (65). In her analysis of *Incidents*, Hazel Carby argues that "many of the relationships portrayed between Linda Brent and white women involve cruelty and betrayal . . . Jacobs's appeal was to a potential rather than an actual bonding between white and black women" (*Reconstructing Womanhood*, 51). Most recently, in a reading of "black and white women in the old South," Elizabeth Fox-Genovese has used *Incidents* to confirm her argument that "slave women did not see their mistresses as oppressed sisters" (48; see epilogue).

bell hooks, however, suggests that the perspectives of black feminist scholars like Wade-Gayles, Gwinn, and Carby come out of the social context of the 1960s, where black women, from both choice and a sense of exclusion, turned against the largely white feminist movement and focused on race oppression. hooks points out that,

> unlike us, black women in 19th century America . . . participated in both the struggle for racial equality and the women's rights movement. When the question was raised as to whether or not black female participation in the women's rights movement was a detriment to the struggle for racial equality, they argued that any improvement in the social status of black women would benefit all black people. (*Ain't I A Woman*, 2)

Jean Fagin Yellin, a scholar who has extensively researched Harriet Jacobs' life, and has recently edited a new edition of *Incidents*, concurs with hooks's analysis. She argues that a vision of interracial sisterhood is the focus of *Incidents*: "A central pattern in *Incidents* shows white women betraying allegiances of race and class to assert their stronger allegiance to the sisterhood of all women" ("Introduction," *Incidents*, xxxiii). William Andrews also agrees: "*Incidents* . . . was written as much to assert the power and potential of women's community in the South and the North as to denounce the state of commonage under which all resided under . . . slavery" (254).

11. Jacobs is even more explicit in suggesting the complicity of Northerners (particularly male) elsewhere. She accuses Northerners generally of being willing to play "bloodhounds" in chasing down escaped slaves (35–36, 44), and she comments on how Northern men are willing both to "give their daughters in marriage to slaveholders" and to become the most avid of slaveholders themselves, turning into "proverbially the hardest masters" (35, 44).

12. I am indebted for this idea to Karen Sanchez-Eppler and Laura Wexler, with whom I shared a stimulating discussion of *Incidents* at the Cornell Sentimentality Conference in February 1990. Their comments challenged me to rethink my arguments about this text in important ways. My particular thanks go to Sanchez-Eppler, who mailed me a copy of her chapter on *Incidents* from her unpublished manuscript.

Bibliography

Primary Sources

Bird, Robert Montgomery. *Nick of the Woods* (1837). New Haven, Conn.: New College and Univ. Press, 1967.

Byrd, William. *Histories of the Dividing Line Betwixt Virginia and North Carolina* (1841, 1929). Rpt. New York: Dover, 1967.

Child, Lydia Maria Francis. *A Romance of the Republic*. Boston: Ticknor and Fields, 1867; rpt. Florida: Mnenosyne, 1969.

———. *The Patriarchal Institution, As Described by Members of Its Own Family*. New York: Anti-Slavery Society, 1860.

———. *Selected Letters, 1817–1880*. Ed. Milton Meltzer and Patricia G. Holland. Amherst: Univ. of Massachusetts Press, 1982.

Cooper, James Fenimore. *The Last of the Mohicans*. Ed. Richard Slotkin. New York: Penguin, 1986.

Cotton, John. "God's Promise to His Plantations" (London, 1630). Rpt. in *Old South Leaflets*, ser. 1, no. 53. New York: Burt Franklin, 1883.

Emerson, Ralph Waldo. "Nature." In *Ralph Waldo Emerson: Selected Prose and Poetry*. New York: Holt, Rinehart and Winston, 1950.

Franklin, Benjamin. "Observations Concerning the Increase of Mankind and the Peopling of Countries" (1751). In *The Complete Works of Benjamin Franklin*. Ed. John Bigelow. Vol. 2. New York: Putnam's, 1887.

Hall, James. *Tales of the Border*. Philadelphia: H. Hall, 1835.

Jacobs, Harriet Ann. *Incidents in the Life of a Slave Girl* (1861). Ed. Jean Fagin Yellin. Cambridge, Mass.: Harvard Univ. Press, 1987.

Jefferson, Thomas. *Notes on the State of Virginia*. Ed. William Peyden. Chapel Hill: Univ. of North Carolina Press, 1955.

Mason, John. *A Brief History of the Pequot War*. Boston, 1736; rpt. in *History of the Pequot War: The Contemporary Accounts of Mason, Underhill, Vincent and Gardener*. Ed. Charles Orr. Cleveland: Helman-Taylor, 1897.

Mather, Cotton. *Bonifacius: An Essay to Do Good* (1710). Gainesville, Fl.: Scholars' Facsimiles and Reprints, 1967.

_____. *Diary of Cotton Mather*. Vol. I (1681–1709). New York: Frederick Ungar Publishing, 1911.

_____. "The Negro Christianized." Boston, 1706.

Melville, Herman. "Benito Cereno" (1855). Rpt. in *The Great Short Works of Herman Melville*. Ed. Warner Berthoff. New York: Harper and Row, 1969.

Morton, Thomas. *The New English Canaan*. Ed. Charles Francis Adams, Jr. New York: Burt Franklin, 1883.

Parkman, Francis. *The Conspiracy of Pontiac*. New York: Collier Books, 1962.

Poe, Edgar Allan. *The Narrative of Arthur Gordon Pym* (1838). *The Imaginary Voyages*. Ed. Burton Pollin. Boston: Twayne, 1981.

Sedgwick, Catherine Maria. *Hope Leslie; Or, Early Times in Massachusetts* (1827). New Brunswick: Rutgers Univ. Press, 1987.

_____. "Old Maids" (1834). Rpt. in *Old Maids: Short Stories by Nineteenth-Century U.S. Women Writers*. Ed. Susan Koppelman. Boston: Pandora Press, 1984.

Simms, William Gilmore. *The Yemassee* (1835). Cambridge: Riverside Press, 1961.

Smith, John. *A True Relation* (London, 1608). Rpt. in *Travel and Works of Captain John Smith*. Ed. Edwin Arber. Edinburgh: John Grant, 1910.

Stowe, Harriet Beecher. *Uncle Tom's Cabin*. New York: Penguin, 1981.

Underhill, John. *Newes from America, or a Late and Experimental Discovery of New England* (London, 1638). Rpt. in *History of the Pequot War: The Contemporary Accounts of Mason, Underhill, Vincent and Gardener*. Ed. Charles Orr. Cleveland: Helman-Taylor, 1897.

Williams, Roger. *A Key into the Language of America*. In *The Complete Writings of Roger Williams*. New York: Russell and Russell, 1963.

Winthrop, John. "A Modell of Christian Charity" (London, 1630). Rpt. in *Old South Leaflets*, ser. 1, no. 207. New York: Burt Franklin, 1883.

_____. "Reasons to be Considered . . . " (London, 1629). Rpt. in *Massachusetts Historical Society Proceedings*, 8 (1864–65): 420–25.

Secondary Sources

Altschuler, Glenn C. "Whose Foot on Whose Throat? A Reexamination of Melville's 'Benito Cereno.'" *College Language Association Journal* 18 (1975): 383–92.

Andrews, William L. *To Tell a Free Story: The First Century of Afro-American Autobiography, 1760–1865*. Urbana: Univ. of Illinois Press, 1986.

Appiah, Anthony. "The Uncompleted Argument: Du Bois and the Illusion of Race." *Critical Inquiry* 12 (1985): 21–37.

Armitage, Susan H. "Women's Literature and the American Frontier: A New Perspective on Frontier Myth." In *Women Writers and the West*. Ed. L. L. Lee and Merrill Lewis. Troy, N.Y.: Whiston, 1979.

Armstrong, Nancy, and Leonard Tennenhouse. *The Violence of Representation: Literature and the History of Violence*. New York: Routledge, 1989.

Axtell, James. *The Invasion Within: The Contest of Cultures in Colonial North America*. New York: Oxford Univ. Press, 1985.

Baines, Barbara J. "Ritualized Cannibalism in 'Benito Cereno': Melville's 'Black-Letter' Texts." *Emerson Studies Quarterly* 30 (1984): 163–69.

Baker, Houston. *The Journey Back: Issues in Black Literature and Criticism*. Chicago: Univ. of Chicago Press, 1980.

Bakhtin, Mikhail M. *The Dialogic Imagination: Four Essays*. Ed. Michael Holquist.

Trans. Michael Holquist and Caryl Emerson. Houston: Univ. of Texas Press, 1981.

Banton, Michael. *Racial Theories*. London: Cambridge Univ. Press, 1987.

Banton, Michael, and Jonathan Harward. *The Race Concept*. New York: Praeger, 1975.

Barker, Martin. "Biology and the New Racism." In *Anatomy of Racism*. Ed. David Theo Goldberg. Minneapolis: Univ. of Minnesota Press, 1990.

Barnett, Louise K. *The Ignoble Savage: American Literary Racism, 1790–1890*. Westport, Conn.: Greenwood Press, 1975.

Barthes, Roland. *Mythologies*. Trans. Annette Lavers. New York: Hill and Wang, 1972.

Baym, Nina. *Novels, Readers and Reviewers: Responses to Fiction in Antebellum America*. Ithaca, N.Y.: Cornell Univ. Press, 1984.

———. *Woman's Fiction: A Guide to Novels by and about Women in America, 1820–1870*. Ithaca, N.Y.: Cornell Univ. Press, 1978.

———. "The Rise of the Woman Author." In *Columbia Literary History of the United States*. Ed. Emory Elliot. New York: Columbia Univ. Press, 1988.

Beard, James Franklin. "James Fenimore Cooper Bibliography." In *Fifteen American Authors Before 1900*. Ed. Earl N. Harvart and Robert N. Rees. Madison: Univ. of Wisconsin Press, 1984.

Becker, Carl. *The Heavenly City of the Eighteenth-Century Philosophers*. New Haven, Conn.: Yale Univ. Press, 1932.

Bell, Michael Davitt. "History and Romance Convention in Catherine Sedgwick's *Hope Leslie*." *American Quarterly* 22 (1970): 213–21.

Belsey, Catherine. *Critical Practice*. London: Methuen, 1980.

Bentley, Nancy. "Poe and the Disfiguring of Travel Writing." Paper delivered at the Modern Language Association Conference held in December 1990 in Chicago, Illinois.

Berger, John. *Ways of Seeing*. New York: Penguin, 1972.

Berkhofer, Robert F., Jr. *The White Man's Indian: Images of the American Indian from Columbus to the Present*. New York: Vintage, 1979.

Berlin, James. "Rhetoric and Ideology in the Writing Class." *College English* 50 (1988): 477–94.

Bernhard, Virginia. "Cotton Mather and the Doing of Good: A Puritan Gospel of Wealth." *New England Quarterly* 49 (1971): 225–41.

Bhabha, Homi. "The Other Question—The Stereotype and Colonial Discourse." *Screen* 24 (1983): 18–36.

———. "Representation and the Colonial Text: A Critical Exploration of Some Forms of Mimeticism." In *The Theory of Reading*. Ed. Frank Gloversmith. Totowa, N.J.: Barnes and Noble, 1984.

Blaney, Michael Stewart. "Roots and the Noble Savage." *North Dakota Quarterly* 54 (1986): 1–17.

Bloom, Harold, ed. *The Tales of Poe*. Modern Critical Interpretations. New York: Chelsea House, 1987.

Bonoparte, Marie. *The Life and Works of Edgar Allan Poe: A Psycho-Analytic Interpretation*. London: Imago, 1949.

Breen, T. H., and Stephen Innes. *"Myne Own Ground": Race and Freedom on Virginia's Eastern Shore, 1640–1667*. New York: Oxford Univ. Press, 1980.

Breitwieser, Mitchell Robert. "Jefferson's Prospect." *Prospects* 10 (1985): 315–52.

Brown, Sterling. "A Century of Negro Portraiture in American Literature." *Massachu-setts Review* 7 (1966): 73–96.

———. "Negro Character as Seen by White Authors." *Journal of Negro Education* 2 (1933): 179–203.

Bruchner, Pascal. *Tears of the White Man: Compassion as Contempt*. Trans. William R. Beer. New York: Free Press, 1986.

Bruns, Roger. *Am I Not A Man and A Brother: The Anti-Slavery Crusade of Revolutionary America, 1688–1788*. New York: Chelsea House, 1977.

Burke, Kenneth. *Attitudes Toward History*. 3rd ed. Berkeley: Univ. of California Press, 1984.

———. *The Philosophy of Literary Form*. Berkeley: Univ. of California Press, 1973.

———. *Rhetoric of Motives*. Berkeley: Univ. of California Press, 1969.

Butterfield, Herbert. *The Origins of Modern Science, 1300–1800*. New York: Free Press, 1957.

Camfield, Gregg. "The Moral Aesthetics of Sentimentality: A Missing Key to *Uncle Tom's Cabin*." *Nineteenth-Century Literature* 43 (1988): 319–45.

———. "Sentimental Liberalism and the Problem of Race in *Huckleberry Finn*." *Nineteenth-Century Literature* 46 (1991). Forthcoming.

Campbell, Mary B. *The Witness and the Other World: Exotic European Travel Writings, 400–1600*. Ithaca, N.Y.: Cornell Univ. Press, 1988.

Carby, Hazel. "The Canon: Civil War and Reconstruction." *Michigan Quarterly Review* 28 (1989): 35–43.

———. *Reconstructing Womanhood: The Emergence of the Afro-American Woman Novelist*. New York: Oxford Univ. Press, 1987.

Cardwell, Guy. "Melville's Gray Story: Symbols and Meaning in 'Benito Cereno.'" In *Herman Melville*. Ed. Harold Bloom. Modern Critical Views. New York: Chelsea House, 1986.

Carlson, Eric W. *Critical Essays on Edgar Allan Poe*. Boston: G. K. Hall, 1987.

Carr, Helen. "Woman/Indian: 'The American' and His Others." In *Europe and Its Others*. Vol. 2. Ed. Francis Barker et al. Essex, Eng.: Essex Sociology of Literature Conference, 1985.

Castiglia, Christopher. "In Praise of Extravagant Women: *Hope Leslie* and the Captivity Romance." *Legacy* 6 (1989): 3–16.

Chase, Richard. *The American Novel and Its Tradition*. Baltimore, Md.: Johns Hopkins Univ. Press, 1957.

Cheyfitz, Eric. *The Poetics of Imperialism: Translation and Colonization from "The Tempest" to "Tarzan"*. New York: Oxford Univ. Press, 1991.

Chomsky, Noam. *The Chomsky Reader*. Ed. James Peck. New York: Pantheon, 1987.

Christian, Barbara. "The Race for Theory." *Cultural Critique* 6 (1987): 51–63.

Collins, Frank M. "Cooper and the American Dream." *PMLA* 81 (1966): 79–94.

Conrad, Susan Phinney. *Perish the Thought: Intellectual Women in Romantic America, 1830–1860*. Seacaucus, N.J.: The Citadel Press, 1978.

Cowie, Alexander. Introduction to *The Yemassee*. New York: American Book Co., 1937.

———. *The Rise of the American Novel*. New York: American Book Co., 1951.

Dahl, Curtis. "Introduction." *Nick of the Woods*, by Robert Montgomery Bird. New Haven, Conn.: New College and Univ. Press, 1967.

D'Avanzo, Mario L. "'Undo It, Cut It, Quick': The Gordian Knot in 'Benito Cereno.'" *Studies in Short Fiction* 15 (1978): 192–94.

Davis, Charles T., and Henry Louis Gates, Jr., eds. *The Slave's Narrative*. New York: Oxford Univ. Press, 1985.

Davis, David Brion. "The Ends of Slavery" (review essay). *New York Review of Books*, March 30, 1989; 29–34.

_____. *The Problem of Slavery in Western Culture*. Ithaca, N.Y.: Cornell Univ. Press, 1966.

Dayan, Joan. *Fables of the Mind: An Inquiry into Poe's Fiction*. New York: Oxford Univ. Press, 1987.

Delacampagne, Christian. "Racism and the West: From Praxis to Logos." In *Anatomy of Racism*. Ed. David Theo Goldberg. Minneapolis: Univ. of Minnesota Press, 1990.

Diggins, John P. "Slavery, Race, and Equality: Jefferson and the Pathos of the Enlightenment." *American Quarterly* 28 (1976): 206–28.

Dirlik, Arif. "Culturalism as Hegemonic Ideology and Liberating Practice." *Cultural Critique* 6 (1987): 13–50.

Dowling, William C. *Jameson, Althusser, Marx: An Introduction to the Political Unconscious*. Ithaca, N.Y.: Cornell Univ. Press, 1984.

Drinnon, Richard. *Facing West: The Metaphysics of Indian-Hating and Empire-Building*. New York: New American Library, 1980.

_____. *White Savage: The Case of John Dunn Hunter*. New York: Schocken Books, 1972.

Dryden, Edgar A. *Melville's Thematics of Form: The Great Art of Telling the Truth*. Baltimore: Johns Hopkins Univ. Press, 1968.

Du Plessis, Rachel Blau. *Writing Beyond the Ending: Narrative Strategies of Twentieth-Century Women Writers*. Bloomington: Indiana Univ. Press, 1985.

Eakin, Paul John. "Poe's Sense of an Ending." *American Literature* 45 (1973): 1–22.

Elliott, Emory, ed. *Columbia Literary History of the United States*. New York: Columbia Univ. Press, 1988.

Ellis, William. *The Theory of the American Romance: An Ideology in American Intellectual History*. Ann Arbor, Mich.: UMI Research Press, 1989.

Emery, Allan Moore. "'Benito Cereno' and Manifest Destiny." *Nineteenth-Century Fiction* 39 (1984): 48–68.

Engel, Leonard W. "Edgar Allan Poe's Use of the Enclosure Device in *The Narrative of Arthur Gordon Pym*." *American Transcendentalist Quarterly* 37 (1978): 34–44.

Erlich, Howard J. *The Social Psychology of Prejudice: A Systemic Review*. New York: John Wiley, 1973.

Fanon, Frantz. *A Dying Colonialism*. Trans. Haako Chevalier. New York: Grove Press, 1965.

_____. *The Wretched of the Earth*. Trans. Constance Farrington. New York: Grove Press, 1963.

Fehrenbacher, Don E. *Slavery, Law, and Politics: The Dred Scott Case in Historical Perspective*. New York: Oxford Univ. Press, 1981.

Ferguson, Robert A. "'Mysterious Obligation': Jefferson's *Notes on the State of Virginia*." *American Literature* 52 (1980): 381–406.

Fiedler, Leslie. *Love and Death in the American Novel*. New York: Stein and Day, 1966.

Fishburn, Katherine. *Women in Popular Culture: A Reference Guide*. Westport, Conn.: Greenwood Press, 1982.

Fisher, Marvin. "'Benito Cereno': Old World Experiences, New World Expectations and Third World Realities." *Forum* (Houston) 13 (1976): 31–36.

_____. *Going Under: Melville's Short Fiction and the American 1850s*. Baton Rouge: Louisiana State Univ. Press, 1977.

Fisher, Philip. *Hard Facts: Setting and Form in the American Novel*. New York: Oxford Univ. Press, 1985.

Fitzpatrick, Peter. "Racism and the Innocence of the Law." In *Anatomy of Racism*. Ed. David Theo Goldberg, Minneapolis: Univ. of Minnesota Press, 1990.

Fogle, Richard Harter. "'Benito Cereno.'" In *Melville: A Collection of Critical Essays*. Ed. Richard Chase. Englewood Cliffs, N.J.: Prentice-Hall, 1965.

Foley, Barbara. "History, Fiction, and the Ground Between: The Uses of the Documentary Mode in Black Literature." *PMLA* 95 (1980): 389–403.

Forclaz, Roger. "A Voyage to the Frontiers of the Unknown." Trans. Gerald Bello, *American Transcendentalist Quarterly* 37 (1978): 45–55.

Foster, Edward Halsey. *Catherine Maria Sedgwick*. TUSAS 233. New York: Twayne, 1974.

Foster, Frances Smith. *Witnessing Slavery: The Development of Ante-bellum Slave Narrative*. Contributions in Afro-American and African Studies, no. 46. Westport, Conn.: Greenwood Press, 1979.

Foucault, Michel. *The History of Sexuality*, vol. 1. Trans. Robert Hurley. New York: Vintage, 1980.

_____. *The Order of Things: An Archeology of the Human Sciences*. New York: Vintage, 1973.

_____. *Power/Knowledge: Selected Interviews and Other Writings*. Ed. Colin Gordon. New York: Pantheon, 1980.

Fox-Genovese, Elizabeth. *Within the Plantation Household: Black and White Women of the Old South*. Chapel Hill: Univ. of North Carolina Press, 1988.

Franklin, H. Bruce. *The Victim as Criminal and Artist: Literature from the American Prison*. New York: Oxford Univ. Press, 1978.

_____. *The Wake of Gods: Melville's Mythology*. Stanford, Calif.: Stanford Univ. Press, 1963.

Fredrickson, George M. *The Arrogance of Race: Historical Perspectives on Slavery, Racism, and Social Inequality*. Middletown, Conn.: Wesleyan Univ. Press, 1988.

_____. *The Black Image in the White Mind: The Debate on Afro-American Character and Destiny*. New York: Harper and Row, 1971.

Freibert, Lucy, and Barbara White, eds. *Hidden Hands: An Anthology of American Women Writers, 1790–1870*. New Brunswick, N.J.: Rutgers Univ. Press, 1985.

Freire, Paulo. *Pedagogy of the Oppressed*. Trans. Myra Bergman Ramos. New York: Seabury Press, 1970.

Fukuchi, Curtis. "Poe's Providential *Narrative of Arthur Gordon Pym*." *Emerson Studies Quarterly* 27.3 (1981): 147–56.

Fuss, Diana. *Essentially Speaking: Feminism, Nature and Difference*. New York: Routledge, 1989.

Fussell, Edwin. *Frontier: American Literature and the American West*. Princeton, N.J.: Princeton Univ. Press, 1965.

Gates, Henry Louis, Jr. "Authority, (White) Power and the (Black) Critic: It's All Greek to Me." *Cultural Critique* 7 (1987): 19–84.

_____. "Editor's Introduction: Writing 'Race' and the Difference It Makes." *Critical Inquiry* 12 (1985): 1–20.

_____. *Figures in Black: Words, Signs and the "Racial" Self.* New York: Oxford Univ. Press, 1987.

Genovese, Eugene. *Roll, Jordan, Roll: The World the Slaves Made.* New York: Vintage, 1976.

Gilmore, Michael T., ed. *Early American Literature: A Collection of Critical Essays.* Englewood Cliffs, N.J.: Prentice-Hall, 1980.

Goldberg, David Theo. Introduction, and "The Social Formation of Racist Discourse." In *Anatomy of Racism.* Ed. David Theo Goldberg. Minneapolis: Univ. of Minnesota Press, 1990.

Gossett, Suzanne, and Barbara Ann Bardes. "Women and Political Power in the Republic: Two Early American Novels." *Legacy* 2.2 (Fall 1987): 13–30.

Gossett, Thomas F. *Race: The History of an Idea in America.* New York: Schocken, 1963.

Gould, Stephen Jay. *The Mismeasure of Man.* New York: Norton, 1981.

Grenander, M. E. "Melville's 'Benito Cereno.'" *Explicator* 39.1 (1980): 33–34.

Gross, Seymour L. *A Benito Cereno Handbook.* Belmont, Calif.: Wadsworth, 1965.

Guillaumin, Collette. "The Idea of Race and its Elevation to Autonomous, Scientific and Legal Status." In *Social Theories: Race and Colonialism.* Ed. Marion O'Callaghan. New York: UNESCO, 1980.

Guthke, Karl S. *The Last Frontier: Imagining Other Worlds from the Copernican Revolution to Modern Science Fiction.* Trans. Helen Atkins. Ithaca, N.Y.: Cornell Univ. Press, 1990.

Gwinn, Minrose. *Black and White Women of the Old South: The Peculiar Sisterhood in American Literature.* Knoxville: Univ. of Tennessee Press, 1985.

Hagan, William T. "Full Blood, Mixed Blood, Generic, and Ersatz: The Problem of Indian Identify." *Arizona and the West* 27 (1985): 309–26.

Hallab, Mary Y. "Victims of 'Malign Machinations': Irving's *Christopher Columbus* and Melville's 'Benito Cereno.'" *Journal of Narrative Technique* 9.3 (1979): 199–206.

Halttunen, Karen. *Confidence Men and Painted Women: A Study of Middle-class Culture in America, 1830–1870.* New Haven: Yale Univ. Press, 1982.

Hammond, Alexander. "The Composition of *The Narrative of Arthur Gordon Pym*: Notes Toward a Reexamination." *American Transcendentalist Quarterly* 37 (1978): 9–20.

Hammond, Dorothy, and Alta Jablow. *The Africa That Never Was: Four Centuries of British Writing About Africa.* New York: Twayne, 1970.

Haraway, Donna. "A Manifesto for Cyborgs: Science, Technology and Socialist Feminism in the 1980s." *Feminism/Postmodernism.* Ed. Linda J. Nicholson. New York: Routledge, 1990.

_____. *Primate Visions: Gender, Race, and Nature in the World of Modern Science.* New York: Routledge, 1989.

Harper, Michael S. "It Is the Man/Woman Outside Who Judges: The Minority Writer's Perspective on Literature." *Tri-Quarterly* 1986 (Winter): 57–65.

Hartsock, Nancy M. *Money, Sex, and Power: Toward a Feminist Historicist Materialism.* Boston, Mass.: Northeastern Univ. Press, 1983.

_____. "Rethinking Modernism: Minority vs. Majority Theories." *Cultural Critique* 7 (1987): 187–206.

Heard, J. Norman. *White into Red: A Study of the Assimilation of White Persons Captured by Indians.* Metuchen, N.J.: Scarecrow Press, 1973.

Herbert, T. Walter, Jr. *Marquesan Encounters: Melville and the Meaning of Civiliza-tion*. Cambridge, Mass.: Harvard Univ. Press, 1980.

Herzog, Kristin. *Women, Ethnics, and Exotics: Images of Power in Nineteenth-Century American Fiction*. Knoxville: Univ. of Tennessee Press, 1983.

Hinz, Evelyn J. "'Tekeli-li': *The Narrative of Arthur Gordon Pym* as Satire." *Genre* 3 (1970): 379–99.

———, and John J. Teunissen. "Poe, Pym, and Primitivism." *Studies in Short Fiction* 14 (1977): 13–20.

Hoch, Paul. *White Hero, Black Beast: Racism, Sexism and the Mask of Masculinity*. London: Pluto Press, 1979.

Holland, Patricia G. "Lydia Maria Child as a Nineteenth-Century Professional Au-thor." *Studies in the American Renaissance* 1981: 157–67.

Holman, C. Hugh. "Introduction." *The Yemassee*, by William Simms. Cambridge, Mass.: Riverside Press, 1961.

hooks, bell (Gloria Watkins). *Ain't I a Woman: Black Women and Feminism*. Boston: South End Press, 1981.

———. *Feminist Theory: From Margin to Center*. Boston: South End Press, 1984.

Horsley-Meacham, Gloria. "Melville's Dark Satyr Unmasked." *English Language Notes* 23.3 (1986): 43–47.

———. "The Monastic Slaver: Images and Meaning in 'Benito Cereno.'" *New England Quarterly* 63.3 (1983): 261–66.

Horsman, Reginald. *Race and Manifest Destiny: The Origins of American Racial Anglo-Saxonism*. Cambridge, Mass.: Harvard Univ. Press, 1981.

Hughs, Merritt Y. Introductions. *John Milton: Complete Poems and Major Prose*. Indianapolis, Ind.: Odyssey Press, 1957.

Irwin, Joel. *American Hieroglyphics: The Symbol of Egyptian Hieroglyphics in the American Renaissance*. New Haven, Conn.: Yale Univ. Press, 1980.

Iser, Wolfgang. "Representation: A Performative Act." In *The Aims of Representation: Subject/Text/History*. Ed. Murray Krieger. New York: Columbia Univ. Press, 1987.

Jameson, Fredric. *The Political Unconscious: Narrative as a Socially Symbolic Act*. Ithaca, N.Y.: Cornell Univ. Press, 1981.

JanMohamed, Abdul R. "The Economy of Manichean Allegory: The Function of Racial Difference in Colonialist Literature." *Critical Inquiry* 12 (1985): 59–87.

———. "Negating the Negation as a Form of Affirmation in Minority Discourse: The Construction of Richard Wright as Subject." *Cultural Critique* 7 (1987): 245–67.

———, and David Lloyd. "Introduction: Toward a Theory of Minority Discourse." *Cultural Critique* 6 (1987): 5–12.

Jennings, Francis. *The Invasion of America: Indians, Colonialism, and the Cant of Conquest*. New York: W. W. Norton, 1975.

Johnson, Barbara. *The Critical Difference: Essays in the Contemporary Rhetoric of Reading*. Baltimore: Johns Hopkins Univ. Press, 1980.

———. *A World of Difference*. Baltimore, Md.: Johns Hopkins Univ. Press, 1987.

Johnson, Paul David. "American Innocence and Guilt: Black White Destiny in 'Benito Cereno.'" *Phylon* 36 (1975): 426–34.

Jordan, Cynthia S. *Second Stories: The Politics of Language, Form, and Gender in Early American Fictions*. Chapel Hill: Univ. of North Carolina Press, 1989.

Jordan, Winthrop. *White Over Black: American Attitudes Toward the Negro, 1550–1812*. New York: W. W. Norton, 1968.

Justman, Stewart. "Repression and Self in 'Benito Cereno.'" *Studies in Short Fiction* 15 (1978): 301–6.

Kaplan, Sidney. "'Benito Cereno': An Apology for Slavery?" *The Journal of Negro History* 41 (1956): 311–38; 42 (1957): 11–37.

_____. "An Introduction to *Pym*." In *Poe: A Collection of Critical Essays*. Ed. Robert Regan. Englewood Cliffs, N.J.: Prentice-Hall, 1967.

Kappeler, Susanne. *The Pornography of Representation*. Minneapolis: Univ. of Minnesota Press, 1986.

Karcher, Carolyn L. "Censorship, American Style: The Case of Lydia Maria Child." *Studies in the American Renaissance* (1986): 283–303.

_____. Introduction to *"Hobomok and Other Writings on Indians,"* by Lydia Maria Child. New Brunswick: Rutgers Univ. Press, 1986.

_____. "Lydia Maria Child's *Romance of the Republic*: An Abolitionist Vision of America's Racial Destiny." In *Slavery and the Literary Imagination*. Ed. Deborah McDowell and Arnold Rampersad. Baltimore, Md.: Johns Hopkins Univ. Press, 1989.

_____. "Rape, Murder, and Revenge in 'Slavery's Pleasant Homes': Lydia Maria Child's Antislavery Fiction and the Limits of Genre." *Women's Studies International Forum* 9 (1986): 323–32.

_____. *Shadow Over the Promised Land: Slavery, Race, and Violence in Melville's America*. Baton Rouge, Louisiana State Univ. Press, 1980.

Keiser, Albert. *The Indian in American Literature*. New York: Oxford Univ. Press, 1933.

Kelley, Mary. "Catherine Maria Sedgwick." *Legacy* 6 (1989): 43–49.

_____. Introduction to *Hope Leslie*. New Brunswick, N.J.: Rutgers Univ. Press, 1987.

_____. *Private Woman, Public Stage: Literary Domesticity in Nineteenth-Century America*. New York: Oxford Univ. Press, 1984.

Kennedy, J. Gerald. *Poe, Death and the Life of Writing*. New Haven, Conn.: Yale Univ. Press, 1987.

_____. "The Preface as a Key to the Satire in *Pym*." *Studies in the Novel* 5 (1973): 191–96.

Ketterer, David. *The Rationale of Deception in Poe*. Baton Rouge: Louisiana State Univ. Press, 1979.

_____. "The Singular *Narrative of Arthur Gordon Pym*." *American Transcendentalist Quarterly* 37 (1978): 21–33.

Kibbey, Ann. *The Interpretation of Material Shapes in Puritanism: A Study of Rhetoric, Prejudice and Violence*. Cambridge, Mass.: Cambridge Univ. Press, 1986.

Kolodny, Annette. *The Land Before Her: Fantasy and Experience of the American Frontiers, 1630–1860*. Chapel Hill: Univ. of North Carolina Press, 1984.

_____. *The Lay of the Land: Metaphor as Experience and History in American Life and Letters*. Chapel Hill: Univ. of North Carolina Press, 1975.

Kopley, Richard. "The Hidden Journey of Arthur Gordon Pym." *Studies in the American Renaissance* (1982): 29–51.

_____. "The Secret of *Arthur Gordon Pym*: The Text and the Source." *Studies in American Fiction* 8 (1980): 203–18.

_____. "The 'Very Profound Under-Current' of *Arthur Gordon Pym*." *Studies in the American Renaissance* (1987): 143–75.

Koppelman, Susan, ed. *The Other Woman: Stories of Two Women and a Man*. Old Westbury, N.Y.: Feminist Press, 1984.

————, ed. *Old Maids: Short Stories by Nineteenth-Century U.S. Women Writers*. Boston: Pandora Press, 1984.

Kuhn, Thomas S. *The Structure of Scientific Revolutions*. 2nd ed., vol. 2, no. 2. Chicago: Univ. of Chicago Press, 1970.

Kupperman, Karen Ordahl. *Captain John Smith: A Select Edition of His Writings*. Chapel Hill: Published for the Institute of Early American History and Culture, Williamsburg, Va., by the Univ. of North Carolina Press, 1988.

————. *Settling with the Indians: The Meeting of English and Indian Cultures in America, 1580–1640*. Totowa, N.J.: Rowman and Littlefield, 1980.

Lawrence, D. H. *Studies in Classic American Literature*. New York: Penguin, 1983.

Lee, Grace Farrell. "The Quest of Arthur Gordon Pym." *Southern Literary Journal* 4.2 (1972): 22–33.

Lee, A. Robert. "'Impudent and Ingenious Fiction': Poe's *The Narrative of Arthur Gordon Pym of Nantucket*." In *Edgar Allan Poe: The Design of Order*. Ed. A. Robert Lee. London: Vision Press, 1987.

Leitch, Thomas M. *What Stories Are: Narrative Theory and Interpretation*. University Park: The Pennsylvania State Univ. Press, 1986.

Lentricchia, Frank. *After the New Criticism*. Chicago: Univ. of Chicago Press, 1980.

————. *Criticism and Social Change*. Chicago: Univ. of Chicago Press, 1983.

Leverenz, David. *Manhood and the American Renaissance*. Ithaca, N.Y.: Cornell Univ. Press, 1989.

Levin, David. *Cotton Mather: The Young Life of the Lord's Remembrancer, 1663–1730*. Cambridge, Mass.: Harvard Univ. Press, 1978.

————. "Cotton Mather's Misnamed Diary: Reserved Memorials of a Representative Christian." *American Literary History* 2 (1990): 183–202.

Levin, Harry. *The Power of Blackness: Hawthorne, Poe, Melville*. New York: Knopf, 1970.

Levine, Richard A. "The Downward Journey of Purgation: Notes on an Imagistic Leit-motif in *The Narrative of Arthur Gordon Pym*." *Poe Studies* 2 (1969): 29–31.

Lewis, R. W. B. *The American Adam: Innocence, Tragedy and Tradition in the Nineteenth-Century*. Chicago: Univ. of Chicago Press, 1955.

Limon, John. *The Place of Fiction in the Time of Science: A Disciplinary History of American Writing*. New York: Cambridge Univ. Press, 1990.

Locke, Mary Stoughton, A. M. *Anti-Slavery in America from the Introduction of African Slaves to the Prohibition of Slave Trade*. Gloucester, Mass.: Peter Smith, 1965.

Lockridge, Kenneth. *The Diary and Life of William Byrd II of Virginia, 1674–1744*. Chapel Hill: Published for the Institute of Early American History and Culture, Williamsburg, Va., by the Univ. of North Carolina Press, 1987.

Marambaud, Pierre. *William Byrd of Westover, 1674–1744*. Charlottesville: Univ. of Virginia Press, 1971.

Martin, Terrence. "Surviving on the Frontier: The Doubled Consciousness of Natty Bumppo." *South Atlantic Quarterly* 75 (1976): 447–59.

Matlack, James. "Attica and Melville's 'Benito Cereno.'" *American Transcendentalist Quarterly* (supplement) 26 (1975): 18–23.

Matthiessen, F. O. *American Renaissance: Art and Expression in the Age of Emerson and Whitman*. New York: Oxford Univ. Press, 1941.

McDowell, Deborah, and Arnold Rampersad, eds. *Slavery and the Literary Imagination*. Selected Papers from the English Institute, 1987. Baltimore, Md.: Johns Hopkins Univ. Press, 1989.

Memmi, Albert. *The Colonizer and the Colonized*. Boston: Beacon Press, 1965.

Merod, Jim. *The Political Responsibility of the Critic*. Ithaca, N.Y.: Cornell Univ. Press, 1987.

Miller, Christopher. *Blank Darkness: Africanist Discourse in French*. Chicago: Univ. of Chicago Press, 1985.

Miller, John C. "Did Edgar Allan Poe Really Sell a Slave?" *Poe Studies* 9 (1976): 52–53.

Miller, Perry. *Nature's Nation*. Cambridge, Mass.: Belknap Press, 1967.

Moldenhauer, Joseph J. "Imagination and Perversity in *The Narrative of Arthur Gordon Pym*." *Texas Studies in Language and Literature* 13 (1971): 267–80.

Morgan, Edmund S. *American Slavery, American Freedom: The Ordeal of Colonial Virginia*. New York: W. W. Norton, 1975.

_____. "Slavery and Freedom: The American Paradox." *Journal of American History* 59 (1972): 5–29.

Morrison, Toni. Address delivered at Princeton University on February 14, 1989.

_____. "Unspeakable Things Unspoken: The Afro-American Presence in American Literature." *Michigan Quarterly Review* 28.1 (1989): 1–34.

Mottram, Eric. "Poe's *Pym* and the American Social Imagination." In *Artful Thunder: Versions of the Romantic Tradition in American Literature in Honor of Howard P. Vincent*. Ed. Robert J. DeMott and Sanford E. Marovits. Kent, Ohio: Kent State Univ. Press, 1975.

Mudimbe, V. Y. *The Invention of African: Gnosis, Philosophy, and the Order of Knowledge*. Bloomington: Indiana Univ. Press, 1988.

Mukarovsky, Jan. *Aesthetic Function, Norm, and Value as Social Facts*. Trans. Mark E. Suino. Ann Arbor: Michigan Slavic Contributions, 1970.

Nash, Gary B. "The Image of the Indian in the Southern Colonial Mind." *William and Mary Quarterly* 29 (1972): 197–230.

_____. *The Great Fear: Race in the Mind of America*. New York: Holt, Rinehart and Winston, 1970.

_____. *Red, White, and Black: The Peoples of Early America*, 2nd ed. Englewood Cliffs, N.J.: Prentice-Hall, 1982.

Neider, Charles, ed. *Short Novels of the Masters*. New York: Rinehart, 1948.

Nelson, Cary. *Repression and Recovery: Modern American Poetry and the Politics of Cultural Memory*. Madison: Univ. of Wisconsin Press, 1989.

Nicholson, Linda, ed. *Feminism/Postmodernism*. New York: Routledge, 1990.

Nielson, Aldon Lynn. *Reading Race: White American Poets and Racial Discourse in the Twentieth Century*. Athens: Univ. of Georgia Press, 1988.

Nikolyukin, A. N. "Past and Present Discussions of American National Literature." *New Literary History* 4 (1973): 575–90.

Nnolim, Charles E. *Melville's "Benito Cereno": A Study in Meaning of Name Symbolism*. New York: New Voices, 1974.

Oakes, James. *The Ruling Class: A History of American Slaveholders*. New York: Vintage, 1983.

Omi, Michael, and Howard Winant. *Racial Formation in the United States from the 1960s to the 1980s*. New York: Routledge, 1986.

Orr, Charles, ed. *The History of the Pequot War: The Contemporary Accounts of Mason, Underhill, Vincent and Gardener*. Cleveland, Ohio: Helman-Taylor, 1897.

Osborne, William S. *Lydia Maria Child*. TUSAS 380. Boston: Twayne, 1980.

Outlaw, Lucius. "Toward a Critical Theory of Race." In *Anatomy of Racism*. Ed. David Theo Goldberg. Minneapolis: Univ. of Minnesota Press, 1990.

Pahl, Dennis. *Architects of the Abyss: The Indeterminate Fictions of Poe, Hawthorne and Melville*. Columbia: Univ. of Missouri Press, 1989.

Papashvily, Helen Waite. *All the Happy Endings*. New York: Harper and Brothers, 1956.

Parrington, Vernon L. *Main Currents in American Thought: The Colonial Mind*. Vol. I (1620–1800). New York: Harcourt, Brace, 1927.

———. *The Romantic Revolution in America, 1800–1860*. New York: Harvest, 1954.

Pattee, Fred Lewis. *The Feminine Fifties*. New York: D. Appleton-Century, 1940.

Patterson, Orlando. *Slavery and Social Death: A Comparative Study*. Cambridge, Mass.: Harvard Univ. Press, 1982.

Pearce, Roy Harvey. *The Savages of America: A Study of the Indian and the Idea of Civilization*. Baltimore, Md.: Johns Hopkins Univ. Press, 1953.

Peck, H. Daniel. "James Fenimore Cooper and the Writers of the Frontier." In *Columbia Literary History of the United States*. Ed. Emory Elliott. New York: Columbia Univ. Press, 1988.

Person, Leland S., Jr. "The American Eve: Miscegenation and a Feminist Frontier Fiction." *American Quarterly* 37 (1985): 669–85.

Peyden, William. "Prologue to a Dark Journey: The 'Opening' to Poe's *Pym*." In *Papers on Poe*. Ed. Richard P. Veler, Springfield, Ohio: Chantry Music Press, 1972.

Pollin, Burton R. "Poe's *Narrative of Arthur Gordon Pym* and the Contemporary Reviewers." *Studies in American Fiction* 2 (1974): 37–56.

———. "*Pym's Narrative* in the American Newspapers: More Uncollected Notices." *Poe Studies* 11 (1978): 8–10.

———. "Three More Early Notices of *Pym* and the Snowden Connection." *Poe Studies* 8 (1975): 32–35.

Porte, Joel. *The Romance in America: Studies in Cooper, Hawthorne, Melville and James*. Middletown, Conn.: Wesleyan Univ. Press, 1969.

Pratt, Mary Louise. "Scratches on the Face of the Country; or, What Mr. Barrow Saw in the Land of the Bushmen." *Critical Inquiry* 12 (1985): 119–43.

Rackett, Tim. "Racialist Social Fantasy and Paranoia." In *Europe and Its Others*. Ed. Francis Barker, et al. Vol. 1. Essex, Eng.: Essex Sociology of Literature Conference, 1984.

Radhakrishnan, R. "Ethnic Identity and Post-Structuralist Difference." *Cultural Critique* 6 (1987): 199–220.

Rampersad, Arnold. "Biography, Autobiography, and Afro-American Culture." *The Yale Review* 73.1 (1983): 1–16.

Reising, Russell J. *The Unusable Past: Theory and the Study of American Literature*. New York: Methuen, 1986.

Ridgely, J. V. "The Continuing Puzzle of *Arthur Gordon Pym*: Some Notes and Queries." *Poe Studies* 2 (1969): 5–6.

———. "The End of Pym and the Ending of *Pym*." In *Papers on Poe*. Ed. Richard P. Veler. Springfield, Ohio: Chantry Music Press, 1972.

Ricardou, Jean. "The Singular Character of the Water." Trans. Frank Towne. *Poe Studies* 9 (1976): 1–6.

Riley, Glenda. *Women and Indians on the Frontier, 1825–1915*. Albuquerque: Univ. of New Mexico Press, 1984.

Ringer, Benjamin B. *We the People and Others: Duality and America's Treatment of its Racial Minorities*. New York: Tavistock, 1983.

Ringer, Benjamin B., and Elinor Lawless. *Race-Ethnicity and Society*. New York: Routledge, 1989.

Robinson, Donald. *Slavery in the Structure of American Politics, 1765–1820.* New York: Harcourt Brace Jovanovich, 1971.

Robinson, Douglas. "Reading Poe's Novel: A Speculative Review of *Pym* Criticism, 1950–1980." *Poe Studies* 14 (1981): 47–54.

Rogin, Michael Paul. "Liberal Society and the Indian Question." *Ronald Reagan, The Movie, and Other Episodes in Political Demonology.* Berkeley: Univ. of California Press, 1987.

_____. *Subversive Genealogy: The Politics and Art of Herman Melville.* Berkeley: Univ. of California Press, 1979.

Root, Deborah. "The Imperial Signifier: Todorov and the Conquest of Mexico." *Cultural Critique* 9 (1988): 197–218.

Rosenthal, Bernard. "Poe, Slavery, and the *Southern Literary Messenger*: A Reexamination." *Poe Studies* 7 (1974): 29–38.

Roundy, Nancy. "Present Shadows: Epistemology in Melville's 'Benito Cereno.'" *Arizona Quarterly* 34 (1978): 344–50.

Rowe, John Carlos. *Through the Custom House: Nineteenth-Century American Fiction and Modern Theory.* Baltimore, Md.: Johns Hopkins Univ. Press, 1982.

Rozat, Guy, and Roger Bartram. "Racism and Capitalism." In *Social Theories: Race and Colonialism.* Ed. Marion O'Callaghan. New York: UNESCO, 1980.

Rozenzweig, Paul. "'Dust Within the Rock': The Phantasm of Meaning in *The Narrative of Arthur Gordon Pym.*" *Studies in the Novel* 14 (1982): 137–51.

_____. "The Search for Identity: The Enclosure Motif in *The Narrative of Arthur Gordon Pym.*" *Emerson Studies Quarterly* 26.3 (1980): 111–26.

Runden, John P. *Melville's "Benito Cereno": A Text For Guided Research.* Boston: D. C. Heath, 1965.

Said, Edward. *Orientalism.* New York: Vintage, 1979.

Salzman, Jack, ed. *Cambridge Handbook of American Literature.* New York: Columbia Univ. Press, 1986.

Sanchez-Eppler, Karen. "Harriet Jacobs: Writing Slavery and Righting Sex." In "Touching Liberty: Abolition, Feminism and the Politics of the Body from the Sentimental to the Lyric." Unpublished manuscript.

Sands, Kathleen. "The Mythic Initiation of Arthur Gordon Pym." *Poe Studies* 7 (1974): 14–16.

Schiffman, Joseph. "Critical Problems in Melville's 'Benito Cereno.'" *Modern Language Quarterly* 11 (1950): 317–24.

_____, ed. *Three Shorter Novels of Herman Melville.* New York: Harper and Brothers, 1962.

Schlissel, Lillian. *Women's Diaries of the Westward Journey.* New York: Schocken Books, 1982.

Sekora, John, and Darwin T. Turner, eds. *The Art of Slave Narrative: Original Essays in Criticism and Theory.* Macomb: Western Illinois Univ. Press, 1982.

Shaner, Richard C. "Simms and the Noble Savage." *American Transcendentalist Quarterly* 30 (1976): 18–22.

Siebert, Donald T. "William Byrd's *Histories of the Line*: The Fashioning of a Hero." *American Literature* 47 (1975): 535–51.

Silverman, Kenneth. *The Life and Times of Cotton Mather.* New York: Harper and Row, 1984.

Simpson, David. *The Politics of American English, 1776–1850.* New York: Oxford Univ. Press, 1986.

Simpson, Lewis P. "The Garden of Chattel: Robert Beverly and William Byrd II." In

Early American Literature. Ed. Michael T. Gilmore. Englewood Cliffs, N.J.: Prentice-Hall, 1980.

Slotkin, Richard. *The Fatal Environment: The Myth of the Frontier in the Age of Industrialization, 1800–1890*. New York: Atheneum, 1985.

———. "Introduction." *The Last of the Mohicans*, by James Fenimore Cooper. New York: Penguin, 1987.

———. *Regeneration Through Violence: The Mythology of the American Frontier, 1600–1860*. Middletown, Conn.: Wesleyan Univ. Press, 1971.

Smith, David. "William Byrd Surveys America." *Early American Literature* 11 (1977): 296–310.

Smith, Henry Nash. "The Scribbling Women and the Cosmic Success Story." *Critical Inquiry* 1 (1974): 47–70.

———. *Virgin Land: The American West as Symbol and Myth*. New York: Vintage Books, 1950.

Smith, Sidonie. *Where I'm Bound: Patterns of Slavery and Freedom in Black American Autobiography*. Contributions in American Studies, no. 16. Westport, Conn.: Greenwood Press, 1974.

Smith, Valerie. *Self-Discovery and Authority in Afro-American Narrative*. Cambridge, Mass.: Harvard Univ. Press, 1987.

Sobel, Mechal. *The World They Made Together: Black and White Values in Eighteenth-Century Virginia*. Princeton, N.J.: Princeton Univ. Press, 1987.

Sollors, Werner. *Beyond Ethnicity: Consent and Descent in American Culture*. New York: Oxford Univ. Press, 1986.

Spivak, Gayatri Chakravorty. *In Other Worlds: Essays in Cultural Politics*. London: Methuen, 1987.

———. *The Post-Colonial Critic: Interviews, Strategies, Dialogues*. Ed. Sarah Harasym. New York: Routledge, 1990.

Stepan, Nancy. *The Idea of Race in Science: Great Britain, 1800–1960*. Hamden, Conn.: Archon Books, 1982.

———. "Race and Gender: The Role of Analogy in Science." In *Anatomy of Racism*. Ed. David Theo Goldberg. Minneapolis: Univ. of Minnesota Press, 1990.

Stroupe, John H. "Poe's Imaginary Voyage: Pym as Hero." *Studies in Short Fiction* 4 (1967): 315–21.

Sundquist, Eric. "Slavery, Revolution, and the American Renaissance." In *The American Renaissance Reconsidered*. Selected Papers from the English Institute, 1982–83. Ed. Walter Benn Michaels and Donald E. Pease. Baltimore, Md.: Johns Hopkins Univ. Press, 1985.

———. "Suspense and Tautology in 'Benito Cereno.'" In *Herman Melville's "Billy Budd," "Benito Cereno," "Bartelby the Scrivener," and Other Tales*. Ed. Harold Bloom. Modern Critical Interpretations. New York: Chelsea House, 1987.

Swann, Charles. "'Benito Cereno': Melville's De(con)struction of the Southern Reader." *Literature and History* 12 (1986): 3–15.

———. "Whodunnit? or, Who did What? 'Benito Cereno' and the Politics of Narrative Structure." *American Studies in Transition*. Ed. David E. Nye and Christen Kold Thomsen. Odense, Denmark: Odense Univ. Press, 1985.

Thompson, G. R. "Edgar Allan Poe and the Writers of the Old South." In *Columbia Literary History of the United States*. Ed. Emory Elliot. New York: Columbia Univ. Press, 1988.

Todorov, Tzvetan. *The Conquest of America: The Question of the Other*. Trans. Richard Howard. New York: Harper and Row, 1984.

_____. "'Race,' Writing and Culture." *Critical Inquiry* 13 (1986): 171–81.

Tompkins, Jane. *Sensational Designs: The Cultural Work of American Fiction, 1790–1860*. New York: Oxford Univ. Press, 1985.

Turner, Frederick. *The Frontier in American History* (1920). Tucson: Univ. of Arizona Press, 1986.

Tynan, Daniel J. "J. N. Reynold's *Voyage of the Potomac*: Another Source for *The Narrative of Arthur Gordon Pym*." *Poe Studies* 4 (1971): 35–36.

Valenti, Peter. "Images of Authority in 'Benito Cereno.'" *College Language Association Journal* 21 (1978): 367–79.

Vanderbilt, Kermit. "'Benito Cereno': Melville's Fable of Complicity." *Southern Review* 12 (1976): 311–22.

Vaughan, Alden T. "From White Man to Redskin: Changing Anglo-American Perceptions of the American Indians." *American History Review* 87 (1982): 917–53.

_____. *New England Frontier: Puritans and Indians, 1625–1675*. Boston: Little, Brown, 1965.

Veler, Richard P. *Papers on Poe: Essays In Honor of John Ward Ostrom*. Springfield, Ohio: Chantry Music Press, 1972.

Wade-Gayles, Gloria. *No Crystal Stair: Visions of Race and Sex in Black Women's Fiction*. New York: Pilgrim Press, 1984.

Walker, I. M. *Edgar Allan Poe: The Critical Heritage*. London: Routledge and Kegan Paul, 1986.

Watson, Charles S. "Portrayals of the Black and the Idea of Progress: Simms and Douglass." *Southern Studies* 20 (1981): 339–60.

Wells, Daniel A. "Engraved Within the Hills: Further Perspectives on the Ending of *Pym*." *Poe Studies* 10 (1977): 13–15.

Welsh, Howard. "The Politics of Race in 'Benito Cereno.'" *American Literature* 46 (1975): 556–66.

Welsh, Sister Mary Michael, O.P. *Catherine Maria Sedgwick: Her Position in the Literature and Thought of Her Time up to 1860*. Washington, D.C.: Catholic Univ. of America, 1937.

Wetherington, Hugh W. *Melville's Reviewers: British and American, 1846–1891*. Chapel Hill: Univ. of North Carolina Press, 1961.

Williams, Michael. *A World of Words: Language and Displacement in the Fictions of Edgar Allan Poe*. Durham, N.C.: Duke Univ. Press, 1988.

Williams, Raymond. *Marxism and Literature*. New York: Oxford Univ. Press, 1977.

Wills, Garry. "Thomas Jefferson and the Equality of Man." In *Early American Literature*. Ed. Michael T. Gilmore. Englewood Cliffs, N.J.: Prentice-Hall, 1980.

Winston, Robert P. "Bird's Bloody Romance: *Nick of the Woods*." *Southern Studies* 23 (1984): 71–90.

Wood, Forrest G. *The Arrogance of Faith: Christianity and Faith in America from the Colonial Era to the Twentieth Century*. New York: Knopf, 1990.

Yellin, Jean Fagin. *The Intricate Knot: Black Figures in American Literature, 1776–1863*. New York: New York Univ. Press, 1972.

_____. "Introduction." *Incidents in the Life of a Slave Girl*, by Harriet Ann Jacobs. Cambridge, Mass.: Harvard Univ. Press, 1987.

_____. "Texts and Contexts of Harriet Jacobs' *Incidents in the Life of a Slave Girl: Written by Herself*." In *The Slave's Narrative*. Ed. Charles T. Davis and Henry Louis Gates. New York: Oxford Univ. Press, 1985.

Zagarell, Sandra A. "Expanding 'America': Lydia Sigourney's *Sketch of Connecticut*,

Catherine Maria Sedgwick's *Hope Leslie*." *Tulsa Studies in Women's Literature* 6 (1987): 225–45.

———. "Reenvisioning America: Melville's 'Benito Cereno.'" *Emerson Studies Quarterly* 30 (1984): 245–59.

Zlatic, Thomas D. "'Benito Cereno': Melville's 'Back-Handed-Well-Knot.'" *Arizona Quarterly* 34 (1978): 327–43.

Index